PEARSON EDEXCEL
INTERNATIONAL AS/A LEVEL
ACCOUNTING
Student Book 1

John Bellwood
Hilary Fortes

Published by Pearson Education Limited, 80 Strand, London, WC2R 0RL.

www.pearsonglobalschools.com

Copies of official specifications for all Edexcel qualifications may be found on the website:
https://qualifications.pearson.com

Text © Pearson Education Limited 2019
Designed by Pearson Education Limited 2019
Typeset by Pearson CSC
Edited by Jess White and Sarah Wright
Original illustrations © Pearson Education Limited 2019
Cover design by Pearson Education Limited 2019
Picture research by Integra

Cover images: *Front*: **Getty Images:** olaser/Getty Images
Inside front cover: Shutterstock.com/Dmitry Lobanov

The rights of John Bellwood and Hilary Fortes to be identified as author of this work have been
asserted by them in accordance with the Copyright, Designs and Patents Act 1988.

First published 2019

2024

10 9 8 7 6 5

British Library Cataloguing in Publication Data
A catalogue record for this book is available from the British Library

ISBN 978 1 292274 61 4

Printed and bound by CPI Group (UK) Ltd, Croydon, CR0 4YY

Acknowledgements
The authors and publisher would like to thank the following individuals and organisations for
permission to reproduce photographs/copyright material:

Text Credit(s):
219: ICAEW Code of Ethics

Image Credit(s):
(Key: b-bottom; c-centre; l-left; r-right; t-top)
2 **Getty Images:** Zanariah Salam/EyeEm/Getty Images; 4 **123RF:** Rob Marmion/123RF;
5 **123RF:** Iakov Filimonov/123RF; 9 **Shutterstock:** Tribalium/Shutterstock;
12 **Shutterstock:** FLariviere/Shutterstock; 16 **123RF:** Lenetsnikolai Lenets/123RF;
18 **123RF:** Iakov Filimonov/123RF; 21 **Shutterstock:** Africa Studio/Shutterstock;
24 **123RF:** Sergiy Tryapitsyn/123RF; 27 **Shutterstock:** Viki2win/Shutterstock;
29 **Shutterstock:** Sergey Ryzhov/Shutterstock; 32 **Shutterstock:** Kenneth William Caleno/
Shutterstock; 36 **Shutterstock:** Itti Ratanakiranaworn/Shutterstock; 40 **Shutterstock:**
Maksimilian/Shutterstock; 41 **123RF:** Apidach Jansawang/ 123RF; 43 **Shutterstock:** Mikbiz/
Shutterstock; 44 **123RF:** Radiantskies/123RF; 45 **Shutterstock:** Matej Kastelic/Shutterstock;
47 **123RF:** Racorn/123RF; 48(cl) **Shutterstock:** Dmitry Kalinovsky/Shutterstock;
48(cr) **Shutterstock:** Brian A Jackson/Shutterstock; 49 **Shutterstock:** Rcarner/Shutterstock;
50 **Shutterstock:** ImagIN.gr photography/Shutterstock; 51 **123RF:** Mark Bowden/123RF;
53(cr) **Shutterstock:** Shutterstock; 53(cl) **Shutterstock:** Baevskiy Dmitry/Shutterstock;
54 **123RF:** Photografier/123RF; 55(tl) **Shutterstock:** ESB Professional/Shutterstock;
55(cr) **Shutterstock:** GuruXOX/Shutterstock; 58 **123RF:** Vereshchagin Dmitry/123RF;
61 **123RF:** Diyana Dimitrova/123RF; 65 **Shutterstock:** S-F/Shutterstock;
68(tl) **Shutterstock:** Oleksandr Lipko/Shutterstock; 68(tr) **Shutterstock:** AlisLuch/Shutterstock;
69(tl) **Shutterstock:** Herbert Kratky/Shutterstock; 69(tr) **Getty Images:** Westend61/Getty

Images; 71 **Shutterstock:** Nishihama/Shutterstock; 72 **Getty Images:** Hinterhaus
Productions/DigitalVision/Getty Images; 74(tl) **Shutterstock:** Curioso/Shutterstock;
74(bl) **Shutterstock:** Baloncici/Shutterstock; 75 **123RF:** Buthsakon Lojanaparb/123RF;
76 **123RF:** Andriy Popov/123RF; 77 **Shutterstock:** Johnny Lye/Shutterstock; 78 **Shutterstock:**
George Rudy/Shutterstock; 81 **Shutterstock:** Lisa S/Shutterstock; 85 **Shutterstock:**
Amble Design/Shutterstock; 86 **123RF:** Dolgachov/123RF 88 **Shutterstock:** Creative Lab/
Shutterstock; 91 **123RF:** Alenin/123RF; 94 **Shutterstock:** Maxx-Studio/Shutterstock;
96 **123RF:** Iakov Filimonov/123RF; 99 **Shutterstock:** Tomasz Szymanski/Shutterstock;
100 **Getty Images:** Paul Bradbury/Caiaimage/Getty Images; 104 **123RF:** Scyther5/123RF;
109 **Shutterstock:** Daxiao Productions/Shutterstock; 115 **Shutterstock:** PzAxe/
Shutterstock; 116 **123RF:** Folewu/123RF; 121 **Shutterstock:** Rawpixel.com/Shutterstock;
123 **Shutterstock:** ESB Professional/Shutterstock; 124 **Shutterstock:** M Taira/Shutterstock;
125 **123RF:** Industryview/123RF; 127 **Shutterstock:** 540631/Shutterstock;
129 **123RF:** Auremar/123RF; 130 **Shutterstock:** Stillfx/Shutterstock;
131 **Shutterstock:** Mark Soon/Shutterstock; 134 **Shutterstock:** Vladimir Volodin/
Shutterstock; 137 **123RF:** Yakov Oskanov/123RF; 140 **Shutterstock:** LouisNguyen/
Shutterstock; 141 **Shutterstock:** Sam72/Shutterstock; 142 **Shutterstock:** Fizkes/
Shutterstock; 145 **Shutterstock:** Zeljkodan/Shutterstock; 148 **Shutterstock:** Shutterstock;
153 **Shutterstock:** Fertas/Shutterstock; 156 **Shutterstock:** Tashatuvango/Shutterstock;
157 **Shutterstock:** Nicholas Rjabow/Shutterstock; 158 **123RF:** Jari Hindstrom/123RF;
166 **Shutterstock:** Suwin/Shutterstock; 168 **Shutterstock:** Alhim/Shutterstock;
171 **123RF:** Ivan Traimak/123RF; 173 **Shutterstock:** Stock-Asso/Shutterstock;
174 **Getty Images:** Runner of Art/Getty Images; 175 **Shutterstock:** Christian Delbert/
Shutterstock; 176 **Shutterstock:** Mavo/Shutterstock; 180(tl) **Shutterstock:** Serezniy/
Shutterstock; 180(tr) **Shutterstock:** Sea Wave/Shutterstock; 182 **Shutterstock:** Pavel L
Photo and Video/Shutterstock; 183 **Shutterstock:** Fizkes/Shutterstock;
186 **123RF:** Kzenon/123RF; 185 **Shutterstock:** VVO/Shutterstock; 187 **123RF:** Dmytro
Tolmachov/123RF; 188 **123RF:** Donyanedomam/123RF; 191 **Shutterstock:** DeSerg/
Shutterstock; 192 **Shutterstock:** Shutterstock; 195 **123RF:** Alexis Bélec/123RF;
198 **Shutterstock:** Dmitry Kalinovsky/Shutterstock; 199 **Shutterstock:** Dzhafarov Eduard/
Shutterstock; 200 **123RF:** Aleksandr Papichev/123RF; 202 **123RF:** Stepan Bormotov/123RF;
203 **Getty Images:** Tom Merton/Caiaimage/Getty Images; 204 **123RF:** Dizanna/123RF;
205 **Shutterstock:** Danielo/Shutterstock; 206 **Shutterstock:** Photographee.eu/Shutterstock;
211 **Shutterstock:** Wachira W/Shutterstock; 214 **Shutterstock:** Olga Popova/Shutterstock;
215 **Getty Images:** Westend61/Getty Images; 216 **Shutterstock:** Eva Kali/Shutterstock;
218 **Shutterstock:** 3D_Creation/Shutterstock; 220 **123RF:** Gnomeandi/123RF.

All other images © Pearson Education

The authors and publisher would like to kindly thank Nicolas Demetriou, Munawar Hameed,
Edwin Ka Hou Lo, Md Mizanur Rahman and Linda Stringer for their valuable assistance in the
development of these materials.

CONTENTS

UNIT 1

ABOUT THIS BOOK

This book is for students following the Edexcel International Advanced Subsidiary (IAS) Accounting course.

The course has been structured so that teaching and learning can take place in any order, both in the classroom and in any independent learning. The book contains full coverage of the IAS unit. The six topic areas within this unit match the titles and order of those in the specification.

Each topic area is divided into chapters to break the content down into manageable chunks. Each chapter features a mix of learning and activities. Global case studies are embedded throughout to show a range of examples within the context of the chapter. Checkpoint questions at the end of each chapter help you to assess understanding of the key learning points. There are exam-style questions at the end of each chapter (except Chapter 1, which is introductory) to provide opportunities for exam practice. Answers are provided in the online eBook version of this textbook.

Topic openers
Introduce each of the key topics in the specification.

Learning objectives
Each chapter starts with a list of key assessment objectives.

Specification reference
The specification reference is given at the start of each chapter and in the running header.

SPECIFICATION 1.1.1–1.1.2   1 ROLE AND PURPOSE OF ACCOUNTING   3

1 ROLE AND PURPOSE OF ACCOUNTING

UNIT 1
1.1.1– 1.1.2

PRINCIPLES OF ACCOUNTING

During the course of your studies of this subject you will read about and work through various aspects of accounting. You will understand that its main purposes are to measure, analyse and communicate transactions. More importantly, accounting is a language for all businesses and it is the intention of this book to teach you how to understand this language and be able to communicate in it.

In this section, you will learn the fundamental principles of accounting; the double-entry system, which forms the basic building blocks of accounting. In addition, you will cover how businesses account for potential non-payment by customers who have bought goods on credit. Finally, there is an introduction to the use of information and communication technology (ICT) in recording financial information.

LEARNING OBJECTIVES

After you have studied this chapter, you should be able to:
■ understand the need for financial information
■ understand and explain the purposes of accounting
■ explain the differences between financial and management accounting
■ identify the main users of accounts and their information needs.

GETTING STARTED

During your accounting studies, you and a friend decide to set up a business selling t-shirts to your fellow students. What financial transactions might you need to write down? What might you need to measure and analyse? What other people might be interested in the information?

TERMINOLOGY – DIFFERENT TYPES OF BUSINESS ORGANISATION

From the start, we need to be clear about a number of terms that we use throughout this book. When we speak about a 'business', we mean a commercial concern. This concern is involved either in manufacturing products, selling products or services, or both. The business invests its capital into resources so that it can make a profit for the owners. Because of this profit motive, organisations such as charities, or even government authorities, are not included in the term. In this book, we will also cover accounting for sole traders and for non-profit-making organisations.

Before going into the detail of the language of accounting, let us examine the basics. We do this by asking a most important question.

WHAT IS ACCOUNTING?

In simple terms, we can say that accounting is about recording, analysing and communicating information. This process allows managers, lenders of finance, shareholders and the many other users of this information the opportunity and ability to make informed judgements and decisions.

Recording
This is the starting point within the accounting system. Once identified, transactions must be recorded in an organised way, as the events take place. To do this, it must be possible to record events and these events must be of a financial nature.

Analysing
We need to be able to measure – whether it is our own wealth, business profits or government spending. To do this, there are rules that establish how events are measured.

You will all have had some experience of using the language of accounting, but many of you will probably not even have realised that you are, or have been, using it.

Individuals measure their wealth in terms of the financial value of their assets (house, car, stocks and shares, cash, etc.). To do this they use value as the means for measurement. This also applies to organisations, which measure their income, expenditure and success (i.e. the profit earned) in financial terms.

Communication
In order for information to be useful, it needs to be communicated to other interested individuals or groups. The information required by users must be presented in a way that the users, who may have little accounting knowledge, can easily understand.

FINANCIAL AND MANAGEMENT ACCOUNTING
Accounting is divided into two parts (see Figure 1). The two areas have differences but are also closely related.
● Financial accounting is concerned with the preparation of financial statements, covering the whole of the activities of the business, for use by external users. This area of accounting is normally regulated by law.
● Management accounting concerns itself with parts of the business, as well as the whole, and is used to help decision making by internal users, such as those in management. The main objective is planning and control.

Key subject terms are colour coded within the text.

Getting started
An activity to introduce the key concepts in each chapter. Questions are designed to stimulate discussion and use of prior knowledge. These can be tackled as individuals, pairs, groups or the whole class.

Skills
Relevant exam questions have been assigned key skills, allowing for a strong focus on particular academic qualities. These transferable skills are highly valued in further study and the workplace.

Activity
Each chapter includes activities to embed understanding through case studies and questions.

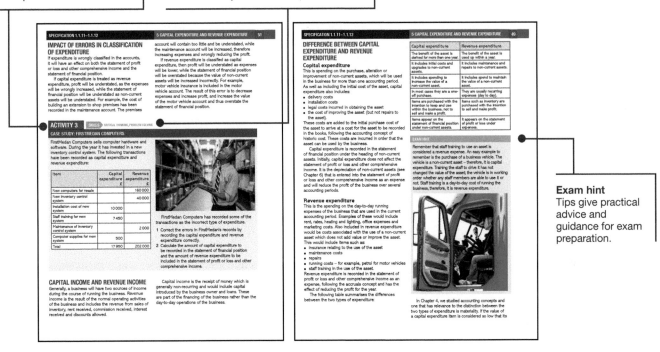

Exam hint
Tips give practical advice and guidance for exam preparation.

Exam practice
Exam-style questions are found at the end of each chapter (except Chapter 1). They are tailored to the Pearson Edexcel specification to allow for practice and development of exam writing technique. They also allow for practice responding to the command words used in the exams.

Subject vocabulary
An alphabetical list of all the subject terms in each chapter with clear definitions for EAL learners. Please note: A collated glossary is available at the back of the book.

Evaluate
See page ix.

Checkpoint
Questions to check understanding of the key learning points in each chapter. These are NOT exam-style questions.

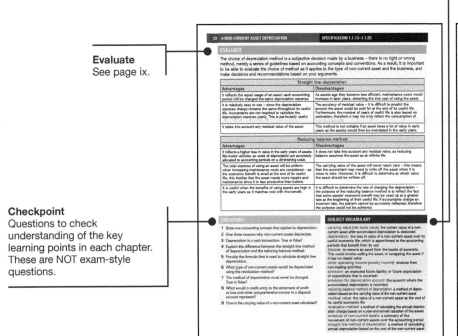

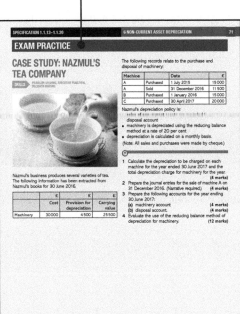

ASSESSMENT OVERVIEW

The following tables give an overview of the assessment for this course. You should study this information closely to help ensure that you are fully prepared for this course and know exactly what to expect in each part of the assessment.

PAPER 1	PERCENTAGE OF IAS	PERCENTAGE OF IAL	MARKS	TIME	AVAILABILITY
THE ACCOUNTING SYSTEM AND COSTING Written exam paper Paper code WAC11 Externally set and marked by Pearson Edexcel Single tier of entry	100%	50%	200	3 hours	January, June & November First assessment: June 2016

ASSESSMENT OBJECTIVES AND WEIGHTINGS

ASSESSMENT OBJECTIVE	DESCRIPTION	% IN IAS	% IN IA2	% IN IAL
AO1	Demonstrate knowledge of accounting procedures and techniques and an understanding of the principles and concepts upon which they are based	30	24–25	27–28
AO2	Select and apply knowledge and understanding of accounting procedures, techniques, concepts and principles to a variety of accounting situations. Present accounting information in an appropriate format	43–44	41–42	42–43
AO3	Analyse financial information, interpret financial data and information and communicate reasoning, showing understanding	17	23–24	20–21
AO4	Evaluate financial and non-financial evidence and make informed recommendations and decisions	9–10	10–11	10

Note: Percentages may not add up to 100 due to rounding.

RELATIONSHIP OF ASSESSMENT OBJECTIVES TO UNITS FOR THE INTERNATIONAL ADVANCED SUBSIDIARY QUALIFICATION

UNIT NUMBER	ASSESSMENT OBJECTIVE			
	AO1	AO2	AO3	AO4
Unit 1	30%	43–44%	17%	9–10%

Note: Percentages may not add up to 100 due to rounding.

ASSESSMENT SUMMARY

PAPER 1	DESCRIPTION	MARKS	ASSESSMENT OBJECTIVES
THE ACCOUNTING SYSTEM AND COSTING Paper code WAC11	**Structure** Paper 1 assesses 100 per cent of the total IAS Accounting qualification and 50 per cent of the IAL Accounting qualification There will be two sections, A and B. Students must answer all questions in Section A and select from a choice of questions in Section B Section A: two compulsory multi-part questions (110 marks); Section B: three multi-part questions from a choice of four (90 marks)	The total number of marks available is 200	Questions will test the following assessment objectives: AO1 – 14% AO2 – 20% AO3 – 7% AO4 – 9%
	Assessment This is a single-tier exam paper The assessment duration is 3 hours Calculators may be used in the examinations		

EVALUATE QUESTIONS

In the exam you will see questions that ask you to 'Evaluate'. In your answer, you will need to compare two methods or ways of working and state which one you think is the most suitable for the scenario given and why. In this book there are 'Evaluate' sections. They give examples of possible methods you might be asked to evaluate, as well as a table showing arguments for and against the method. You could use these tables to help you plan an essay answer on the topic.

Remember in the exam to always develop your points; the examiner will not award full marks if you only write bullet points. To achieve the highest marks, you will need to write a conclusion in which you decide which method is best. You need to justify your decision with reasons and you will also be expected to show a chain of reasoning – how your points have helped you to come to your conclusion.

CURRENCY

All of the examples in this textbook use GBP £ because all the examination papers also use GBP £ only. However, you might want to challenge yourself by creating examples using the currency from your own country or other major currencies, such as USD $.

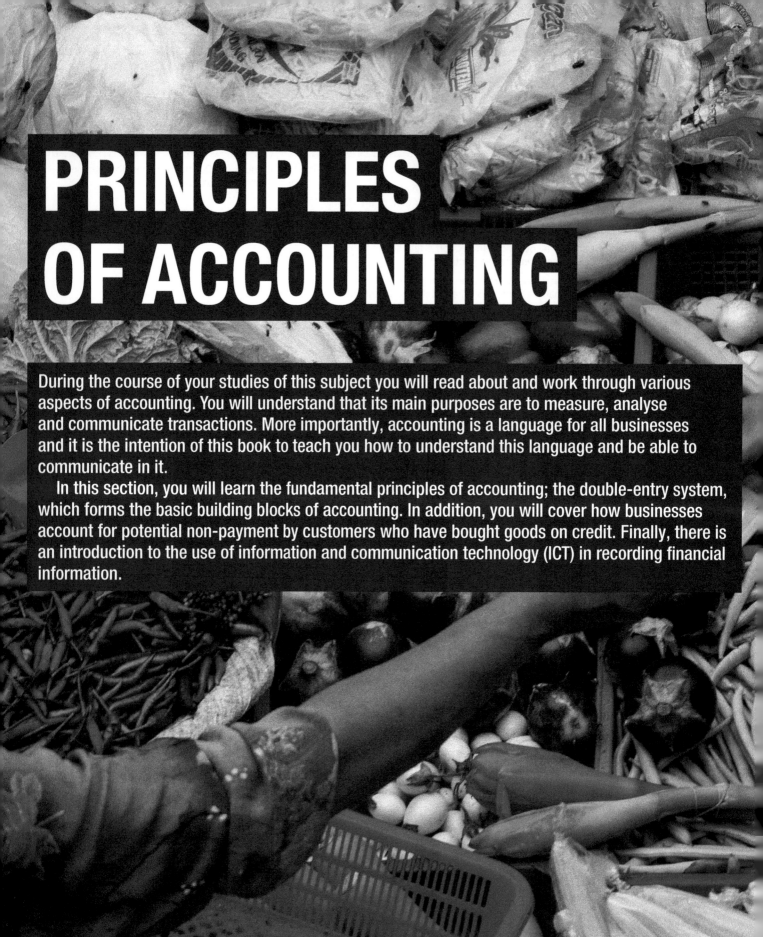

PRINCIPLES OF ACCOUNTING

During the course of your studies of this subject you will read about and work through various aspects of accounting. You will understand that its main purposes are to measure, analyse and communicate transactions. More importantly, accounting is a language for all businesses and it is the intention of this book to teach you how to understand this language and be able to communicate in it.

In this section, you will learn the fundamental principles of accounting; the double-entry system, which forms the basic building blocks of accounting. In addition, you will cover how businesses account for potential non-payment by customers who have bought goods on credit. Finally, there is an introduction to the use of information and communication technology (ICT) in recording financial information.

1 ROLE AND PURPOSE OF ACCOUNTING

LEARNING OBJECTIVES

After you have studied this chapter, you should be able to:
- understand the need for financial information
- understand and explain the purposes of accounting
- explain the differences between financial and management accounting
- identify the main users of accounts and their information needs.

GETTING STARTED

During your accounting studies, you and a friend decide to set up a business selling t-shirts to your fellow students. What financial transactions might you need to write down? What might you need to measure and analyse? What other people might be interested in the information?

TERMINOLOGY – DIFFERENT TYPES OF BUSINESS ORGANISATION

From the start, we need to be clear about a number of terms that we use throughout this book. When we speak about a 'business', we mean a commercial concern. This concern is involved either in manufacturing products, selling products or services, or both. The business invests its capital into resources so that it can make a profit for the owners. Because of this profit motive, organisations such as charities, or even government authorities, are not included in the term. In this book, we will also cover accounting for sole traders and for non-profit-making organisations.

Before going into the detail of the language of accounting, let us examine the basics. We do this by asking a most important question.

WHAT IS ACCOUNTING?

In simple terms, we can say that accounting is about recording, analysing and communicating information. This process allows managers, lenders of finance, shareholders and the many other users of this information the opportunity and ability to make informed judgements and decisions.

Recording

This is the starting point within the accounting system. Once identified, transactions must be recorded in an organised way, as the events take place. To do this, it must be possible to record events and these events must be of a financial nature.

Analysing

We need to be able to measure – whether it is our own wealth, business profits or government spending. To do this, there are rules that establish how events are measured.

You will all have had some experience of using the language of accounting, but many of you will probably not even have realised that you are, or have been, using it.

Individuals measure their wealth in terms of the financial value of their assets (house, car, stocks and shares, cash, etc.). To do this they use value as the means for measurement. This also applies to organisations, which measure their income, expenditure and success (i.e. the profit earned) in financial terms.

Communication

In order for information to be useful, it needs to be communicated to other interested individuals or groups. The information required by users must be presented in a way that the users, who may have little accounting knowledge, can easily understand.

FINANCIAL AND MANAGEMENT ACCOUNTING

Accounting is divided into two parts (see Figure 1). The two areas have differences but are also closely related.
- Financial accounting is concerned with the preparation of financial statements, covering the whole of the activities of the business, for use by external users. This area of accounting is normally regulated by law.
- Management accounting concerns itself with parts of the business, as well as the whole, and is used to help decision making by internal users, such as those in management. The main objective is planning and control.

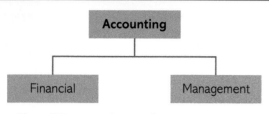

▲ Figure 1 The areas of accounting

These distinctions do not mean that the basic data is different. The sources are the same, but they are analysed and reported in different ways in order to be useful for different purposes.

We will now examine the two areas in more detail.

Financial accounting

As financial accounts are required by law, the following applies.

- The disclosure of information must conform to legal requirements and some businesses may show only the minimum requirements.
- Reports should contain financial information which is useful to users.
- The information provided is designed for external users.
- The results are based on past activities.
- All of the information presented is based on accounting concepts and conventions.
- The results are shown in a set of accounts, which are published annually in a standard, summarised format.
- For any event to be shown, it must be measurable in monetary terms.

Management accounting

Management accounts provide specific information to managers for a very definite purpose. It may be for the introduction of a new product or the purchase of a new machine. It could include the preparation of quotations and the costing of specific jobs. The prepared accounts will assist with planning, control, monitoring, decision making and investment.

All of the above can only be possible because management accounting information has certain standards. These can be summarised as follows.

- The information is detailed and up to date. Reports could be weekly, monthly, etc.
- The statements are usually forward looking (although some may look back). Examples of management accounting reports include budgets and cost reports.
- Accounts are confidential and for internal use only.
- There is no standard format and the accounts are not subject to external regulation.
- The information is both financial and non-financial (quantitative and qualitative).

People often ask if two systems are necessary within an organisation because of these differences. As we see from the above, each gives different information, so we can say that both are needed, but they can be done through a good integrated system which is linked to one database. The larger the company, the greater the need for good strategic management information, but the more information given, the greater the cost. Therefore, we must consider the costs and the benefits of preparing management accounts.

THE NEED FOR FINANCIAL ACCOUNTING

Having reviewed the definition, let us now examine the need for financial accounting. Accounts are prepared for a variety of reasons:

- to assess the trading activities of a business
- to enable external owners to see how managers are performing
- to control the activities of the business
- to plan future activities
- to assist in raising finance
- to report on the activities of the business to interested parties.

USERS OF FINANCIAL ACCOUNTS

The efficiency and sustainability of a business is very important to many groups of people. These groups will have a different level of understanding of accounts. Nevertheless, attempts must be made to ensure effective communication to a broad range of users.

At this stage, it is essential that we identify the main users of financial accounting. However, not all of the users listed below can study the financial statements of a business, since some businesses (such as a sole trader business) are not required by law to publish their accounts publicly.

Owners

The owners of a business and the existing and potential shareholders of a company will want to know how effectively the directors and managers are performing their stewardship function; that is, how they control and organise the company. This is important in all businesses where the owners and shareholders are not involved in the day-to-day running, so they can rely on the financial statements to communicate the results. They will use the financial statements as the basis for their decisions – to sell some, or all, of their shares or perhaps to buy some additional shares. In addition, they will also use the financial statements to decide how profits are to be shared out and allocated.

Small-business owners also use financial statements to assess profitability. They may need to adjust their expenses if the profit target cannot be met. They may also look for extra finance by looking at the ratio between assets and liabilities.

Trade creditors

These include the various businesses that supply goods and services to the reporting business – they are usually called 'suppliers'. Suppliers usually study the amount of debts that are due in the short term, as they need to obtain payment from businesses within one to three months. They would want to know if they are able to provide credit to a business and, if so, whether they will be paid on the due date. A supplier would also consider whether to provide credit in the future in order to continue a business relationship.

Long-term creditors

The second type of creditors are those who provide finance to a business. These advances (loans) are usually repaid over an extended (long) period of time. Long-term creditors will look at the assets and liabilities, particularly the non-current liabilities (liabilities that need to be repaid over a long period of time). Lenders look at assets to see whether they could be sold for cash if one day the business cannot repay the debt. Lenders look at non-current liabilities to assess whether the business already has too many debts to repay.

The loan creditors will want to ensure that interest payments will be made promptly and that capital repayments on loans will be made as agreed.

Employees

This group includes existing, potential and past employees, as well as trade unions whose members are employees. Past employees will be mainly concerned with ensuring that any pensions paid by the business are maintained. Present employees will be interested in ensuring that the business is able to keep on operating – and therefore maintaining their jobs and paying them acceptable wages – and that any pension contributions are paid. In addition, they may want to ensure that the business is being fair to them, so that they get a reasonable share of the profits made by the business as a result of their efforts. Trade unions will protect the interests of their members and will, possibly, use the financial statements in wage and pension negotiations.

Potential employees will also be interested in assessing whether or not it would be worth seeking employment with that particular business.

Bankers

Where a bank has not given a loan or an overdraft, there will be no great need to see the financial statements. However, where money is owed to the bank, they will want to ensure that the payment of interest will be made when it is due, and that the business will be able to repay the loan or overdraft on the due date.

Bankers are also interested in profit so that they can see whether a business can pay the interest on a loan on time. Furthermore, they will also look at the amount of assets and liabilities. Bankers require some form of security from a business when it takes out a loan or applies for an overdraft, and so the quality and amount of a business's assets will affect the final amount of loan available.

Customers

Customers want to know whether or not a business is a secure supply source of goods and services. If customers buy warranty services for products such as electronic goods, they may also want to know whether the business will provide after-sales service.

Competitors

Business rivals will use the information to assess their own position, compared with that of the rival business. The information will serve as a benchmark for them to use. Potential takeover bidders will also want to assess the desirability of any such move.

The analyst and/or adviser group

Financial journalists need information for their readers, while stockbrokers need it to advise current and potential investors. Credit agencies want the information in order to advise present and possible suppliers of goods and services to the business as to its ability to get credit.

Governments

Governments will need to know the financial position to assess the tax payable by the business. Large businesses are required to publish annual financial details, including annual revenue, annual salaries, expenses and profit details. Governments may also use the information to decide their future policies.

Other official agencies

Various organisations that are concerned with the supervision of industry and commerce may want financial statements for their specific purposes. These organisations vary from country to country.

Management

In addition to the internally produced management accounts, management are also concerned with any financial statements. This is because the financial statements give an overall view of the financial situation of the business. This allows them to evaluate the performance of the business. Management would then consider the effect of such financial statements on the local community and the world at large.

The public

This section of users consists of groups such as taxpayers, political parties, pressure groups and consumers. The needs of these parties will vary accordingly. It should be noted that in a local community the businesses can be very important to the local economy.

ACTIVITY 1   SKILLS   CRITICAL THINKING

CASE STUDY: PRINCIPLES OF ACCOUNTING

This book shows you how accounts are prepared. It also shows how the information provided is used.

1 List the six reasons for preparing accounts.
2 There are many users of accounts and the information that they provide. Identify six such users.

ACTIVITY 2   SKILLS   CRITICAL THINKING, REASONING

CASE STUDY: DEFINING ACCOUNTING

Accounting is defined differently by many organisations, but it is agreed that there are three key words that are associated with accounting.

1 What are the three key words associated with accounting?
2 In your own words, state how you would describe accounting.

ACTIVITY 3   SKILLS   CRITICAL THINKING, REASONING

CASE STUDY: FINANCIAL AND MANAGEMENT ACCOUNTING

1 Draw a table to show the differences between financial accounting and management accounting.
2 While thinking about the differences that exist, write down a list of the things they have in common.

CHECKPOINT

1 What is accounting?
2 Explain the difference between financial accounting and management accounting.
3 Accounting information is used to control the activities of a business. True or false?
4 Accounting information is used to report on the activities of a business. True or false?
5 Competitors are not interested in the accounting information for a business. True or false?
6 Identify two internal and two external business users of accounting information.
7 Explain the difference between financial recording and financial accounting.

SUBJECT VOCABULARY

accounting the process of recording, classifying, analysing and communicating financial information

accounting concepts guidelines for the treatment of accounting transactions

capital investment (cash, resources or other assets) provided by the owner of the business

external user a person outside the business organisation

financial accounting the recording and presentation of past financial information to external users for their decision making

financial statements (final accounts) produced by the business to provide a summary of the performance of the business (the statement of profit or loss and other comprehensive income) and the financial position of the business (the statement of financial position)

financial transaction a business event or action that has a monetary impact on the business

internal user a person inside the business organisation

management accounting the preparation of past and future, financial and non-financial information for internal users

profitability the ability of a business to generate profit

quotation a document prepared in response to an enquiry from a customer detailing the price that will be charged for the product or service requested

sole trader a business owned by a single person

transaction a business event, such as the sale of inventory, which can be measured in monetary terms and which must be recorded in the books of accounts

2 DOUBLE-ENTRY SYSTEM 1

LEARNING OBJECTIVE

After you have studied this chapter, you should be able to:
■ record transactions in the books of account.

GETTING STARTED

You buy a new computer with some cash you have saved. Write down two things that have happened. You sell some computer games to a friend who promises to pay you next month. Again, write down two things that have happened. Can you think of other business transactions that take place and the two effects these have?

CLASSIFICATION OF ACCOUNTS

Accountants classify transactions (i.e. events that can be measured in monetary terms) into six elements.

- Capital is the amount of owner's interest in the business, it represents the owner's investment in the business.
- Liabilities are amounts due by the business; in other words, debts that must be paid. For example, these can be amounts due to suppliers for goods or services or rent and telephone. Any amount owing and to be paid within one year is a short-term liability (also called current liability). Any amount to be paid for a time period of greater than one year is called a non-current liability.
- Expenses – when running a business all firms will have to make payments for expenses, which include, for example, wages, electricity and motor expenses. All these costs are recorded in separate ledger accounts so that the business can see the total of each expense.
- Assets are items of value that a business possesses. This could be the building it occupies, its delivery vehicles, or the computers and other office equipment (termed non-current assets). In addition, the business also has its inventory, trade receivables (people that owe it money for goods or services) and cash in the bank or on hand (all of which are termed current assets).

- Revenue (or income) is usually derived from the receipt of money for goods or services provided by the business. If, for example, the business is a dress shop, then the sale of dresses to its customers would generate revenue to the business. Other forms of revenue could be any interest received from investment accounts, rent received from letting out premises owned by the business, and even commission received for arranging the sale of a product for someone else.
- Drawings – the owner of a business takes money from the business for his/her private needs which is called drawings. This also includes the withdrawal from the business of goods as well as cash. As these withdrawals are of a private nature they are not classed as an expense of the business.

EXAM HINT

You will notice that the first letters of each word above – Capital, Liabilities, Expenses, Assets, Revenue, Drawings – spell out 'CLEARD'. You can use this to help you remember the terms in your exam.

ACTIVITY 1   SKILLS   CRITICAL THINKING

CASE STUDY: ASSETS OR LIABILITIES?

You should now be able to fill in the tables below:

Identify the following:	Asset	Liability
1 Delivery vehicle		
2 Bank loan		
3 Inventory		
4 Cash on hand		
5 Trade payables		
6 Trade receivables		
7 Office equipment		
8 Cash at bank		

Identify the following:	Expense	Revenue
1 Rent received		
2 Telephone charges		
3 Sales of goods or services		
4 Wages and salaries		
5 Commission paid		
6 Advertising costs		
7 Rent payable		
8 Purchases		

DOUBLE-ENTRY SYSTEM

Accounting is based on transactions. There are two effects for every transaction, as can be seen from the example below. Accountants use the following accounting equation:

> Assets = Capital − Drawings + Liabilities

This accounting equation then evolved into the double-entry system:

	Assets, expenses, drawings	Liabilities, capital & revenue
Balance	Dr	Cr
Increase	Dr	Cr
Decrease	Cr	Dr

We have an existing business which has £1 000 in the bank and an inventory of goods purchased for £200. We now buy an additional £300 of goods, for cash.

Account	Element	Increase/decrease	Dr or Cr
Cash	Asset	Decrease	Cr
Inventory	Asset	Increase	Dr

From Figure 1, we can see that the original amount of cash and inventory is reflected in the first section of the graph. You then see the increase in the **purchases** and the relevant decrease in the cash balance.

You can see that at least two accounts are affected when a transaction occurs. It is this dual effect (duality) that lies behind the double-entry system. We can say, therefore, that double entry is the system by which the books of account reflect the fact that every transaction has two sides:

- receiving a benefit by one or more accounts
- giving a benefit.

This means that each transaction made in the books of account is made twice (that's the reason for the term 'duality'), a debit and a credit.

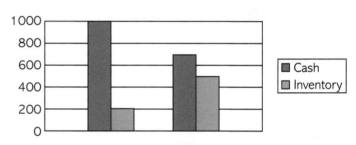

▲ Figure 1 Movement of cash and inventory

BASIC RULES FOR DOUBLE-ENTRY TRANSACTIONS

It is vital that accounting transactions are recorded correctly in the books. **Debit entries** are always recorded on the left-hand side of the ledger and the **credit entry** on the right-hand side, as shown below:

Debit side (Dr)			Credit side (Cr)		
		Account name			
Date	Details	£	Date	Details	£

If we now take each of the six types of account, we can see how the transactions are recorded.

Capital

Debit side (Dr)			Credit side (Cr)		
		Capital			
Date	Details	£	Date	Details	£
Decreases on the debit side			Increases on the credit side		

Liabilities

Debit side (Dr)		Credit side (Cr)	
	Liability account		
Date	Details £	Date	Details £
Decreases on the debit side		Increases on the credit side	

Expenses

Debit side (Dr)		Credit side (Cr)	
	Expense account		
Date	Details £	Date	Details £
Increases on the debit side		Decreases on the credit side	

Assets

Debit side (Dr)		Credit side (Cr)	
	Asset account		
Date	Details £	Date	Details £
Increases on the debit side		Decreases on the credit side	

Revenue

Debit side (Dr)		Credit side (Cr)	
	Revenue account		
Date	Details £	Date	Details £
Decreases on the debit side		Increases on the credit side	

Drawings

Debit side (Dr)		Credit side (Cr)	
	Drawings		
Date	Details £	Date	Details £
Increases on the debit side		Decreases on the credit side	

ACTIVITY 2   SKILLS ▷ CRITICAL THINKING

CASE STUDY: DEBITS AND CREDITS

Answer the following questions on debits and credits.

Does a debit item:	Yes	No
1 decrease capital?		
2 decrease income?		
3 decrease liabilities?		
4 decrease assets?		
5 decrease expenses?		

Does a credit item:	Yes	No
1 increase capital?		
2 increase income?		
3 increase liabilities?		
4 increase assets?		
5 increase expenses?		

SOURCE OF TRANSACTIONS

A transaction is the act which involves a transfer of money or value from one person or business to another. It is this which is recorded in the books of account for the business. The accounts of a business are contained in a book, or a number of books, called ledger(s) (covered in more detail later in this chapter).

In order to record the transaction, we need to have some record or proof of it having taken place, otherwise we cannot simply record a transaction. This proof can come from one of two sources:

- external – from another person or business, e.g. an invoice for purchases
- internal – from documents prepared by the business to record transactions, e.g. petty cash vouchers, cheque counterfoils, etc.

ACCOUNTING FOR INVENTORY

Inventory refers to the goods or stock that a business buys with the intention of selling at a later time and for a profit. While inventory is an asset, the purchase and sale are not recorded as inventory. When inventory is bought it is recorded as a purchase and when it is sold it is recorded as a sale. This is a very important concept that you must remember.

Purchase of inventory

A business buys inventory to the value of £500, paying in cash. The effect would be:

Account	Element	Increase/ decrease	Dr/Cr	£
Purchases	Asset	Increase	Dr	500
Cash	Asset	Decrease	Cr	500

If the purchases were paid by means of a bank transaction (a cheque or credit transfer) then the 'cash' entry would change to 'bank' to reflect that the funds for the purchase were taken from the bank account. If the purchases were made on credit, when payment for the goods will be made after the transaction has taken place, then the following would be recorded:

Account	Element	Increase/ decrease	Dr/Cr	£
Purchases	Asset	Increase	Dr	500
Trade payables	Liability	Increase	Cr	500

As the business has not paid for the asset, it now owes the supplier £500 and so a liability increases.

Sales of inventory

The business now sells all of the inventory for £900. Let us assume it receives the money immediately, so either the bank or cash increases:

Account	Element	Increase/ decrease	Dr/Cr	£
Cash or bank	Asset	Increase	Dr	900
Sales	Revenue	Increase	Cr	900

If the business does not receive the money immediately, then a trade receivable is created as an asset of the business:

Account	Element	Increase/ decrease	Dr/Cr	£
Trade receivables	Asset	Increase	Dr	900
Sales	Revenue	Increase	Cr	900

Make sure you fully understand double entry, its duality, and debit and credit entries. Let's get started and look at some basic transactions.

WORKED EXAMPLE

You are given the following list of transactions:
1 The business buys a car for cash, paying £3 600.
2 The business sells goods on credit to Mr Brown, for £320.
3 The business pays £68 cash for an advertisement in the local newspaper.
4 The business pays, in cash, the weekly wages of £190.
5 The business buys £197 worth of goods on credit from Mr Green, for resale.

Remember that every transaction must be posted to a ledger account and all these accounts have a heading (or name). Each transaction will have two effects. Given the above information, we will identify the accounts for the above transactions as follows:

1 The business buys a car for cash, paying £3 600:

Account	Element	Increase/ decrease	Dr/Cr	£
Motor car	Asset	Increase	Dr	3 600
Cash	Asset	Decrease	Cr	3 600

2 The business sells goods on credit to Mr Brown, for £320:

Account	Element	Increase/ decrease	Dr/Cr	£
Mr Brown	Asset	Increase	Dr	320
Sales	Income	Increase	Cr	320

Mr Brown is a trade receivable account for the business.

3 The business pays £68 cash for an advertisement in the local newspaper:

Account	Element	Increase/ decrease	Dr/Cr	£
Advertising	Expense	Increase	Dr	68
Cash	Asset	Decrease	Cr	68

4 The business pays, in cash, the weekly wages of £190:

Account	Element	Increase/ decrease	Dr/Cr	£
Wages	Expense	Increase	Dr	190
Cash	Asset	Decrease	Cr	190

5 The business buys £197 worth of goods on credit from Mr Green, for resale:

Account	Element	Increase/ decrease	Dr/Cr	£
Purchases	Expense	Increase	Dr	197
Mr Green	Liability	Increase	Cr	197

Mr Green is a trade payable account.

You will see from the above that each account has its own name, e.g. motor car, purchases, wages, etc. We do not mix the transactions into a single account. However, all transactions for one account are shown in that account, e.g. the cash account will have three entries in the example above.

THE LEDGER

From the above examples, you can see that all the transactions of a business are posted into a ledger or ledgers. The ledger can be described as a collection of accounts of a business (in simple terms, it is a book with one page for each account or, if the accounts are computerised, they be will part of the software package), and it is in the principal book of account where all financial transactions are recorded. We commonly talk about 'keeping the books' or 'writing up the books'. In this instance, the word 'books' means the ledger (or ledgers).

An account is the place where all the information relating to one type of asset, liability, income or expense is to be found. It reflects a detailed record of all transactions as they relate to a particular expense, receipt, asset or liability.

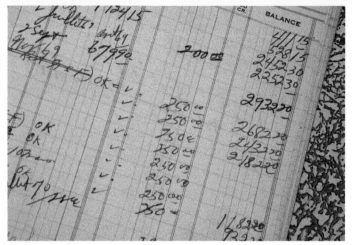

▲ An old-fashioned paper ledger

A LEDGER ACCOUNT

Each ledger account has its own name, e.g. motor expenses, advertising, trade receivables, and all are similar in appearance.

A typical ledger account that we would expect to see in a business is illustrated in Figure 2. The name of the account is placed at the top of the account. This describes the nature of the transaction contained in the account. From its title, we can work out if it is an expense or income account, an asset or a liability.

The page is divided into two halves by a central vertical line. The left-hand side is the debit side (Dr) and the right-hand side is the credit side (Cr). Each side is ruled in exactly the same way, with a number of vertical columns.

The first column is for the date of the transaction. The next column gives the details of that transaction. The third column is the folio column. A folio number (that is, a page number) is used in cross-referencing between the subsidiary books (see page 15) and the ledger. As the folio is not used in exams, this column is ignored throughout this text. It is hoped that in this way you will get to understand the principles of the accounting system without having to deal with too much detail.

Throughout this book we will show a simplified ledger account – commonly known as a 'T' account (it takes the form of the capital letter 'T'). This shows the date of the transaction, description of the transaction and the amount.

Through the use of these two sides of the ledger – and depending on the type of account (e.g. asset, liability, etc.) – we are able to show increases on the one side and decreases on the other. This does not mean that increases are always on the debit side or decreases are always on the credit side. This depends on the type of account that we are dealing with. To illustrate this, using the simplified T account, let us look at the examples below, starting with T accounts from the worked example on page 11:

Motor car

Date	Details	£	Date	Details	£
Date	Cash [1]	3 600			

Cash account

Date	Details	£	Date	Details	£
			Date	Motor car [1]	3 600
				Advertising [3]	68
				Wages [4]	190

Revenue

Date	Details	£	Date	Details	£
			Date	Mr Brown [2]	320

Mr Brown (Trade receivable)

Date	Details	£	Date	Details	£
Date	Sales [2]	320			

Advertising

Date	Details	£	Date	Details	£
Date	Cash [3]	68			

Wages

Date	Details	£	Date	Details	£
Date	Cash [4]	190			

Purchases

Date	Details	£	Date	Details	£
Date	Mr Green [5]	197			

Mr Green (Trade payable)

Date	Details	£	Date	Details	£
			Date	Purchases [5]	197

Dr			(Name of Account)		Cr
Date	Details	£	Date	Details	£

▲ Figure 2 Ledger account

WORKED EXAMPLE

The first account is for wages and shows the amounts that have been paid in January and February. We see that two wages payments (by cheques) occurred in January and February.

Account	Element	Increase/decrease	Dr/Cr
Wages	Expense	Increase	Dr
Bank	Asset	Decrease	Cr

When a business pays wages, the total amount of wages paid increases, therefore the wages account has been debited to reflect this increase.

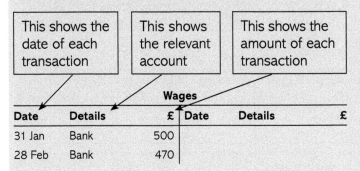

This shows the date of each transaction	This shows the relevant account	This shows the amount of each transaction

Wages

Date	Details	£	Date	Details	£
31 Jan	Bank	500			
28 Feb	Bank	470			

The second account is one that relates to a non-current asset – a computer – and shows the purchase of a computer in April. In this account we see that we paid £1 200 by cheque on 30 April for a computer.

Account	Element	Increase/decrease	Dr/Cr
Computer	Asset	Increase	Dr
Bank	Asset	Decrease	Cr

Computer (office equipment)

Date	Details	£	Date	Details	£
30 April	Bank	1 200			

The third account is the **capital account** of the business. It shows how the business was started with a capital investment of £5 000 and another amount, some three months later, of £11 000.

Account	Element	Increase/decrease	Dr/Cr
Bank	Asset	Increase	Dr
Capital	Capital	Increase	Cr

In this account we see that capital increased from £5 000 at the end of January to £16 000 at the end of April. In this instance we credited the capital account to reflect the increase.

Capital

Date	Details	£	Date	Details	£
			31 Jan	Bank	5 000
			30 April	Bank	11 000

From the worked examples, we learn that we can increase expenses, e.g. wages, by debiting the named account. This will also apply to assets, e.g. a computer, as they are on the debit side of the ledger.

We can increase a liability or capital by crediting the named account. This will also apply to revenue, e.g. sales, which is a credit to the relevant ledger accounts.

We also see how the accounting system records the many transactions. Clearly, we must record all transactions in at least two separate ledger accounts. You must always ask yourself an important question when posting transactions, and that is:

'Have I recorded this transaction in two accounts?'

If not, you have not entered the transaction according to the double-entry system. We will see the problem this causes when we discuss the trial balance in Chapter 7.

From now on, do not think that a credit means an increase or that a debit means a decrease. In accounting, this is far from the truth! As an additional guide, we must remember that assets and expenses are debits, while liabilities and income are credits. To illustrate this, we look at the following worked examples of double entry.

WORKED EXAMPLE

1 A motor vehicle is purchased for £1 145 cash on 2 June 2017.

Account	Element	Increase/ Decrease	Dr/Cr	£
Motor Vehicle	Asset	Increase	Dr	1 145
Cash	Asset	Decrease	Cr	1 145

Motor vehicle

Date	Details	£	Date	Details	£
2 June 2017	Cash	1 145			

Cash

Date	Details	£	Date	Details	£
			2 June 2017	Motor vehicle	1 145

2 The owner of the business funded it with a cash deposit of £2 000 on 2 June 2017.

Account	Element	Increase/ decrease	Dr/Cr	£
Cash	Asset	Increase	Dr	2 000
Capital	Capital	Increase	Cr	2 000

Capital

Date	Details	£	Date	Details	£
			2 June 2017	Cash	2 000

Cash

Date	Details	£	Date	Details	£
2 June 2017	Capital	2 000			

3 To start its trading activities, the business purchased £1 600 of goods on 4 June 2017 from A Wholesaler. An amount of £840 was paid in cash and the balance due for goods purchased was on credit.

Account	Element	Increase/ decrease	Dr/Cr	£
Purchases	Expenses	Increase	Dr	1 600
A Wholesaler (trade payable)	Liability	Increase	Cr	760
Cash	Asset	Decrease	Cr	840

Purchases

Date	Details	£	Date	Details	£
4 June 2017	Cash	840			
	A Wholesaler	760			

A Wholesaler (Trade payable)

Date	Details	£	Date	Details	£
			4 June 2017	Purchases	760

Cash

Date	Details	£	Date	Details	£
			4 June 2017	Purchases	840

4 A business purchased office equipment from A Supplier on 11 July 2018. This was a credit purchase of £543.

Account	Element	Increase/ decrease	Dr/Cr	£
Office equipment	Asset	Increase	Dr	543
A Supplier (trade payable)	Liability	Increase	Cr	543

Office equipment

Date	Details	£	Date	Details	£
11 July 2018	A Supplier	543			

A Supplier (trade payable)

Date	Details	£	Date	Details	£
			11 July 2018	Equipment	543

We can see that each of the items above are entered using a debit and a credit entry. We also note that in certain instances (items 1, 2 and 3) the cash account has been credited with part of the double entry. Instead of having three separate accounts for cash, we would have a single one. This account, showing all three transactions will appear as follows:

Cash

Date	Details	£	Date	Details	£
2 June 2017	Capital	2 000	2 June 2017	Motor vehicle	1 145
			4 June 2017	Purchases	840

It is important to note that the posting of transactions to the ledger accounts is done in a very formal way. The date of the transaction must be shown, as well as the description of the transaction. This description is normally the title of the other account of the double entry and allows anyone reading the ledger the opportunity to find the transaction on the opposite side.

All these accounts are collected together into a ledger and we will see later that it is from this ledger (or ledgers) that the financial statements are prepared.

TYPES OF LEDGER ACCOUNTS

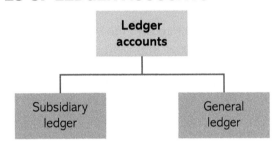

▲ Figure 3 The types of ledger accounts

The ledger can be divided into a number of smaller ledgers. These smaller ledgers are additional to the main (general) ledger and record transactions prior to entry (or posting) to the main ledger, which is why they are called subsidiary books. Examples of these subsidiary books are:

- the trade receivables (or sales) ledger (which records individual trade receivables who owe us money)
- trade payables (or purchase) ledger (where we record what we buy and how much we owe to each individual trade payable).

All of these subsidiary books will be discussed later.

ACTIVITY 3   SKILLS   CRITICAL THINKING

CASE STUDY: LEDGERS

Transactions	General ledger	Trade receivables ledger	Trade payables ledger
Cash sales			
Rent			
Bank			
Credit purchases			
Credit sales			
Wages paid			
Rent received			

1 Identify the ledger in which the above transactions would be shown.

UNDERSTANDING LEDGER ENTRIES

You should also be able to interpret and understand what each ledger account tells you. It sets out a transaction and you need to interpret it. Take the following ledger accounts and, by looking at each transaction, interpret what has happened.

Example 1

In the below account, we can 'read', for example, that rent of £500 was paid by the business on 1 March 2019. We also see that £10 000 was paid into the business as capital. We received £21 500 in cash sales and paid out various other items shown in the account below.

Bank

Date	Details	£	Date	Details	£
1 Mar 2019	Capital	10 000	1 Mar 2019	Rent	500
11 Mar 2019	Sales	21 500	3 Mar 2019	Gibson Wholesalers	1 000
			29 Mar 2019	Drawings	1 000
			30 Mar 2019	Motor expenses	1 900
				Other operating expenses	1 050
				Salaries	4 000

Example 2

Trade payable – J Smith

Date	Details	£	Date	Details	£
31 May 2019	Bank	15 300	31 May 2019	Purchases	45 990

Purchases

Date	Details	£			
31 May 2019	J Smith	45 990			
	Cash	38 961			

In the accounts above, we see that the credit purchase from J Smith amounted to £45 990. In addition, we paid £38 961 for cash purchases. We also see that we paid J Smith £15 300 by cheque.

Example 3

Revenue

Date	Details	£	Date	Details	£
			31 May 2019	Cash	6 900
				J Jones	41 000

The above account shows us that we sold goods on credit to J Jones to the value of £41 000. A further amount of £6 900 was sold for cash.

Trade receivable – J Jones

Date	Details	£	Date	Details	£
31 May 2019	Sales	41 000			

Once we are able to interpret the various ledger accounts, we are closer to having a full understanding of double entry.

Before we continue, let us work through some examples which will help illustrate the duality of transactions and highlight the accounts that we debit and those that we credit.

WORKED EXAMPLE

Alex starts a new business selling office supplies on 1 January 2018. The first thing she does is to invest £8 000 into the business bank account.

Bank account

Date	Details	£	Date	Details	£
1 Jan 2018	Capital	8 000	2 Jan 2018	Purchases	1 200
4 Jan 2018	Sales	2 100	8 Jan 2018	Purchases	1 500
				Wages	110

On 1 January 2018, we debit the bank account (money paid into the bank, which is the receiver) and credit the owner's (Alex) capital account. This transaction tells us that Alex contributed additional cash to the business.

Capital account

Date	Details	£	Date	Details	£
			1 Jan 2018	Bank	8 000

We are now in a position to start up the business, having received the necessary capital from the owner.

On 2 January, Alex purchases, by cheque, some inventory for resale. Let us assume that she buys goods to the value of £1 200.

Purchases

Date	Details	£	Date	Details	£
2 Jan 2018	Bank	1 200			
8 Jan 2018	ABC	3 800			
	Bank	1 500			

We debit purchases with £1 200 and credit the bank account with a similar amount (note: we use one bank account for all transactions).

The important thing to notice in this last transaction is that we credit the bank account to decrease the value of the asset. We do not show a minus figure on the debit side, but a credit to the ledger account. After these transactions there is a positive bank balance of £6 800 and this will show as an asset of the business.

Having bought goods for resale, Alex then sells the goods on 4 January for £3 500. Of this amount, she receives a cheque for £2 100. The remainder of the transaction is a credit sale to G Bush.

Revenue

Date	Details	£	Date	Details	£
			4 Jan 2018	Bank	2 100
				G Bush	1 400

Trade receivable – G Bush

4 Jan 2018	Sales	1 400	

We credit the revenue account with the £3 500 (total) and debit the bank account with £2 100 and the trade receivable of G Bush with £1 400.

On 8 January, Alex buys additional goods for £5 300, of which £3 800 is bought on credit from I Supply & Co. She issues a cheque for £1 500 for the other purchases.

Trade payable – I Supply & Co.

Date	Details	£	Date	Details	£
			8 Jan 2018	Purchases	3 800

She hires D Smith to work with her and agrees to pay him a wage of £110 per day.

Wages

Date	Details	£	Date	Details	£
8 Jan 2018	Bank	110			

At the end of that day she would debit purchases with £5 000, credit the trade payable account of I Supply & Co. with £3 800 and credit the bank account with £1 200. She pays D Smith his wages for the day and so we debit the wages account and credit the bank account with £110.

Work through the worked example very carefully and make sure that you understand why we debit and why we credit various accounts. Once you are confident that you understand this example, you are ready to work through a number of additional activities on your own. You must at all times make sure that you are familiar with the debit and credit concept of the double-entry system.

ACTIVITY 4   SKILLS   ANALYSIS, PROBLEM SOLVING, EXECUTIVE FUNCTION

CASE STUDY: AKSHAY'S SPORTS GOODS STORE

Akshay has set up his business and is preparing to commence trading in his sports goods store as from 1 April 2019. Before he started to trade, he introduced capital of £30 000. This was by way of a cheque paid into the business on 25 March 2019. On the same day, he purchased a motor van and paid out £7 400 by cheque. In addition, he paid for shop fittings (£2 900), purchases (£7 100) and half the rent for April for the shop (£2 000). All these payments were made by cheque. He purchased, on credit, goods for resale from Tennis Ltd to the value of £3 400.

Akshay's business transactions for the first week in April 2019 are as follows:

1 April	Paid £150 by cheque to the local newspaper for an advertisement.
2 April	Paid £2 000 for the balance of rent due by cheque.
3 April	Sold goods for cash, £150.
4 April	Sold goods for cash, £210.
5 April	Sold goods for cash, £80.
6 April	Sold goods for cash, £153.
6 April	Purchased additional goods from Tennis Ltd on credit for £1 500.
7 April	Cash sales, £197.
7 April	Paid £120 wages to shop assistant in cash.
7 April	Paid £600 cash into the bank.

1 Open the necessary ledger accounts for all the above transactions and post the entries to those accounts. Make sure that both the debit and credit entries are made for each transaction.

At the end of this period, you would balance the cash and bank accounts. (If you have entered the accounts correctly, you will see that an amount of £70 remains in the cash account and that the bank account shows a balance of £9 050.)

ACTIVITY 5   SKILLS   ANALYSIS, PROBLEM SOLVING, EXECUTIVE FUNCTION

CASE STUDY: LARRY'S ANTIQUES

On 1 September 2018 Larry started an antiques business. The transactions for September 2018 were as follows:

1 September	Paid £40 000 into the business bank account.
2 September	Purchased antiques for £26 000. Cheque issued from the bank account.
4 September	Paid insurance premium of £980 for the year ending 31 September 2019. Payment was made by cheque.
10 September	Larry was charged £1 200 for packing material by Upack.
12 September	A bill was sent to Acquire for goods sold, £12 900.
19 September	A cheque for £8 000 was received from Acquire.
25 September	A bill for £5 300 was sent to Okay for antiques sold.
27 September	Larry paid D Brown, by cheque, wages of £1 100 for the month. Larry withdrew £2 000 from the bank account for personal use.
28 September	Goods invoiced for £1 900 were damaged and sent back by Okay for credit.

1 Prepare the ledger accounts for the month of September 2018.

ACTIVITY 6   SKILLS   ANALYSIS, PROBLEM SOLVING, EXECUTIVE FUNCTION

CASE STUDY: JACK'S COSMETICS STORE

On 1 July 2017, Jack opened a cosmetics store. He transferred £20 000 cash from a personal bank account to the business. During the remainder of the month he completed the following transactions, all of which were by cheque:

10 July	Paid rent, £900.
11 July	Purchased a delivery truck from MotoTrade for £15 000. He paid £7 000 on the date of purchase. The balance due is to be paid on 31 December 2017.

12 July	Purchased shelving and other fixtures, £3 700.
14 July	Purchased goods, £885.
14 July	Paid insurance premiums, £750.
15 July	Sold goods and received immediate payment of £1 200.
16 July	Purchased £1 240 worth of goods on credit from Hilcom Cosmetics.
17 July	Paid wages, £600.
24 July	Sold goods on credit for £3 100, to Monica.
27 July	Paid telephone expenses, £1 205.
27 July	Paid gas expenses, £173.
28 July	Received payment from Monica, £1 350.
31 July	Paid wages, £1 350.
31 July	Withdrew money for personal use, £1 500.

1 Write up all the above transactions to the relevant ledger accounts.

ACTIVITY 7　　SKILLS　ANALYSIS, PROBLEM SOLVING, EXECUTIVE FUNCTION

CASE STUDY: MEI'S CLOTHING BUSINESS

On 1 June 2018, Mei started a clothing business. During the month, Mei completed the following transactions, all of which were by cheque unless stated otherwise:

5 June　　Mei transferred £15 000 from a personal bank account to an account to be used for the business.

5 June　　Paid rent for the month, £1 950.

7 June　　Purchased office equipment on credit from File & Co. for £6 250.

8 June　　Purchased a used car for £16 000 from NuVan Ltd and paid £9 500 on account. The balance was payable in 6 months.

10 June　　Purchased goods, £725.

12 June　　Cash sales of £1 600.

15 June　　Paid wages to employees, £800.

20 June　　Paid insurance premiums of £725.

22 June　　Invoiced A Lu for clothes bought, £1 950.

24 June　　Received an invoice from NuVan Ltd for motor expenses, £310.

26 June　　Cash sales of £1 650.

28 June　　Purchased goods, £590.

29 June　　Paid gas and electricity expenses, £490.

29 June　　Paid other operating expenses, £195.

30 June　　Received from A Lu on account, £1 200.

30 June　　Paid wages to employees, £200.

30 June　　Paid File & Co. on account, £1 500.

30 June　　Withdrew money for personal use, £500.

1 Show the transactions in the ledger accounts.

ACTIVITY 8　　SKILLS　CRITICAL THINKING

CASE STUDY: DEBITS OR CREDITS?

You have learned a lot in this chapter. It is a good time to test your understanding. How many of these can you complete correctly without looking back?

	Debit	Credit
Trade payables		
Capital		
Loan from bank		
Postages		
Drawings		
Liability		
Revenue		
Non-current asset		
Purchases		
Trade receivables		

1 Indicate whether the above ledger accounts are normally debits or credits.

WHAT THE BOOKS TELL US

The various records contained in the books of account assist in providing an understanding of the financial health and growth potential of the business. In particular, they set out:

- how much the business owes to others, and how much others owe the business
- the details of income, expenses, assets and liabilities
- the source of profits or losses
- the profit or loss for any given period
- the value of the business.

Accounting does not, and cannot, be kept separate from other business activities – it reflects the activities of the business, which reacts and interacts with the external environment. This is influenced by many different forces which may be political, social, legal or economic.

Business decisions have social as well as economic consequences. Businesses must accept responsibility for the social implications of their activities, such as their impact on the environment or the extent to which employment opportunities are provided.

BALANCING THE LEDGER ACCOUNTS

After all transactions are entered (posted), the ledger accounts are balanced – i.e. the difference between the debit side and the credit side is calculated. This is usually done at the end of a trading period.

The balance is transferred, as a single amount, to the following period, or to the **statement of profit or loss and other comprehensive income**, and to the **statement of financial position** (see Chapter 10).

Wages

Date	Details	£	Date	Details	£
31 March	Cash	800	30 June	Statement of profit or loss	2 700
30 April	Cash	600			
31 May	Cash	900			
30 June	Cash	400			
		2 700			2 700

In the above example, wages have been paid from March until June. At the end of June, a statement of profit or loss and other comprehensive income is to be prepared and therefore the total of the ledger account is transferred to the statement of profit or loss and other comprehensive income at that date. As the full amount (£2 700) is transferred, there is no balance on this account.

The balance is the amount by which one side of the account exceeds the other side. This allows you to see, at a glance, a single amount for each ledger account – what is in the bank, the value of trade receivables, or what we owe.

To balance an account there are a number of steps that we have to take. These are:
- add the money columns on the debit and credit sides and find the difference (the balance)
- enter the balance on the side where the total is less than the other. This is the balance carried down (c/d)
- the two sides are now equal, and the totals are written on the same line on each side and ruled off with a single line above and a double line below the total
- the balance is brought down (b/d) to the side with the higher total. Write this balance immediately below the total. This completes the double entry which is inherent in the balancing process
- the balance b/d is the opening balance for the next period.

The following account illustrates the above process:

Cash account

Date	Details	£	Date	Details	£
3 April	Sales	150	7 April	Bank	600
4 April	Sales	210	7 April	Wages	120
5 April	Sales	80	7 April	Balance c/d	70
6 April	Sales	153			
7 April	Sales	197			
		790			790
8 April	Balance b/d	70			

We have referred to the balancing of the accounts 'at the end of a period'. We must, however, understand that accounts can be balanced at any time, even when the ledger page is full and we need to carry the balance forward on to a new page. Usually, we balance the accounts at the end of a month, or year, as it is then that we prepare the financial statements.

EXAM HINT

When balancing off accounts with a balance c/d figure, ensure you complete the double entry by entering the balance b/d in the ledger account.

Do not use abbreviations for balances carried down and brought down. The minimum acceptable is likely to be Bal c/d and Bal b/d.

ACTIVITY 9   SKILLS   ANALYSIS, PROBLEM SOLVING, EXECUTIVE FUNCTION

CASE STUDY: OLIVIER

Olivier commenced business on 1 January 2018. He paid an amount of £11 000 by cheque as capital and he also received a cheque for £7 000 as a loan from A Turner. The transactions for the six months, ending 30 June, were as follows:

Account	Amount £
Drawings	9 000
Cash received from trade receivables	12 500
Cash paid to trade payables	15 300
Expenses paid	7 900
Credit purchases	34 200
Cash purchases	21 900
Payment for motor vehicle	18 000
Cash sales	9 400
Credit sales	32 000
Returns inward	325
Returns outward	197

1 Show the bank account (all cash is banked immediately) as well as ledger accounts of the sales and purchases for the six months. The trade receivables and trade payables accounts at 30 June 2018 should also be shown.
2 Balance off the accounts at 30 June 2018 and bring down the balances at 1 July.

(Note: you can ignore dates in this answer. However, in most exam questions you must show the dates and carry down balances on the ledger accounts.)

Once we have balanced off the ledger accounts, the balances are then transferred to the trial balance. All debit balances are shown on the left side of the trial balance and all credit balances are on the right. After entering all the balances, we total them to ensure that it balances. For more details on this, see Chapter 7.

From this balanced trial balance we are then in a position to prepare the financial statements. We no longer have to go through the various ledger accounts to find information – it is all in one place: the trial balance.

At this stage it is important that you practise balancing off various ledger accounts. In the following examples you are given ledger accounts with opening balances and details of transactions for the following month. Enter these transactions and then balance off the accounts as explained above.

ACTIVITY 10   SKILLS ANALYSIS, PROBLEM SOLVING, EXECUTIVE FUNCTION

CASE STUDY: ANN

Ann owns a travel agency. You are presented with the following ledger account in Ann's books. The account gives details of the bank transactions for the month of July 2019.

Bank

Date	Details	£	Date	Details	£
1 Jul 2019	Capital	40 000	10 Jul 2019	Rent	1 900
15 Jul 2019	Sales	3 587	11 Jul 2019	Computer	2 100
28 Jul 2019	Trade receivables	2 984	12 Jul 2019	Phone	156
31 Jul 2019	Interest	143	14 Jul 2019	Purchases	1 123
	Sales	1 988		Drawings	1 200
			17 Jul 2019	Wages	950
			27 Jul 2019	Printer	287
				Electricity	342
			31 Jul 2019	Wages	1 980
				Insurance	3 500

1 Balance this account and show the opening balance at 1 August 2019.

ACTIVITY 11   SKILLS ▶ ANALYSIS, PROBLEM SOLVING, EXECUTIVE FUNCTION

CASE STUDY: CASH ACCOUNT

Cash account

Date	Details	£	Date	Details	£
1 Sept 2018	Loan	4 000	10 Sept 2018	Wages	1 000
15 Sept 2018	Revenue	2 000	11 Sept 2018	Rent	2 000
28 Oct 2018	Commission	500	12 Oct 2018	Postage	100
31 Oct 2018	Interest	850	14 Nov 2018	Purchases	2 300
11 Nov 2018	Revenue	2 300	19 Nov 2018	Wages	500
			24 Nov 2018	Purchases	900
			27 Nov 2018	Rent	1 000

1 Balance the cash account for September, October and November 2018.
2 Post the payments made for purchases and wages and show the balances on each of those accounts at 30 November 2018.

CARRY FORWARDS

Do not confuse the various terms used. We have read about the terms 'b/d' and 'c/d' earlier in the chapter. In addition, you will come across two other terms – carried forward (c/f) and brought forward (b/f). These terms are not used in carrying down a balance on an account. The only time they are used is when we carry an amount forward, from one page of the ledger to another. We add the two sides and carry forward the total of each side to the next page. At the top of the next page we show each total as having been brought forward. An example is shown below.

Cash account

Date	Details	£	Date	Details	£
3 April	Sales	150	7 April	Bank	600
4 April	Sales	210	7 April	Wages	120
5 April	Sales	80			
	Balance c/f	440		Balance c/f	720

As the ledger account continues on to the following page, we need to transfer the balances at the end of page one to page two. We do this by 'carrying forward' the balances from one page to the next.

Cash account

Date	Details	£	Date	Details	£
5 April	Balance b/f	440	7 April	Balance b/f	720
6 April	Sales	153	8 April	Balance c/d	70
7 April	Sales	197			
		790			790
8 April	Balance b/d	70			

ACTIVITY 12   SKILLS ▶ ANALYSIS, PROBLEM SOLVING, EXECUTIVE FUNCTION

CASE STUDY: MARIA'S GIFT SHOP

Maria started a gift shop on 1 March 2019. The following cheque payments were made during the month:

1 March	Maria transferred £10 000 to the business.
1 March	Paid rent for office, £500.
3 March	Purchased goods from Gift Wholesalers, £2 900.
8 March	Paid Gift Wholesalers on account, £1 000.
11 March	Cash sales, £21 500.
29 March	Withdrew cash for personal use, £1 000.
30 March	Paid motor expenses, £1 900, and other operating expenses, £1 050.
30 March	Paid office salaries, £4 000.

1 Prepare all the ledger accounts for the above transactions and balance them at the month end.
2 What is the total revenue recorded in the ledger?
3 State the amount of total expenses for the month.
4 What is the net income for March? (Assume that all goods purchased have been sold.)

EXAM HINT

You must remember to make two entries for each double-entry transaction – one Dr entry and one Cr entry. The debit entry values must equal the credit entry values.

There are a number of mnemonics which can be used to help you remember the rules of double entry. It is important you choose the one that works for you.

DEAD CLIC **Dr** Expenses, Assets and Drawings

Cr Liabilities, Income and Capital

CLEAR **C**apital, **L**iability, **E**xpenses, **A**ssets and **R**evenue

PEARLS **Dr** PEA **P**urchases, **E**xpenses and **A**ssets

Cr RLS **R**evenue, **L**iabilities and **S**ales

Given that accounting terminology is always being amended, none are perfect, but all offer some help.

CHECKPOINT

1 Every transaction requires a debit entry and a credit entry. True or false?

2 What is a ledger?

3 What are drawings?

4 What are assets?

5 If a business receives cash, on what side of the cash account is the entry?

6 Wages are an asset. True or false?

7 State three possible expenses.

8 State three possible assets.

9 Explain how ledger accounts are balanced.

SUBJECT VOCABULARY

assets resources that are owned and used by the business

bring down (or carry down) the amount entered as the opening balance in the next accounting period, which is the balancing figure calculated for the current financial period. It is entered on the opposite side in the new financial period, this maintains the double entry

capital account the fixed account of a partner showing capital introduced or withdrawn

credit entry (Cr) an entry on the right-hand side of the ledger account

current assets resources which are converted to cash within one year

current liabilities amounts owed that are payable within one year

debit entry (Dr) an entry on the left-hand side of the ledger account

drawings resources removed from the business by the owner; these could be cash or inventory

expenses cost incurred by the business in generating revenue

inventory (stock) raw material, work in progress and finished goods held by a business

ledger account an account containing the double entry

liabilities the debts of a business owed to others

non-current assets (fixed assets) assets held by a business for more than one year

non-current liabilities (long-term liabilities) amounts owed with a repayment date greater than one year

purchases inventory bought for resale

revenue (or income) the monetary value of sales made by a business

sales inventory sold in the normal course of business to customers

statement of financial position one of two financial statements that shows the assets, capital and liabilities of a business

statement of profit or loss and other comprehensive income one of two financial statements which shows the profits or losses of the business

trade payables the total of all the individual persons and businesses that a business owes money to and will pay within one year

trade receivables the total of all the individual persons and businesses that owe money and will repay within one year

EXAM PRACTICE

CASE STUDY: FRAN'S CANDLE SHOP

SKILLS   EXECUTIVE FUNCTION, CRITICAL THINKING, REASONING

Fran opens a shop selling candles and home decorations. The following cheque transactions have been made by Fran during the month of August 2018. The opening balance in the bank account was £225 Dr.

Account	£
Capital introduced	20 000
Computer	1 500
Drawings	2 000
Electricity	415
Insurance	1 200
Interest paid	55
Purchases	4 000
Rent	15 000
Revenue	3 500
Wages	1 100

Q

1 Prepare the ledger account for this bank account. Balance the account and show the opening balance at 1 September 2018. (Dates not required.) **(12 marks)**
2 Explain the significance of the credit balance brought down (b/d) in the bank account. **(4 marks)**
3 Explain the difference between drawings and expenses. **(4 marks)**

3 DOUBLE-ENTRY SYSTEM 2

LEARNING OBJECTIVES

After you have studied this chapter, you should be able to:
- record transactions in the books of prime entry
- account for end-of-period transfers and adjustments
- create and maintain ledger accounts for the allowance/provision for irrecoverable debts
- evaluate the use of information and communication technology in the recording of transactions and the preparation of reconciliations and financial statements.

GETTING STARTED

Your business has a lot of transactions covering buying products and raw materials from different suppliers, so you sell and raise invoices to many suppliers. This generates many original documents. How do you record them? Where do you record them? Would it be better to use paper records, or could you use information and communication technology to record and process your paperwork?

RECORDING TRANSACTIONS IN THE BOOKS OF PRIME ENTRY

Most businesses issue and receive vast numbers of invoices, receipts, credit notes and paying-in slips. These documents are known as source documents. In order to keep track of all this information, a business will summarise and record these on a daily basis. In fact, books of prime entry are also referred to as day books or subsidiary books. The books used by most businesses are shown below.

Book of prime entry	Transactions recorded
Purchases day book	Credit purchases from suppliers
Purchase returns (returns outwards)* day book	Returns out of purchases
Revenue day book	Credit sales to customers
Revenue returns (returns inwards)** day book	Returns in of goods sold
Cash book	Bank and cash transactions and cash discounts
The journal	For all transactions not covered by the other day books

*Purchase returns are also known as returns outwards – either term is acceptable in the exam.
**Revenue returns are also known as returns inwards – either term is acceptable in the exam.

Except for the cash book, all these books of prime entry are memorandum books and are used to collect transactions of a similar nature. By doing this, we can reduce the number of entries in the ledger accounts.

These books are used to record the first details of business transactions. What are these details? They are invoices for goods purchased or sold by the business. When goods are returned, either by the business, or by a customer of the business, a credit note is issued. These credit notes are also transactions that have to be recorded. All these transactions are listed in the relevant subsidiary books as they occur.

At the month end, the totals are posted to the relevant ledger accounts, e.g. revenue, purchases, returns inwards (revenue returns) and returns outwards (purchase returns).

PURCHASES DAY BOOK

A large majority of the transactions of a business consist of buying goods for resale. This results in a considerable number of purchase invoices, which are recorded in the purchase day book. These purchases are entered in total, to the debit of the purchases account and a credit to the individual trade payable accounts.

The ruling of the purchases day book is as follows:

Date	Supplier	Total of invoice £
1 July	ABC	1 175.50
4 July	XYZ	2 350.00

WORKED EXAMPLE

We are going to write up the purchases day book for Julian for April 2019. The following is a list of purchases made by him during the month.

1 April	Bought goods on credit from Thomas for £3 400.
5 April	Bought goods on credit from Geoffrey. The price was £1 600.
11 April	Bought goods on credit from Jay for £900.
19 April	Bought goods on credit from Thomas for £600.
28 April	Bought goods on credit from Geoffrey. The price was £900.

We add these figures together and rule off the total with a single line above and a double line below. From the total columns of the day book, we can then post in a single figure to the appropriate ledger accounts. The total net amount of £7 400 is posted to purchases. At the end of each line, the total invoice amount will be posted to the individual trade payables accounts.

Purchases day book

Date	Supplier	Net amount £
01 Apr 2019	Thomas	3 400
05 Apr 2019	Geoffrey	1 600
11 Apr 2019	Jay	900
19 Apr 2019	Thomas	600
28 Apr 2019	Geoffrey	900
	Total for April 2019	7 400

Purchases

Date	Details	£	Date	Details	£
	Purchase journal	7 400			

Jay

				Purchases	900

Thomas

				Purchases	3 400
				Purchases	600

Geoffrey

				Purchases	1 600
				Purchases	900

PURCHASES RETURNS BOOK

When goods are returned to a supplier, a credit note is received from them and this is recorded in a purchases returns book. The full amount of the credit note is debited to the supplier's account, with the totals entered to the purchases returns (returns outwards) account.

Date	Supplier	Net amount £
1 July	ABC	1 000

WORKED EXAMPLE

Based on the information provided, we will write up the purchases returns book for Julian for April 2019. The following returns of goods were made by Julian during the month.

6 April	Julian returned goods to Geoffrey and a credit note was issued for £100.
20 April	Julian returned goods to Thomas and a credit note was issued for £300.

Purchases return day book

Date	Supplier	Net amount £
06 Apr 2019	Geoffrey	100
20 Apr 2019	Thomas	300
	Total April 2019	400

Thomas

Date	Details	£	Date	Details	£
	Returns out	300			

Geoffrey

	Returns	100			

Purchases returns

				Purchases returns day book	400

From the total columns of the day book we can post to the respective ledger account. The total amount of £400 is posted to the credit of the purchases returns account. At the end of each line, the total of each credit note is debited to the individual trade payables account.

ACTIVITY 1   SKILLS   PROBLEM SOLVING, EXECUTIVE FUNCTION

CASE STUDY: BORIS

Boris owns a building and decorating business. He purchased goods to install a kitchen. The following is a list of transactions for Boris in July 2018.

| 5 July | Bought goods on credit from Jay & Co., £260. |

8 July	Bought goods on credit from T Williams, £660.
21 July	Bought goods on credit from H Henry, £540.
26 July	Bought goods on credit from J Jones, £200.
29 July	Bought goods on credit from Green & Co., £900.

In addition to the above transactions, Boris also returned certain goods to various suppliers:

| 2 July | Returned goods to H Henry, £140. |
| 23 July | Returned goods to J Jones, £80. |

1 Enter the above transactions into the purchases day book and the purchases returns day book and indicate the accounts to be debited and credited.

ACTIVITY 2   SKILLS   PROBLEM SOLVING, EXECUTIVE FUNCTION

CASE STUDY: LEON

Leon owns a shop selling stationery. The following transactions show his purchases for the month of March 2019.

2019	Transaction	£
3 March	Bought goods on credit from Jay	914
6 March	Bought goods on credit from Emma	432
	Returned goods to Jay	106
8 March	Bought goods on credit from Jay	317
18 March	Bought goods on credit from Jay	204
	Paid cash for goods for resale	123
	Returned goods purchased for cash	119
22 March	Bought goods on credit from Emma	543
25 March	Bought goods on credit from Zanc	802
26 March	Returned goods purchased for cash	105
	Discount received on purchase from Jay	182
31 March	Bought goods on credit from Jay	167
	Returned goods to Jay	198

1 Write up the purchases and purchases returns day books for Leon to record the relevant transactions shown above. You also need to show the ledger account for purchases for March 2019.
2 Using the relevant day books, record all the above transactions and then enter the totals to the purchases account and the purchases returns account.

ACTIVITY 3   SKILLS   PROBLEM SOLVING, EXECUTIVE FUNCTION

CASE STUDY: BELLA

Bella's business sells homemade soaps and other bath products. The transactions below are for her business in the month of August 2018.

2018	Transaction	£
3 Aug	Bought goods on credit from Jay & Co.	1 200
6 Aug	Bought goods on credit from T Singh	1 400
	Returned goods to Jay & Co.	400
8 Aug	Bought goods on credit from Green & Co.	1 000
18 Aug	Bought goods on credit from Jay & Co.	400
22 Aug	Bought goods on credit from Jay & Co.	500
25 Aug	Bought goods on credit from H Henry	800
31 Aug	Bought goods on credit from T Singh	1 800
	Returned goods to Jay & Co.	120

1 Write up the purchases and purchases returns day books for Bella to record all the transactions set out above. You also need to show the ledger account for purchases and purchases returned.

REVENUE DAY BOOK

As sales are the most important and frequent transactions for a business, some form of summary needs to be kept so that there aren't too many entries and repetitive detail. This summary is kept in the revenue day book, which lists all the credit sales and only the total amount is posted to the trade receivables account and the control account.

All credit sales made by a business are invoiced and these invoices are posted to the credit of the revenue account with the relevant debit to the trade receivables control account. (In the case of a cash sale, the debit is shown in the cash book as the money is received immediately.)

The ruling of the revenue day book would be as follows:

Date	Invoice no.	Customer	Net amount £
1 July	1234	XYZ	100
4 July	5678	ABC	200
			300

WORKED EXAMPLE

You are given Jason's transactions for the month of July 2019:

8 July	Inv. 2	Sold goods on credit to Colin, £160.
11 July	Inv. 3	Sold goods on credit to Ari, £360.
21 July	Inv. 4	Sold goods on credit to Christelle, £240.
24 July	Inv. 5	Sold goods on credit to Jacques, £300.
31 July	Inv. 6	Sold goods on credit to Sophia, £180.

You will need to enter the above transactions into the revenue day book, as shown below, and indicate the accounts to be debited and credited.

Revenue day book

Date	Invoice no.	Customer	Net amount £
8 July	2	Colin	160
11 July	3	Ari	360
21 July	4	Christelle	240
24 July	5	Jacques	300
31 July	6	Sophia	180
	Totals		£1 240

The total of each invoice is posted to the debit of the individual customer and the net invoice amount of £1 240 is credited to revenue.

REVENUE RETURNS BOOK

When goods are returned by a customer the business issues a credit note. The credit note is entered into the revenue returns book and posted to the credit of the trade receivables control account. Details of each credit sales return transaction are shown in the revenue returns day book. The totals, usually at month end, are posted to the debit of the revenue returns account.

Date	Credit note no.	Customer	Net amount £
1 July	987	XYZ	10
9 July	432	ABC	20
			30

WORKED EXAMPLE

Jason owns a toy shop. During July 2019, a number of customers returned goods to him:

10 July	Credit note (CN) 6	Goods of £40 were returned by Ari.
22 July	CN 7	Goods of £60 were returned by Christelle.
29 July	CN 8	Goods of £180 were returned by Jacques.

Revenue returns book

Date	CN no.	Customer	Net amount £
10 July	6	Ari	40
22 July	7	Christelle	60
29 July	8	Jacques	180
		Totals	£280

A debit would be entered to the revenue returns account for £280. The trade receivables accounts would be credited individually with the total amount of the credit notes.

Returns in

Date	Details	£	Date	Details	£
31 July	Revenue returns	280			

Ari

Date	Details	£	Date	Details	£
			10 July	Returns in	40

Christelle

Date	Details	£	Date	Details	£
			22 July	Returns in	60

Jacques

Date	Details	£	Date	Details	£
			29 July	Returns in	180

ACTIVITY 4   SKILLS ▸ EXECUTIVE FUNCTION, PROBLEM SOLVING

CASE STUDY: SHAY

2019	Transaction	£
6 Mar	Sold goods on credit to Dee	375
	Cash sales banked	874
	Cash sale customer returned damaged goods	114
11 Mar	Sold goods on credit to Gert	192
12 Mar	Sold goods on credit to Henry	109
26 Mar	Sold goods on credit to Gert	147
29 Mar	Sold goods on credit to Gert	314
	Sold goods on credit to Henry	719

1 Write up the revenue and revenue returns day books for Shay, to record the relevant transactions set out above.
2 Using the relevant day books, record all the transactions in the correct ledger account.

ACTIVITY 5   SKILLS ▸ PROBLEM SOLVING, EXECUTIVE FUNCTION

CASE STUDY: JASON

2019	Transaction	£
5 Aug	Sold goods on credit to Jacques	2 400
11 Aug	Sold goods on credit to Ari	1 600
12 Aug	Sold goods on credit to Sophia	440
18 Aug	Sophia returned goods	240
26 Aug	Sold goods on credit to Sophia	1 440
	Ari returned goods	480
29 Aug	Sold goods on credit to Christelle	860
31 Aug	Sold goods on credit to Ari	640

1 Write up the revenue and revenue returns day books for Jason, to record all the transactions set out above. You also need to show the ledger account for revenue and revenue returns.

THE JOURNAL

Journals are often called day books and are not part of the double-entry system. They store details of the transactions that are entered into the accounts. The journal is used for transactions that are not regular, for example, the sale of a non-current asset. We will deal with this form of journal in the following paragraphs.

WHY USE A JOURNAL?

No transaction can be entered straight into the ledger. They must first be recorded in a book of prime entry and then posted to the ledger. The journal is used for items which cannot be conveniently entered into any other books of prime entry. All journals are books of original entry because they record the first details of the transactions.

There are many instances when we would make use of the journal instead of another subsidiary book. For example:

- when we buy or sell a non-current asset on credit (if we paid cash, then it would be entered via the cash book)
- to write off any irrecoverable debts
- to correct errors
- when we adjust entries, such as adjustments for other payables and other receivables
- for any year-end adjustments for depreciation
- to transfer amounts between accounts (inter-ledger transfers).

Figure 1 gives an example of a journal. Here, the first money column is for the debit entry and the second money column is for the credit entries.

When we enter items into the journal, we must decide which account is to be debited and which account is to be credited. An important part of the journal entry is the narration – that is, the 'story'. This describes the reason for making the journal entry. Without this we would often not know or understand why the journal entry was made.

It is extremely important that you familiarise yourselves with the journal as you have to plan, in advance, the account(s) to be debited and the account(s) to receive the relevant credit. To be a complete entry, you must ensure that it is properly dated and described (the narration). All too often in answering examination questions, a near-perfect journal entry loses marks because the student has failed to put in the date or narration.

Date		Details	Folio	DR		CR	

▲ Figure 1 Example of a journal

WORKED EXAMPLE

On 1 August 2019, A Ltd purchased from X Motors a delivery van for the business. The purchase price was £8 000 and X Motors agreed that the total amount was payable over eight months. We are going to record this transaction.

As payment is not made by cheque (and therefore there is no cash book entry), we must record it via the journal.

		£	£
		Dr	Cr
1 Aug 2019	Delivery van	8 000	
	X Motors		8 000
	Purchase price of new van		
	from X Motors payable over		
	8 months as from 1 August		
	2019*.		

*This statement is known as the narration.

We have a trade receivable, J Smith, who owes us £300. He became insolvent (unable to pay his debt) on 30 June 2019 and therefore we need to write off the amount owing to us. To do this, we can only use the journal.

		£ Dr	£ Cr
30 Jun 2019	Irrecoverable debts	300	
	J Smith		300
	Amount owing by J Smith on his account now written off due to his insolvency.		

On 31 August 2019, we buy a new machine for our factory from Planters Ltd. The purchase price is £1 500 and the payment will be made on 30 November 2019.

		£ Dr	£ Cr
31 Aug 2019	Plant and machinery	1 500	
	Planters Ltd		1 500
	Purchase of plant and machinery.		
	Payment due on 30 Nov 2019.		

J Smith owes us £130 for goods that we sold to him. At the same time, we also purchased goods from him for the business. On 30 June 2019, we owe J Smith a total of £90 on his trade payables account. On the same day, he sends us a cheque for £40 to settle his account. In the entry below, we use the journal to offset the £90 credit balance with the £90 debit balance. This is called set-off.

The journal entry would be:

		£ Dr	£ Cr
30 Jun 2019	J Smith (trade payable)	90	
	J Smith (trade receivable)		90
	An offset of the trade receivables and trade payables accounts at 30 June 2019.		

ACTIVITY 6   SKILLS   ANALYSIS, PROBLEM SOLVING, EXECUTIVE FUNCTION

CASE STUDY: DEE'S JOURNAL

Dee owes £162. She pays £102 on 31 July 2018 but makes no further payments. On 3 October 2018 she is declared bankrupt and we are informed that we will receive 20p in the £ on whatever is still owing. We receive this amount on 30 November 2018.

1 Calculate the amount of the irrecoverable debt for the year ended 31 December 2018. Show the journal entry for the irrecoverable debt and also the trade receivables ledger account.

ACTIVITY 7   SKILLS   ANALYSIS, PROBLEM SOLVING, EXECUTIVE FUNCTION

CASE STUDY: RAJESH'S NEW BUSINESS

Rajesh starts up a new business on 11 May 2017. He purchased a homewares shop, including certain assets and liabilities from the previous owner. The following is the list of assets and liabilities purchased:

	£
Property	15 000
Electricity due	170
Inventory	7 960
Trade payables	960
Trade receivables	410
Overdraft	3 420
Equipment	11 640

Rajesh paid for the net assets from his personal bank account. The net amount paid is regarded as his capital in the business.

1 Make the necessary journal entries to record the transactions.

THE CASH BOOK

Two very important accounts are the cash account and the bank account. We need to know on a daily basis what funds the business has and watch the flow of funds closely. These two accounts are kept in the cash book. The cash book is classed as a ledger.

Details of receipts and payments are kept in a separate book (or ledger) – the cash book, which is a book of prime (original) entry and a division of the ledger. Only the cash book can properly be described as a ledger account and the balances in the cash book are taken directly to the trial balance.

Importantly, the cash book is part of the double-entry system. All cash and bank transactions are first entered into this book and then afterwards posted to the ledger to complete the double entry.

All entries on the debit side of the cash book are posted to the credit side of the relevant accounts and vice versa. To check the cash balance and make sure it is correct we can count the cash on hand and see that it agrees with the balance shown in our ledger account (cash book).

In the case of the bank account in the cash book there are other transactions such as bank charges that the bank may be taking from our bank account, but we do not yet know about them. Therefore, we need to reconcile (agree) our bank balance in the cash book with that of the records kept by the bank.

THE THREE-COLUMN CASH BOOK

This shows receipts and payments by cash and bank but also has an additional column on each side for cash discounts. By using the extra column for recording the discount we are able to post both discount received and discount allowed, in total, instead of individually.

Discount received occurs when a supplier allows us to pay a little less for the goods ordered because we have made a prompt payment. Discount allowed is when we accept a smaller amount than originally invoiced (billed) from a customer for prompt payment. Discount received and discount allowed are known as 'cash discounts' even though the invoice may be paid by cheque.

WORKED EXAMPLE

The following example illustrates a three-column cash book and two ledger accounts to which items in the cash book are posted. For this example you would also need to making postings to the revenue, trade payables, wages, purchases and discount received ledgers.

Note that the item for discount allowed (shown on the debit side of the cash book) is posted to the **DEBIT** side of discount allowed in the ledger. The credit entry for this discount is posted to the trade receivables ledger account.

In a similar way the discount received entry from the credit side of the cash book is posted to the **CREDIT** side of the discount received account, with a corresponding debit entry to the trade payables' account.

Cash book

Date	Details	Discount allowed	Cash	Bank	Date	Details	Discount received	Cash	Bank
4 Jul 19	Receivable	20		103	3 Jul 19	Payable	14		139
9 Jul 19	Revenue		9	51	6 Jul 19	Wages			140
31 Jul 19	Revenue		89	404	31 Jul 19	Purchase		35	200
						Balance c/d		63	79
		20	98	558			14	98	558
1 Aug 19	Balance b/d		63	79					

Trade receivables

					Date	Details			
					4 Jul 19	Bank			103
						Disc allowed			20

Discount allowed

Date	Details			
31 Jul 19	Cash book			20

We must remember that the discount column is a 'memorandum' column and as such is not part of the double-entry system. The total of the discount columns must be entered to the relevant ledger accounts, e.g. total discount received will be posted to the credit side of the discount received account. The total of the discount allowed column will be debited to the discount allowed account.

TRADE DISCOUNTS

When we buy goods, we are sometimes given a **trade discount**, which is a reduction in the list price because we are buying large quantities or reselling to an end user. This discount is not shown in the books as it is deducted before the purchase is entered. It must not be confused with a cash discount, which is when the supplier offers an incentive for a prompt payment.

CASH DISCOUNTS

A business tries to collect its outstanding trade receivables as quickly as possible. To do this it sometimes offers an incentive – a discount for cash. In effect, the business tells the customer that if the amount owing is paid within a certain time (e.g. 30 days from invoice), the customer would be entitled to an additional discount (over and above any trade discount already given).

END-OF-PERIOD TRANSFERS AND ADJUSTMENTS

At the end of the accounting period the double-entry accounts need to be balanced so that the financial statements can be prepared. As we have seen, the balance carried down on an account arises when the debit and credit entries are unequal. The balances in the ledgers and cash book are used to produce the trial balance (see Chapter 7), which acts as an arithmetical check on the accuracy of the double-entry system and helps in the preparation of the financial statements.

The **general ledger** accounts that record the revenues (sales, rent received) and expenses (insurance, motor vehicle expenses) of a business will have the balances transferred to the statement of profit or loss and other comprehensive income. Not all accounts will be closed down, as they are needed for the next accounting period. The asset and liability accounts will have the balances carried down to the next period and these balances will be transferred into the statement of financial position.

The balances for the revenue and expense accounts are transferred to the statement of profit or loss and other comprehensive income, while the balance on the bank account, an asset, is carried forward to the next accounting period.

The receipts of revenue (income) and the payment of expenses do not always happen at the same time

WORKED EXAMPLE

The following transactions took place during the month of December for Bilal. All transactions were paid by cheque:

2 Dec	Sold all inventory for £3 750.
14 Dec	Paid wages of £1 000 and general expenses of £500.
28 Dec	Paid wages of £500.

At the start of December, Bilal had a bank balance of £1 000 (Dr). We will prepare the ledger accounts for the end of December, showing the transfers to the statement of profit or loss and other comprehensive income and the balances carried forward to the next financial period.

Wages

Date	Details	£	Date	Details	£
14 Dec	Bank	1 000	31 Dec	Statement of profit or loss	1 500
28 Dec	Bank	500			
		1 500			1 500

General expenses

Date	Details	£	Date	Details	£
14 Dec	Bank	500	31 Dec	Statement of profit or loss	500
		500			500

Revenue

Date	Details	£	Date	Details	£
31 Dec	Statement of profit or loss	3 750	2 Dec	Bank	3 750
		3 750			3 750

Bank

Date	Details	£	Date	Details	£
1 Dec	Balance b/d	1 000	14 Dec	Wages	1 000
2 Dec	Revenue	3 750	14 Dec	General expenses	500
			28 Dec	Wages	500
			31 Dec	Balance c/d	2 750
		4 750			4 750
1 Jan	Balance b/d	2 750			

as the business's financial year end. Sometimes an expense will still be owing at the end of the year – wages may have been **incurred** but not paid for, or insurance may have been paid in advance for a period of months, some of which are in the next financial period. These are known as other payables and other receivables and are covered in detail in Chapter 11.

In order to provide accurate and useful information, year-end adjustments to these accounts must be made so that only the expense or revenue relevant to that financial period is included in the financial statement. The accounting concepts behind this treatment are covered in Chapter 4.

At the end of the accounting period, a business will prepare financial statements. The end-of-period transfers and adjustment will ensure that:

- all revenue earned in the period has been accounted for
- all expenses relating to that revenue have been accounted for
- all assets and liabilities at the period end are accurately recorded in the ledgers.

IRRECOVERABLE DEBTS AND ALLOWANCE/ PROVISION FOR IRRECOVERABLE DEBTS

We sell on credit and expect to be paid. But this does not always happen, and businesses often have to write off amounts owing to them because of irrecoverable debts. To do this, we debit the irrecoverable debt account and credit the trade receivables account.

The balance on the irrecoverable debts account is then written off to the statement of profit or loss and other comprehensive income at the year end as an expense for the period. The trade receivables balances, as shown in the statement of financial position, are reduced by the amount of the irrecoverable debt written off.

WORKED EXAMPLE

Hilda Hardware sells goods to Smythe during the 2018 financial year. The total sales to 30 April 2018 were £872. On 12 May 2018, Smythe pays Hilda Hardware £220 on account. In September 2018 Hilda Hardware is informed that Smythe is insolvent and no further payments can be expected.

You are asked to show the ledger accounts for the above transactions.

Smythe

Date	Details	£	Date	Details	£
30 April	Sales	872	12 May	Bank	220
			30 Sept	Irrecoverable debt	652
		872			872

Irrecoverable debts

Date	Details	£	Date	Details	£
30 Sept	Smythe	652	31 Dec	Statement of profit or loss	652

After balancing off Smythe's account, we have transferred the irrecoverable debt – £652 – to the irrecoverable debts account. We rule off the totals with a double line underneath.

ALLOWANCE/PROVISION FOR IRRECOVERABLE DEBTS

We do not always know that a trade receivable is or will become irrecoverable – there is sometimes just a risk that we may not get paid. Based on this, we estimate the percentage of trade receivables that may not pay in the future because prudence (being sensible and careful) demands that we do so. (The concept of prudence is discussed fully in Chapter 4.)

This estimate is known as an **allowance/provision for irrecoverable debts**. This, like other financial arrangements, is an amount set aside for a known expense where the amount is not definite.

In a way, this financial arrangement is similar to writing off an irrecoverable debt as it serves to reduce the total trade receivables as shown in the statement of financial position, and any change in the allowance is also shown in the statement of profit or loss and other comprehensive income as an expense.

The allowance that we create is only an estimate of the possible amount of future irrecoverable debts. We could examine each and every trade receivable account and see if the amount is likely to be paid. If not, then we could allow for that trade receivable to form part of the allowance. This can be very time-consuming and can also only be an estimate.

We could analyse the trade receivables balances into an age category. The longer a trade receivable is outstanding, the more likely it is that it will ultimately become irrecoverable. By doing this, we are able to allocate a fixed percentage to the different 'ages' of the trade receivables and so arrive at an amount for the allowance. Here, too, the amount is an estimate but less time-consuming than the first alternative.

In the table below, an age analysis of trade receivables and the calculation of the amount of the allowance is shown.

Analysis of trade receivables by age

Months outstanding	Amount of trade receivables £	Percentage doubtful	Allowance amount £
Under 1 month	8 800	0.5%	44
1 to 3 months	11 200	1.5%	168
4 to 6 months	2 000	3.0%	60
6 to 12 months	1 000	5.0%	50
Over 12 months	1 500	10.0%	150
Totals	24 500		472

Each year, after writing off all known irrecoverable debts, we calculate the amount of the allowance. The difference is either an additional expense (when the allowance increases) or is shown as a credit to the statement of profit or loss and other comprehensive income (when the allowance is reduced).

In accounting terms, we can say that if the allowance is greater than it was in the previous year then we must debit the statement of profit or loss and other comprehensive income with the additional amount and credit the allowance account. On the other hand, if the allowance is less, then the excess must be credited to the statement of profit or loss and other comprehensive income and deducted (debited) from the allowance account.

A decrease in the allowance/provision for irrecoverable debts is an income and added to **gross profit**. An increase in the allowance/provision for irrecoverable debts is an expense and increases expenses and decreases profit for the year.

WORKED EXAMPLE

A business has trade receivables of £250 000 on 31 December 2018. It anticipates that 5 per cent of them will not pay their debts. You are required to calculate the amount to be charged in the statement of profit or loss and other comprehensive income and show the presentation of trade receivables as it would appear in the statement of financial position.

Trade receivables

Date	Details	£	Date	Details	£
31 Dec 2018	Balance b/d	250 000			

Allowance/provision for irrecoverable debts

Date	Details	£	Date	Details	£
			31 Dec 2018	Statement of profit or loss	12 500

The statement of profit or loss and other comprehensive income is charged with £12 500 as an allowance/provision for irrecoverable debts. In the statement of financial position, we would show trade receivables of £250 000 − £12 500 = £237 500.

Any increase in the allowance in later years is shown as an expense in the statement of profit or loss and other comprehensive income.

1 A business has a balance of £900 000 of outstanding trade receivables on 31 December 2018. Each year, it calculates an allowance of 5 per cent of year-end trade receivables. On 31 December 2017 the allowance amounted to £30 000. We will calculate the amount to be shown in the statement of profit or loss and other comprehensive income and show the presentation of the trade receivables in the statement of financial position as of 31 December 2018.

Trade receivables

Date	Details	£	Date	Details	£
31 Dec 2018	Bal b/d	900 000			

Allowance/provision for irrecoverable debts

Date	Details	£	Date	Details	£
			31 Dec 2017	Statement of profit or loss	30 000
			31 Dec 2018	Statement of profit or loss	15 000

In 2017 the allowance/provision was £30 000, while in 2018 we are told that the allowance is 5 per cent of £900 000 = £45 000. Therefore, we only need increase the existing allowance by an additional amount of £15 000. In the 2018 statement of financial position, we would show trade receivables as follows:

	£
Trade receivables	900 000
Less allowance/provision for irrecoverable debts	(45 000)
	855 000

From this we see that it is the total allowance of 5 per cent of the closing trade receivables balances (£45 000) that is shown in the statement of financial position in 2018. In the statement of profit or loss and other comprehensive income, however, only the additional amount of £15 000 is shown as a current year's expense.

Extract from statement of profit or loss and other comprehensive income 31 Dec 2018

Details	£
Allowance/provision for irrecoverable debts	15 000

WORKED EXAMPLE

A business has trade receivables at its year end of £40 000. One trade receivable of £2 500 is in liquidation and it is also thought that there could be other trade receivables, estimated as being 4 per cent of the outstanding balances, who may not pay. The business would write off the £2 500 as an irrecoverable debt and would then calculate an allowance of 4 per cent on the remaining trade receivables of £37 500. The statement of financial position would show trade receivables of £37 500 − £1 500 = £36 000.

The irrecoverable debts (£2 500) and the allowance (£1 500) are both treated as expenses in the statement of profit or loss and other comprehensive income.

Irrecoverable debts

Date	Details	£	Date	Details	£
Year 1	Trade receivable A	2 500	Year 1	Statement of profit or loss	2 500

The following year, the allowance is recalculated and a new one is created. Only the increased amount (say £400) is charged to the statement of profit or loss and other comprehensive income in the new period. There may, of course, be a reduction in the allowance, and in this case the amount is credited to the statement of profit or loss and other comprehensive income.

Allowance/provision for irrecoverable debts

Date	Details	£	Date	Details	£
			Year 1	Statement of profit or loss	1 500
			Year 2	Statement of profit or loss	400

We can define an allowance as an amount deducted from profit to provide for expenses that are not known accurately at the time the accounts are prepared. If legal action is being brought against a business, it might make an allowance for legal costs and claims. This is acting prudently, recognising the possible costs as soon as possible.

ACTIVITY 8   SKILLS   ANALYSIS, PROBLEM SOLVING, EXECUTIVE FUNCTION

CASE STUDY: AJAX ELECTRICAL

Ajax Electrical decides that 5 per cent of all trade receivables are assumed to be irrecoverable debts and makes an allowance accordingly. You are told that the trade receivables balances are as follows:

	£
31 December 2016	50 000
31 December 2017	60 000
31 December 2018	40 000

1 Show the relevant ledger account for the allowance/provision for irrecoverable debts for each year. Also indicate what amounts will appear in the statement of profit or loss and other comprehensive income and statement of financial position at the end of each year.

RECOVERY OF IRRECOVERABLE DEBTS

Sometimes a trade receivable amount that has been written off as an irrecoverable debt will be paid at some point in the future. This could be voluntarily by the trade receivable or because of the debt collection procedures of the business. When this happens, we call it an irrecoverable debt recovered. The journal entries for this will be as follows.

To reinstate the debt:

Dr   The individual trade receivables account
Cr   Irrecoverable debts recovered account*

To record the payment:

Dr   Bank or cash
Cr   The individual trade receivables account

*If the irrecoverable debt is recovered in the same financial year as it is written off, some businesses will credit the irrecoverable debts account to reduce this, rather than post it to the irrecoverable debts recovered account. If the debt is recovered after the end of the financial year in which it occurred, then the correct treatment is always to credit the irrecoverable debts recovered account.

At the end of the period, the credit balance in the irrecoverable debts recovered account is entered as a recovery of an expense in the profit and loss account.

WORKED EXAMPLE

From the earlier example of an irrecoverable debt, let us assume that Smythe paid Hilda Hardware £420 on 20 July 2019. Using the information, the ledger account would be as follows:

Smythe

Date	Details	£	Date	Details	£
30 April 2018	Sales	872	12 May 2018	Bank	220
			31 Dec 2018	Irrecoverable debt	652
		872			872

Note that the trade receivables account is not altered in any way. The recovery (in this case only a part recovery) is credited to the Irrecoverable debts recovered account on the date it is received. At the end of the year, the balance on this account is transferred to the statement of profit or loss and other comprehensive income, where it shows as an income item.

Irrecoverable debt recovered

Date	Details	£	Date	Details	£
31 Dec 2019	Statement of profit or loss	420	20 Jul 2019	Smythe	420

INFORMATION AND COMMUNICATION TECHNOLOGY

Traditionally, accounts have been maintained by means of handwritten records. With the decrease in the cost of computers and the software required, increasing numbers of businesses have computerised their accounting function. As a result, many businesses today maintain much or all of their accounting transactions and information on specialised accounting software, from the very simple to highly complex and sophisticated systems which integrate all elements of the accounting process.

Simple systems may just record details of cash book transactions, while others will provide a full set of formal books, from daybooks to ledgers, and from ledgers into control procedures (see Unit 2), and finally financial statements (Unit 3).

USES OF ICT IN ACCOUNTING

At a basic level, ICT can be used to record accounting transactions from source documents, entering the data into the various books of prime entry. From here, the data can be automatically entered into the formal books of account – the ledgers.

In addition to posting the double entry into the ledgers, control procedures can be automatically prepared. These control procedures are extremely useful in checking the accuracy of the information provided by the accounting system and allow effective management decisions to be made.

An important control procedure is the preparation of control accounts (covered in Chapter 8). This looks at information that relates to total trade receivables and trade payables, and therefore helps with the management of the working capital cycle. The process should allow for the preparation of the schedule of trade receivables and could reduce the level of irrecoverable debts and allow for an accurate allowance/provision for irrecoverable debts.

A further use is the preparation of a trial balance (Chapter 7), which checks the accuracy of the double entry, allows for errors to be identified and corrected and, finally, allows for the preparation of the financial statements – the statement of profit or loss and other comprehensive income, and the statement of financial position.

Benefits of ICT accounting systems

- They utilise the single entry of accounting transactions, with simultaneous updating of accounting records. One advantage of using accounting software is that once a transaction is recorded in the book of original entry (sometimes source documents if the system links source documents to accounting records), the remaining parts of the accounting records will be updated. For instance, when a sales transaction is entered in the Revenue day book, it automatically updates the ledger accounts.
- They provide increased accuracy of accounting data, as errors are minimised by the software used. Arithmetical errors, which can be found quite often in manual accounting, can be eliminated.
- Accounting software is faster in comparison to processing the data manually.
- Information is provided in a timely manner because the system can generate financial reports whenever required. This helps to improve decision making.
- The security of financial information will be improved as passwords are required in order to access the information.

Limitations of ICT accounting systems

- The initial capital cost of the hardware and software might be too high for many small businesses. In addition, the hardware and software may become out of date quickly, requiring more expense.
- The cost of maintaining the system may be high – staff will need to be trained and the software updated regularly.
- There is a significant risk of data loss if the system fails, and back-ups may not be available. Security breaches may also occur.
- Not all errors will be removed (see Chapter 9), expert staff will still be needed to correct these.
- Staff morale may be affected if they see the introduction of computerised systems as a threat to their job security.

As you can see, there are many positives and negatives that relate to the use of ICT accounting software. Ultimately, the decision whether to use ICT or maintain a manual accounting system will depend on the nature of each individual business. It is clear that, whatever approach a business chooses, it will require staff with an excellent level of accounting knowledge!

ACTIVITY 9

 SKILLS PROBLEM SOLVING, EXECUTIVE FUNCTION

CASE STUDY: FAIZAN

On 31 December 2017, Faizan's ledger contained the following balances:

	£
Trade receivables	20 000
Allowance/provision for irrecoverable debts	3 340

The allowance/provision for irrecoverable debts consisted of a general allowance of £800 and specific allowances for the following trade receivables:

	£
D Swart	420
J Cohen	1 200
L Beck	920

During the year ended 31 December 2018, the following transactions took place:

- On 30 April, D Swart was declared bankrupt and a payment of £95 was received on 18 July 2018.
- On 15 June, Faizan was advised that the full debt due from J Cohen included in the trade receivables at 31 December 2017 was irrecoverable.
- On 3 August, L Beck paid the amount he owed in full.

Faizan wishes to make allowance for future irrecoverable debts by providing a general allowance/provision for irrecoverable debts of 5 per cent of the year-end trade receivables.

1 Show the ledger accounts for the above items. You can assume that no other transactions took place on the trade receivables ledger, other than those given in the question. Indicate clearly what changes are to be made to the statement of profit or loss and other comprehensive income for the year.

ACTIVITY 10

SKILLS PROBLEM SOLVING, EXECUTIVE FUNCTION

CASE STUDY: JAYA

Jaya commenced her business on 1 June 2016. She sells most of her goods on credit and therefore ensures that there is always an adequate allowance/provision for irrecoverable debts. She considers that the allowance should be equal to 5 per cent of the outstanding trade receivables at the end of the financial year.

On 31 May 2017, the trade receivables outstanding were £14 800. Included in these trade receivables was an amount of £620 due by Martin, who had been declared bankrupt. Jaya decided she would write this amount off as an irrecoverable debt.

On 31 May 2018, the outstanding trade receivables amounted to £18 900. Jaya received a payment of 15p in the £ from Martin's liquidators. This amount has not yet been recorded in her books. During the year Winston was unable to pay the £280 due and Jaya decided that the amount should be treated as an irrecoverable debt.

On 31 May 2019, the trade receivables outstanding were £21 000. Jaya considered that the allowance/ provision for irrecoverable debts should be increased to 6 per cent of the trade receivables balances.

1 Show the entries to be made to the statement of profit or loss and other comprehensive income for the years ending 2017, 2018 and 2019.
2 Show the trade receivables figure that is to be shown in the statement of financial position for each year.

EXAM HINT

You need to understand the difference between trade discounts and cash discounts. When accounting for an allowance/provision for irrecoverable debts when an existing allowance exists, you only need to account for the difference as an expense or other income.

CHECKPOINT

1 What are the six books of prime entry?
2 Cash sales are recorded in the revenue day book. True or false?
3 Identify one transaction that would be entered in to the journal day book.
4 Explain the difference between a trade discount and a cash discount.
5 A decrease in the allowance/provision for irrecoverable debts is an expense. True or false?

EVALUATE

An allowance/provision for irrecoverable debts is an example of using prudence (see Chapter 4). The debt may or may not be received from a trade receivable. This provision is put in place because of the possibility that the amount will not be received. As there is no certainty, it is generally accepted that we should account for this uncertainty by 'providing' for it. However, as it is not certain, there is always an element of judgement involved in providing for an allowance/provision for irrecoverable debts.

Reasons for creating an allowance/provision for irrecoverable debts	Reasons for only accounting for irrecoverable debts
Applies the prudence concept to the accounts	May be difficult to accurately assess likely future irrecoverable debts with any accuracy, so better to wait for them to occur
Profit will not be overstated, as expenses will be increased	Actual irrecoverable debts are known with precision, no estimation required
Current assets will not be overstated in the statement of financial position	Simple to apply entries as they only need to be made as the irrecoverable debts occur
Providing for future irrecoverable debts requires a review of trade receivables accounts. Actions to prevent them can then be taken more easily, and might prevent sudden shocks	

SUBJECT VOCABULARY

allowance/provision for irrecoverable debts an amount put aside from profits for possible irrecoverable debts

books of prime entry where transactions are classified and recorded before posting to the ledger accounts

cash book a book of prime entry in which all cash and bank transactions are recorded. It is also part of the double-entry system

cash discount a reduction in the amount owing in return for early payment of the debt

control accounts accounts which prove the transactions of a set of accounts: the trade receivables control account and the trade payables control account

depreciation the loss in value of a non-current asset over its useful economic life, which is apportioned to the accounting periods that benefit from its use

discount received the cash discount a business obtains for early payment to a trade payable

general ledger a book containing all impersonal accounts

gross profit the difference between the revenue and the cost of sales

incurred a term used in accounting to show that a business transaction has taken place and needs to be recognised in the books of accounts

irrecoverable debt amount deducted from a trade receivable when the amount owed is not recoverable

schedule of trade receivables a list of outstanding trade receivables by the age of the debt

trade discount reduction in the invoice total given to a customer

trade payables ledger a ledger containing individual personal accounts of credit suppliers

trade receivables ledger a ledger containing the accounts of the individual credit customers

EXAM PRACTICE

CASE STUDY: DEJOHN'S COMPUTER REPAIRS

SKILLS ▶ PROBLEM SOLVING, EXECUTIVE FUNCTION, REASONING

Dejohn repairs computer hardware. The following were recorded in the books at 1 August 2017:
- trade receivables £25 500
- allowance/provision for irrecoverable debts £755

At the year end, 31 July 2017, Dejohn produced the following schedule of trade receivables:

Age of debt	Trade receivables (£)
0–1 month	22 000
1–2 months	10 000
2–3 months	3 200
Over 3 months	1 200

Dejohn applies the following percentages relating to potential future irrecoverable debts:

0–1 month	Nil
1–2 months	2%
2–3 months	4%
Over 3 months	10%

Q

1 Prepare a statement of financial position extract for 31 July 2017, showing how the two accounts would be presented. **(4 marks)**
2 Calculate the allowance/provision for irrecoverable debts at 31 July 2018. **(4 marks)**
3 Prepare the allowance/provision for irrecoverable debts account for the year ended 31 July 2018. **(4 marks)**
4 State whether the account indicates an expense for the year or other income. **(1 mark)**

The following information relates to Hytek Supplies, a supplier to Dejohn, for the month of July 2018:

1 July – Dejohn owed Hytek Supplies £350.
4 July – Dejohn purchased goods to the value of £510, after deducting a trade discount of 7.5 per cent.
21 July – Dejohn settled the account in full by cheque, obtaining a cash discount of 5 per cent.

5 Prepare the ledger account for Hytek Supplies for July 2018 in Dejohn's books. **(4 marks)**
6 Explain the difference between a trade discount and a cash discount. **(4 marks)**

4 ACCOUNTING CONCEPTS AND CONVENTIONS

LEARNING OBJECTIVES

After you have studied this chapter, you should be able to:
- explain the purpose of accounting concepts and conventions
- understand the meaning of different accounting concepts and conventions
- explain and evaluate the use of International Accounting Standards (IAS).

GETTING STARTED

Both you and your friend buy and sell t-shirts. You each buy £50 worth of t-shirts and you pay cash while your friend buys them on credit. You both sell all the t-shirts for £80 cash and your friend records a profit of £80, while you record a profit of £30.

Your friend appears to have a more successful business. Is this true? Is it possible to compare the performance? How might the difference be sorted out?

We have shown that accounts are prepared for various users. In preparing these accounts, we must follow certain rules and guidelines, called **accounting concepts**, or accounting principles or conventions. These rules are used by accountants and are intended to maintain objective accounting. In the example above, you and your friend followed different rules and, therefore, there's a difference in the reported profits.

Some principles are found in law and in accounting standards (such as International Accounting

Standards [IAS]). Because we all use the same rules when we prepare accounts, we know that we can rely on the information and the way in which items are shown in the accounts will be the same for all businesses.

No personal preferences must exist when we prepare accounts. Whatever is done in the accounts must be based on facts and not on an opinion. For example, if we buy a non-current asset on the last day of the year, then this asset would be shown in the statement of financial position at cost. We know this is a fact and not our own interpretation on how we think the particular asset should be reflected in the accounts. As a result, any user of the accounts can be sure that the original figure came from a cost value and not some imaginary estimate.

This means that objectivity is extremely important in accounting, so that financial statements show no personal preference and all users can accept them with confidence.

FUNDAMENTAL CONCEPTS

There are rules that establish the way in which we record all transactions. These rules are known as accounting concepts. These are broken down further, and we have a group of accounting concepts that are known as the fundamental accounting concepts (or accounting principles), and these are incorporated

▲ Figure 1 The four fundamental accounting concepts

into the accounting standards issued by the various accountancy bodies.

We will discuss each of these concepts in more detail in the paragraphs below.

Going concern

This refers to an entity (business) that will continue its present operation for the foreseeable future. If an entity claims that it is a going concern entity, it is assumed that it is not likely to stop trading in the near future.

A business advertising itself as a going concern might report the value of its assets at its carrying amount (cost less depreciation), rather than its market value. If a business reports its assets at market value, it indicates that the business is forced to close down, so it will be useful to users by showing how much can be received from selling the assets.

Consistency

Consistency means that we must treat similar items in the same way; for example, we depreciate all motor vehicles at a rate of 25 per cent per annum, using straight line method. This rate and method would be applied year after year. Although we are allowed to change a method if it provides a fair view (for example, we can move from straight line depreciation to the reducing balance method), we cannot change every year and we must recalculate previous figures so that profit can be compared on the same basis.

Prudence

Prudence is a key accounting principle which makes sure that assets and income are not overstated, and liabilities and expenses are not understated. In preparing any financial statement we must adopt a cautious approach. We must ensure that the assets are not overvalued and that the liabilities are not understated when using this approach. As a result, all anticipated losses and expenses are shown, even if they are uncertain. For example, an allowance/provision for irrecoverable debts may need to be shown (see Chapter 3). Similarly, revenue is not taken into account by anticipating sales. This recognition of profits is covered in an additional concept known as the realisation concept. Prudence is an important concept when it comes to the valuation of non-current assets (Chapter 6). It ensures that non-current assets are not overvalued by the business.

Accruals

The accounts should show the revenues earned in an accounting period matched against the expenses involved in earning those revenues.

We record sales in the statement of profit or loss and other comprehensive income when they are earned and not when we receive the cash. This also applies to expenses, which we disclose when they are incurred and not when we pay for them.

Accruals is a fundamental principle which must be followed when preparing financial statements. For example, a business makes sales of £1 000 in the last month of the financial year but does not receive the money until the following financial year. The £1 000 would appear in the current financial year rather than the following year when the cash is received. For expenses, if the business paid for one year's insurance in the final month of a financial period, only one month's value of insurance would be included in the expenses for the year, the remaining 11 months would be matched to the revenue earned in the following year.

OTHER CONCEPTS

In addition to these fundamental concepts there are further accounting concepts that are adopted and applied in financial statements through good accounting practice. These concepts are:

- historic cost
- money measurement
- business entity
- materiality
- realisation.

Historic cost

This concept deals with the way in which the valuation of transactions is done. If the value is based on the amount actually paid, it is objective and can be proved. As an example, it means that a non-current asset is normally shown at its cost less accumulated depreciation. The historic cost concept ensures that the cost of an asset is a known fact and can be verified.

Arguments against placing a historic cost value on assets are that no allowance is made for the changing value of money or for reflecting the current value of the resources available to the business. For this reason, the historic cost rule is not always applied. For example, property can be accounted for at fair value rather than at its historic cost.

Money measurement

Items are only shown in the accounts if they can be measured in money terms. As a result of this concept, we cannot expect to read about the quality of the management of a business in the financial statements, or whether the labour workforce is properly trained. We may form an opinion about some indicators, but there can be no monetary value placed on any positive aspects, nor can there be a deduction in monetary terms for any negative situation.

Business entity

This concept states that the financial affairs of the business should remain separate from the financial affairs of the owner. Only business revenues and expenditures are recorded in the books of account and not private items (drawings). However, when the owner introduces new capital or withdraws capital, this is recorded within the business records. Difficulties can arise when the same resource is used by both the business and the owner for personal reasons; for example, a motor vehicle. When this happens, the costs must be apportioned (shared) between the business and owner.

Materiality

Any item appearing in the financial statements is governed by one major rule which is that the item should be material to that business. If the exclusion of an item would mislead users, then it is material. If the item is not material then it is better to exclude it, otherwise the report is confusing and makes for difficult reading. No useful purpose is served by adding non-material items into the financial statements.

Any item appearing in the financial statements is regarded as a material item. This follows the principle of materiality. Materiality states that financial information is material if omitting (excluding) or misstating the information can influence users' decision making. This means that if an omitted or misstated item could influence a user's decision, then the information is important. Material information should be shown individually.

The size or nature of the item can make the information material. For example, many businesses may not report each individual motor vehicle in financial statements because the amount of each motor vehicle is small for decision making. Therefore, all motor vehicles will be grouped together and only the total value of motor vehicles will be reported.

Another example – a business owner only withdrew £100 cash from the business for his personal use (total revenue is £1 million). Since the nature of the transaction is important (showing how much funds the owner took from the business), it needs to be shown separately.

In many businesses, materiality is decided by a monetary amount. We may say that any item under £100 is not material to the financial statements of that firm. In a large multinational business, the amount may be set at £10 000 or even higher.

Realisation

This concept states that revenue should only be recognised when the exchange of the goods and services is certain. We should not anticipate sales; we only show items in any account if it has been realised. One important aspect of this is that we only recognise profits when the goods pass to the customer, who accepts liability to pay for the goods. We do not inflate any value in the statement of financial position, nor do we show profit if it is not yet realised. We saw in the prudence concept that, regarding assets, we err on the side of caution.

ACTIVITY 1   SKILLS   CRITICAL THINKING, ANALYSIS, REASONING

CASE STUDY: CONCEPTS AND ADJUSTMENTS

The table below lists various adjustments that need to be made to a trial balance before the preparation of financial statements.

An amount of £4 000 due from trade receivable A was written off as an irrecoverable debt.
Inventory of £9 000 was written down to its net realisable value of £8 000.
£1 000 paid for private travel was debited to drawings.
Motor vehicles were depreciated at 20 per cent on cost.
£2 100 insurance was paid for the following financial year.
A tablet was written off as an expense even though it could last 3–5 years.
An electronic goods business has staff to show customers how to operate certain tools. This is considered to be worth £50 000 but is not recorded in the books.
Depreciation is charged at 20 per cent but we want to increase it to 25 per cent for this year only.

1 State the relevant accounting concept that applies to each item listed.
2 What is meant by the term 'fundamental concepts'? Give three examples.

QUALITATIVE CHARACTERISTICS – A SUMMING UP

It is important that all accounts have certain characteristics. These are:

- relevance – requires the financial information be relevant to the decision-making needs of the users
- comparability – requires the financial information to be comparable between different accounting periods and between different businesses

- understandability – requires the financial information to be clearly understood by users with reasonable knowledge of business and accounting activities
- materiality – requires the financial information to focus on that which is expected to affect the decisions of the users of the information
- faithful representation – requires the financial information to be true, fair and free from error
- timeliness – requires the financial information to be provided for users when it is needed and not unduly delayed.

Whenever you are required to prepare accounts, make sure you take notice of the concepts detailed in the paragraphs above. These rules, or guidelines, must be used in the preparation of the financial statements. They have developed gradually over time and have been adopted for practical rather than theoretical purposes. The application of these concepts is often subjective and relies on your own judgement.

ACTIVITY 2   SKILLS ▷ CRITICAL THINKING, REASONING

CASE STUDY: ACCOUNTING CONCEPTS

1 Define the use of each of the accounting concepts and illustrate your definitions with an example:
   (a) going concern
   (b) prudence
   (c) accrual
   (d) consistency
   (e) historic cost
   (f) materiality.

ACTIVITY 3   SKILLS ▷ CRITICAL THINKING, REASONING

CASE STUDY: CONCEPTS IN PRACTICE

1 Identify the concepts that apply to the following:
   (a) subtracting an amount paid for rent because it relates to the next accounting period
   (b) keeping the same method of depreciation from year to year.
2 Identify which accounting concepts are being ignored in the following:
   (a) a sole trader includes an amount in his factory insurance that relates to his own house insurance
   (b) a sole trader decides to value some inventory at the selling price after a customer said they would buy some in the near future.

INTERNATIONAL ACCOUNTING STANDARDS (IAS)

The use of accounting standards enables financial statements to be produced in a way and format that allows them to be compared both between companies and over time. In a global economy, this is becoming more and more important.

A number of accounting standards have been produced to provide a regulatory framework for financial accounting. This reduces the variety of accounting treatments that companies can use when preparing financial statements. It has reduced the ability of companies to act unethically (ethical accounting is covered in Chapter 22).

The main purpose of international accounting standards is to ensure that the qualitative characteristics of accounts are maintained at all times. The International Accounting Standard 1 (IAS1) covers the presentation of financial statements (see Chapter 10). Not only does it identify the components of financial statements (for your studies, these cover the statement of comprehensive income and the statement of financial position) but it requires businesses to comply with the accounting concepts you have studied. Although, legally, international accounting standards only apply to corporate bodies, it is perhaps beneficial that they should be applied, where it is reasonable to do so, to the financial statements of sole traders, partnerships and clubs.

The second purpose of international accounting standards is to eliminate the differences in accounting rules between countries. The benefit of this is to encourage international investment, since the same rules and standards are used.

ACTIVITY 4   SKILLS ▶ CRITICAL THINKING

CASE STUDY: INTERNATIONAL ACCOUNTING STANDARDS

IAS require that all accounts must contain certain qualitative characteristics. This allows users to compare one business with another.

1 Describe four such characteristics.

ACTIVITY 5   SKILLS ▶ CRITICAL THINKING, CREATIVITY, COMMUNICATION

CASE STUDY: APPLICATION OF ACCOUNTING CONCEPTS TO DIFFERENT SCENARIOS

Accounting concepts ⇒ Accounting transactions ⬇	Going concern				
Drawings					

1 Create a table that you can complete as your knowledge of concepts and accounting transactions develops over the course of your studies. The table above shows the format you should use.

(a) In the first column, list the accounting transactions you have learned.

(b) Along the top row of the table, write in the accounting concepts you have learned.

(c) Every time you learn a new accounting transaction, add a row to your table, enter the new transaction type in the first column and then identify which accounting concepts apply to this transaction. Get your fellow students and teachers to help you with this.

EVALUATE

Adilah operates a small business selling spices. She has begun to prepare her financial statements and is not sure whether she should use accounting concepts in the preparation of these. Here are some suggestions relating to this issue.

Arguments for	Arguments against
Gives a more accurate profit figure when revenues and expenses are calculated using accounting concepts. This might allow Adilah to take out an appropriate amount of **drawings** from the business.	Concepts and conventions are open to interpretation and may not result in financial statements that are perfectly comparable.
Provides consistency between different businesses so they can be compared effectively.	Their use requires staff to be skilled in accounting techniques – this has staff training and cost implications for the business.
Users of financial statements can rely on the information and so make informed decisions.	They ignore non-financial factors, such as the skills of the workforce.

▲ Table 1 Evaluating the use of accounting concepts and conventions

Adilah is aware that she does not have to legally prepare her financial statements in accordance with International Accounting Standards, but is keen to prepare for the future should the business become more successful.

Arguments for IAS	Arguments against
Users of financial information can rely on the information; comparisons can be made between different companies.	Only applies to corporate bodies, so the time and cost may not be justified.
They provide a common standard that can be applied across the world, this makes them more understandable.	IAS only cover financial factors, so non-financial implications of business activities are ignored – for example, the effects on the environment.

▲ Table 2 Evaluating the use of International Accounting Standards

CHECKPOINT

1 State the four fundamental accounting concepts.

2 State three other accounting concepts.

3 Identify the accounting concept relating to the recording of non-current assets.

4 A business buys some calculators for use over several years. It decides to treat these as an expense in the year. Identify the relevant accounting concept.

5 Which IAS covers the preparation of financial statements?

6 Identify four characteristics of accounts addressed by International Accounting Standards.

EXAM HINT

Questions on accounting concepts and conventions will often require you to evaluate their use. If this is the case, just providing a detailed description of all the concepts will gain few, if any, marks. You should explain the benefits and limitations of them and reach a conclusion based on your arguments.

SUBJECT VOCABULARY

accounting concepts guidelines for the treatment of accounting transactions

accruals the concept that income and expenditure for goods and services is matched to the same accounting period when calculating profit

accumulated the total to date

business entity only the transactions relating to the business are recorded in the books of account for the business

consistency the concept that after a business has adopted a particular policy for recording financial transactions, the policy should not be changed without a valid reason

drawings resources removed from the business by the owner; these could be cash or inventory

going concern the assumption that the business will continue to trade in the foreseeable future

historic cost this concept states that transactions should be recorded in the books of account using the actual cost at the time the transaction took place

International Accounting Standards (IAS) accounting standards, which apply globally, enabling users of accounting information to make reliable judgements and decisions about businesses from a range of countries

materiality allows for the correct accounting treatment to be ignored if the amount involved is insignificant relative to the size of the business

money measurement items should only be recorded in the books of accounts if they can be measured in monetary terms

overstate to state more than the actual sum

prudence states that accounts should reflect a cautious view of the business, that losses should be accounted for as they are anticipated, but profits should not be recognised until realised

realisation the concept that revenues should only be recognised when the exchange of goods and services has taken place

understate to state less than the actual sum

EXAM PRACTICE

CASE STUDY: HOLBORN PRODUCTS

SKILLS   REASONING, DECISION MAKING

Holborn Products specialises in glasses for reading. The owner is proposing changes to the way in which financial statements are prepared. There are four proposals.

Proposal 1   Include a sum for the skill of the workforce as a non-current asset in the statement of financial position.

Proposal 2   Charge the full cost price of non-current assets to the year in which they are purchased.

Proposal 3   No longer provide for unrealised profit by removing the provision for unrealised profit on manufactured goods from the accounts.

Proposal 4   Charge the drawings of the owner to the statement of profit or loss and other comprehensive income.

Q

1   State, giving reasons for your answer, an accounting principle or concept that would not be complied with if each of the proposals 1, 2, and 3 were introduced.
(9 marks)

2   Evaluate the use of International Accounting Standards in the preparation of financial statements.
(12 marks)

5 CAPITAL EXPENDITURE AND REVENUE EXPENDITURE

LEARNING OBJECTIVES

After you have studied this chapter, you should be able to:
- explain the difference between capital expenditure and revenue expenditure
- identify the correct accounting treatment for capital expenditure and revenue expenditure, referring to appropriate accounting concepts
- explain the difference between capital income and revenue income.

GETTING STARTED

You have just purchased a new delivery vehicle. Your bookkeeper has added the amount of insurance to the value of your motor vehicle in your books of account. What has happened to the value of your motor vehicle? Do you think that this is the correct accounting treatment for this transaction? What might the correct treatment be?

In Chapter 3, we looked at the accounting distinction between the purchase of items for use within the business over several accounting periods (non-current assets). We also looked at the purchase of items for resale (current assets), and the expenses incurred by the business in its daily operation (wages, insurance, heating and lighting). These expenses are required to support the sales of the product and therefore help generate revenue for the business. To calculate the correct profit for the year figure and the correct value of the business in the financial statements, it is essential that the correct distinction is made between two very different types of spending – capital expenditure and revenue expenditure.

DIFFERENCE BETWEEN CAPITAL EXPENDITURE AND REVENUE EXPENDITURE

Capital expenditure

This is spending on the purchase, alteration or improvement of non-current assets, which will be used in the business for more than one accounting period. As well as including the initial cost of the asset, capital expenditure also includes:

- delivery costs
- installation costs
- legal costs incurred in obtaining the asset
- the cost of improving the asset (but not repairs to the asset).

These costs are added to the initial purchase cost of the asset to arrive at a cost for the asset to be recorded in the books, following the accounting concept of historic cost. These costs are incurred in order that the asset can be used by the business.

Capital expenditure is recorded in the statement of financial position under the heading of non-current assets. Initially, capital expenditure does not affect the statement of profit or loss and other comprehensive income. It is the depreciation of non-current assets (see Chapter 6) that is entered into the statement of profit or loss and other comprehensive income as an expense and will reduce the profit of the business over several accounting periods.

Revenue expenditure

This is the spending on the day-to-day running expenses of the business that are used in the current accounting period. Examples of these would include rent, rates, heating and lighting, office expenses and marketing costs. Also included in revenue expenditure would be costs associated with the use of a non-current asset which does not add value or improve the asset. This would include items such as:

- insurance relating to the use of the asset
- maintenance costs
- repairs
- running costs – for example, petrol for motor vehicles
- staff training in the use of the asset.

Revenue expenditure is recorded in the statement of profit or loss and other comprehensive income as an expense, following the accruals concept and has the effect of reducing the profit for the year.

The following table summarises the differences between the two types of expenditure:

Capital expenditure	Revenue expenditure
The benefit of the asset is derived for more than one year.	The benefit of the asset is used up within a year.
It includes initial costs and upgrades to non-current assets.	It includes maintenance and repairs to non-current assets.
It includes spending to increase the value of a non-current asset.	It includes spend to maintain the value of a non-current asset.
In most cases they are a one-off purchase.	They are usually recurring expenses (day to day).
Items are purchased with the intention to keep and use within the business, not to sell and make a profit.	Items such as inventory are purchased with the intention to sell and make profit.
Items appear on the statement of financial position under non-current assets.	It appears on the statement of profit or loss under expenses.

EXAM HINT

Remember that staff training to use an asset is considered a revenue expense. An easy example to remember is the purchase of a business vehicle. The vehicle is a non-current asset – therefore, it is capital expenditure. Training the staff to drive it has not changed the value of the asset; the vehicle is in working order whether any staff members are able to use it or not. Staff training is a day-to-day cost of running the business, therefore, it is revenue expenditure.

In Chapter 4, we studied accounting concepts and one that has relevance to the distinction between the two types of expenditure is materiality. If the value of a capital expenditure item is considered so low that its treatment as revenue expenditure would not affect the financial statement's validity, it is acceptable to classify capital expenditure as revenue expenditure, under the concept of materiality. An example of this is low-value office equipment, which would be used over several accounting periods, and could be entered into the books of account as 'general expenses' or 'office expenses'.

CLASSIFYING CAPITAL EXPENDITURE AND REVENUE EXPENDITURE

When preparing financial statements, it is important that these expenditures are correctly classified in the accounts. If they are not recorded correctly, both the value of assets and profit will be wrong.

WORKED EXAMPLE

Lalaina Water Taxis has recorded the following amounts for the current financial year, relating to the purchase of a new speedboat for use in its water taxi service.

	£
Purchase of speedboat	100 000
Delivery costs	10 000
Painting of company logo on boat	1 500
Insurance	5 000
Fuel costs	12 000
Cost of increasing seating capacity	15 000

Below, you can see how the amounts have been classified into capital and revenue expenditure.

	Capital expenditure £	Revenue expenditure £	Reason
Purchase of speedboat	100 000		Bought new asset
Delivery costs	10 000		Delivery required before asset can be used
Painting of company logo on boat	1 500		Adding value/improving asset
Insurance		5 000	Day-to-day expense
Fuel costs		12 000	Day-to-day expense
Cost of increasing seating capacity	15 000		Adding value/improving asset
Total	126 500	17 000	

ACTIVITY 1   SKILLS CRITICAL THINKING, REASONING

CASE STUDY: CLASSIFYING CAPITAL EXPENDITURE AND REVENUE EXPENDITURE

1 Classify each of the following as either capital expenditure or revenue expenditure:

(a) installation costs of new machinery
(b) carriage inwards on goods for resale
(c) carriage inwards on delivery of new machinery
(d) wages to warehouse staff
(e) power costs of operating machinery
(f) legal costs on the purchase of an office building or land for some warehouses.

ACTIVITY 2   SKILLS CRITICAL THINKING, REASONING

CASE STUDY: MOTOR VEHICLE BUSINESS EXPENDITURE

1 Identify whether each of the following is capital expenditure or revenue expenditure:

(a) cost of delivery
(b) road licence/tax
(c) insurance
(d) fitting shelving to the vehicle
(e) fuel costs
(f) sign writing of company name onto vehicle
(g) wages for the driver.

IMPACT OF ERRORS IN CLASSIFICATION OF EXPENDITURE

If expenditure is wrongly classified in the accounts, it will have an effect on both the statement of profit or loss and other comprehensive income and the statement of financial position.

If capital expenditure is treated as revenue expenditure, profit will be understated, as the expenses will be wrongly increased, while the statement of financial position will be understated as non-current assets will be understated. For example, the cost of building an extension to shop premises has been recorded in the maintenance account. The premises account will contain too little and be understated, while the maintenance account will be increased, therefore increasing expenses and wrongly reducing the profit.

If revenue expenditure is classified as capital expenditure, then profit will be understated as expenses will be lower, while the statement of financial position will be overstated because the value of non-current assets will be increased incorrectly. For example, motor vehicle insurance is included in the motor vehicle account. The result of this error is to decrease expenses and increase profit, and increase the value of the motor vehicle account and thus overstate the statement of financial position.

ACTIVITY 3   SKILLS ▶ CRITICAL THINKING, PROBLEM SOLVING

CASE STUDY: FIRSTMEDAN COMPUTERS

FirstMedan Computers sells computer hardware and software. During the year it has invested in a new inventory control system. The following transactions have been recorded as capital expenditure and revenue expenditure:

Item	Capital expenditure £	Revenue expenditure £
New computers for resale		160 000
New inventory control system		40 000
Installation cost of new system	10 000	
Staff training for new system	7 450	
Maintenance of inventory control system		2 000
Computer supplies for new system	500	
Total	17 950	202 000

FirstMedan Computers has recorded some of the transactions as the incorrect type of expenditure.

1 Correct the errors in FirstMedan's records by recording the capital expenditure and revenue expenditure correctly.
2 Calculate the amount of capital expenditure to be recorded in the statement of financial position and the amount of revenue expenditure to be included in the statement of profit or loss and other comprehensive income.

CAPITAL INCOME AND REVENUE INCOME

Generally, a business will have two sources of income during the course of running the business. Revenue income is the result of the normal operating activities of the business and includes the revenue from sales of inventory, rent received, commission received, interest received and discounts allowed.

Capital income is the receipt of money which is generally non-recurring and would include capital introduced by the business owner and loans. These are part of the financing of the business rather than the day-to-day operations of the business.

EXAM HINT

When asked to explain how capital expenditure will be treated in the financial statements, it is important to remember that the cost will be recorded in the statement of financial position, and that an amount of the asset value – the depreciation – will be charged as an expense in the statement of profit or loss and other comprehensive income.

CHECKPOINT

1 What is meant by the term 'revenue expenditure'?

2 Identify two examples of capital expenditure.

3 Identify three examples of revenue expenditure.

4 How are revenue and capital expenditure treated in the financial statements?

5 What will happen to total assets if revenue expenditure is classified as capital revenue?

6 Identify one accounting concept that applies to the treatment of capital expenditure.

7 Identify one source of revenue income, other than the sale of products.

SUBJECT VOCABULARY

capital expenditure spending on non-current assets or their improvement
capital income receipts from the sale of non-current assets
carriage inwards the expense incurred in the transporting of items into the business
revenue expenditure spending on the day-to-day running expenses of a business
revenue income receipts resulting from the normal trading activities of a business

EXAM PRACTICE

CASE STUDY: SANBORN FOODS

SKILLS   CRITICAL THINKING, PROBLEM SOLVING, EXECUTIVE FUNCTION

Sanborn Foods are planning to expand their operations. As a result, they expect to:

- purchase an additional shop
- install new shelves and counters in the shop
- purchase additional inventory
- employ additional sales staff
- insure the new premises.

Q

1 State whether each of the above is capital expenditure or revenue expenditure. **(5 marks)**

The accountant has discovered an error in the books of account. Motor vehicle expenses of £2 500 had been recorded in the motor vehicles account.

2 Prepare the journal entry to correct the error. **(2 marks)**

3 Calculate the effect on profit after the error is corrected. **(2 marks)**

6 NON-CURRENT ASSET DEPRECIATION

LEARNING OBJECTIVES

After you have studied this chapter, you should be able to:

- explain the causes of depreciation
- explain the reasons for charging depreciation
- calculate the depreciation charge using straight line, reducing balance and revaluation methods
- prepare ledger accounts for non-current assets and provisions for depreciation
- calculate and explain the effect on profit of different methods of depreciation and from a change in the method of depreciation
- account for the disposal of non-current assets
- understand the format of a schedule of non-current assets.

GETTING STARTED

When a business purchases a non-current asset, does it incur an expense? Over time, what happens the value of a non-current asset? How might a business record the cost of using a non-current asset?

Non-current assets are long-term assets that will be used by a business over several accounting periods. This investment is classified as capital expenditure. The journal entry for the purchase of non-current assets is:

Dr   Non-current assets
Cr   Bank/trade payables

From this, it can be seen that both entries are entered into the statement of financial position, therefore no expense has been recorded. Nevertheless, these assets do cost the business some form of expense. They have a limited life and, over time, suffer from a loss in value due to business using the asset.

This loss in value is known as **depreciation**. It can be defined as the loss in value of a non-current asset over its useful economic life. This cost is apportioned (shared out) to all accounting periods that benefit from the use of the asset. This is not the same as a reduction in the market value of an asset. Depreciation relates to cost, rather than the value of an asset.

CAUSES OF DEPRECIATION

Non-current assets depreciate for several reasons. These include:

- the condition of an asset progressively getting worse over a period of time
- technical obsolescence; for example, a computer becomes outdated with the development of newer and faster technology
- reduction of natural resources
- the passage of time in the case of leasehold property (buildings).

▲ Outdated equipment which is no longer fit for purpose is one example of depreciation

However, at this point we must remember that land is the one non-current asset that does not normally depreciate. In fact, it often rises in value. Even so, we may still apply depreciation to buildings.

REASONS FOR CHARGING DEPRECIATION

The charging of depreciation for each accounting period that benefits from the use of a non-current asset is an example of the application of the accruals concept, whereby revenue and expenses are matched to the accounting period to which they relate. If the cost of a non-current asset was classified as revenue expenditure at the time of purchase, the profit reported would not be a true and fair view of the performance of the business. This is because the expenses for the period would be overstated and the profit would be understated in the year of purchase but would then be overstated in future years. This would make it difficult for users of financial information to make comparisons over time.

Depreciation ensures that a part of the cost of a non-current asset is matched to the revenue generated from the use of the asset. In this way, each accounting period that benefits from the use of the non-current asset includes an element of the original cost of the asset.

At this point, note that depreciation:
- is a non-cash accounting transaction
- is not a method of valuing non-current assets but a method of calculating the cost of using them
- is not a fund for the replacement of a non-current asset.

METHODS OF DEPRECIATION

The methods of depreciation include:
- straight line method
- reducing balance method
- revaluation method.

STRAIGHT LINE METHOD

This method allows for the same amount to be charged each year as an expense. The business estimates the fall in economic value of the non-current asset and takes into account any value that it may receive for that asset at the end of its life.

Examples of non-current assets using the straight line method include buildings, machinery, fixtures and fittings. It is common to understand how machinery is depreciated using the straight line method because it is assumed that the economic benefit of the machinery decreases constantly over the useful life. It implies that machinery wears out at the same rate every year and it is collectively known as the residual value.

Formula for straight line method

$$\text{Depreciation per year} = \frac{\text{Cost} - \text{residual value}}{\text{Useful economic life}}$$

or

$$\text{Depreciation per year} = (\text{Cost} - \text{residual value*}) \times \text{Depreciation rate (\%)}$$

(*In this case, the residual value is usually zero.)

WORKED EXAMPLE

Jacintha's film production company buys a camera at a cost of £55 000. The cost includes the delivery charge which is added to the capital amount of the machine. It is expected to use the machine for five years and at the end of the period it will be sold for £5 000 (the residual value).

To calculate the depreciation the following formula is used:

$$\text{Depreciation per year} = \frac{\text{Cost} - \text{residual value}}{\text{Useful economic life}}$$

This formula divides the cost of the asset (original cost − residual value) into equal proportions according to its estimated useful life.

$$\text{Depreciation charge for the year} = \frac{£55\,000 - £5\,000}{5}$$
$$= £10\,000 \text{ p.a.}$$

The depreciation charge remains fixed every year. This charge is shown in the statement of profit or loss and other comprehensive income as an expense, although we must note that there is no payment for depreciation (hence, no cash flows out of the business). The statement of financial position shows the net carrying value of the asset, which is the original cost minus the accumulated (total to date) depreciation.

In the worked example above, we see that after one year the value of the non-current asset is its cost minus the accumulated depreciation which, in this case, is the depreciation for one year only. The balance is known as the carrying value. The effect of depreciation can be seen in the table below.

Year	Cost £	Depreciation £	Accumulated depreciation £	Carrying amount £
0	55 000	0	0	55 000
1	55 000	10 000	10 000	45 000
2	55 000	10 000	20 000	35 000
3	55 000	10 000	30 000	25 000
4	55 000	10 000	40 000	15 000
5	55 000	10 000	50 000	5 000

This final balance equates to the anticipated scrap value of the non-current asset. When it is sold, the cash received will be credited to a disposal account, together with the original cost and accumulated depreciation of the asset. Any balance will be a profit or loss on disposal.

To illustrate fully how the non-current asset depreciates in value, the following table is given:

Detailed schedule of the machine over 5 years

	£	£	£	£	£
	Year 1	Year 2	Year 3	Year 4	Year 5
Original cost	55 000	55 000	55 000	55 000	55 000
Accumulated depreciation at beginning of the year		10 000	20 000	30 000	40 000
Opening balance	55 000	45 000	35 000	25 000	15 000
Depreciation for year	10 000	10 000	10 000	10 000	10 000
Accumulated depreciation	10 000	20 000	30 000	40 000	50 000
Carrying value	45 000	35 000	25 000	15 000	5 000

The following shows how depreciation is reported in a statement of comprehensive income, for each of the next five years:

Expenses	£ Year 1	£ Year 2	£ Year 3	£ Year 4	£ Year 5
Depreciation (machine)	10 000	10 000	10 000	10 000	10 000

In the statement of financial position, the following would be shown after five years:

	£ Cost	£ Accumulated depreciation	£ Carrying value
Non-current assets			
Machine	55 000	50 000	5 000

The full format of the statement of comprehensive income and the statement of financial position are covered in detail in Chapter 10, the extracts given here are to show you what happens after the depreciation has been calculated and entered into the ledger accounts.

In some cases, a residual value of zero is used. It is common practice in these cases to express the deprecation as a percentage of the cost of the non-current asset.

WORKED EXAMPLE

Prabath Joinery has the following non-current assets at the end of May 2016.

	Cost £	Accumulated depreciation £
Fixtures and fittings	20 000	5 000
Equipment	30 000	10 000

Fixtures and fittings are depreciated at the rate of 10 per cent per annum using the straight line method. Equipment is depreciated at the rate of 20 per cent per annum using the straight line method.

We will calculate the depreciation to be charged on the fixtures and fittings, and the equipment, for the year ended 31 May 2016:

Fixtures and fittings cost = £20 000 × 10% = £2 000 depreciation charge per annum

Equipment cost = £30 000 × 20% = £6 000 depreciation charge per annum

These figures would be recorded as expenses in the statement of profit or loss and other comprehensive income and added to the existing accumulated depreciation in the statement of financial position.

REDUCING BALANCE METHOD

Under this method, a fixed percentage of depreciation is applied to the asset each year based on the carrying value. Some non-current assets do not fall in value equally over their lives. For example, when we buy a vehicle it loses a lot of value within the first year but less and less over the next few years. We attempt to account for this by using the reducing balance method.

To use this method, we need to have a fixed annual depreciation rate (%) which is then applied to the carrying value each year. The carrying value is calculated by subtracting the accumulated depreciation from the cost of the non-current asset.

WORKED EXAMPLE

For the purposes of this method, we use a percentage that has been calculated before and then apply this percentage to the carrying value of the non-current asset to arrive at a charge for the year.

Using the same value non-current asset (which cost £55 000) as in the straight line method, we apply the fixed percentage for this asset of 20 per cent each year calculated on the reducing balance.

At the end of the first year, the depreciation equals £11 000. This is calculated by taking the fixed rate of 20 per cent and multiplying it by the cost of £55 000.

This then gives us the carrying value of £55 000 − £11 000 = £44 000.

At the end of the second year, the depreciation for the year equals the fixed rate multiplied by the reduced balance. This is calculated as £44 000 × 20% = £8 800. We now have a carrying value at the end of year 2, as the cost minus the accumulated depreciation (year 1 and year 2). This is shown as £55 000 − £19 800 (i.e. £11 000 + £8 800) = £35 200.

Year	Cost £	Depreciation £	Accumulated depreciation £	Carrying value £
0	55 000	0	0	55 000 [W1]
1	55 000	11 000	11 000	44 000 [W2]
2	55 000	8 800	19 800	35 200 [W3]
3	55 000	7 040	26 840	28 160 [W4]
4	55 000	5 632	32 472	22 528 [W5]
5	55 000	4 506	36 978	18 022 [ ]

Calculation:

W1: £55 000 × 20% = £11 000
W2: £44 000 × 20% = £8 800
W3: £35 200 × 20% = £7 040
W4: £28 160 × 20% = £5 632
W5: £22 258 × 20% = £4 506

	£	£	£	£	£
	Year 1	Year 2	Year 3	Year 4	Year 5
Original cost	55 000	55 000	55 000	55 000	55 000
Accumulated depreciation at beginning of the year		11 000	19 800	26 840	32 472
Opening balance – carrying value	55 000	44 000	35 200	28 160	22 528
Depreciation for year	11 000	8 800	7 040	5 632	4 506
Accumulated depreciation	**11 000**	**19 800**	**26 840**	**32 472**	**36 978**
Carrying value	44 000	35 200	28 160	22 528	18 022

Above is a detailed schedule of the machine over the five years using the reducing balance method. We can see that the carrying value as calculated using this method is greater than that using the straight line method.

The following table shows how depreciation is reported in a statement of comprehensive income: We can see that the depreciation expense decreases every year.

Expenses	£	£	£	£	£
	Year 1	Year 2	Year 3	Year 4	Year 5
Depreciation on machine	11 000	8 800	7 040	5 632	4 506

REVALUATION METHOD

This method is used where there are many small but important items, e.g. an electrician's tools. Under the concept of materiality (see Chapter 4, page 43) small-value items, such as a home office printer, are likely to be written off. To use this method, the assets are valued each year and the fall in value is the depreciation for that year. No fixed percentage is used to reduce the value but the carrying value is calculated by valuation. In this method only the reduction in value is taken into account in the statement of profit or loss and other comprehensive income and there is no increase in the value of the asset.

WORKED EXAMPLE

A garage which repairs motor vehicles has a large range of low-value tools it uses when repairing customer cars:

1 June 2016 – tools were valued at £5 500.

Purchase of new tools during the year was £1 000.

31 May 2017 – tools were valued at £5 350.

Depreciation is calculated as follows:

Value at start of year	£5 500
Add purchases	£1 000
Less value at end of year	(£5 350)
Depreciation charge for year	£1 150

(The depreciation charge of £1 150 will be charged as an expense.)

CALCULATING DEPRECIATION WHEN ASSETS ARE PURCHASED OR SOLD DURING THE YEAR

Businesses rarely purchase or dispose of non-current assets at the beginning of the financial year. Therefore, the calculation of depreciation for the year needs to be changed to take this into account. Generally, one of the following three rules is applied:

- depreciation is calculated on a monthly basis for the year, if an asset was owned for three months of the financial year, the depreciation charge would be 3/12 of the annual charge

- a full year's depreciation is charged in the year of purchase and none in the year of disposal
- a full year's depreciation is charged in the year of disposal and none in the year of purchase.

LEDGER ACCOUNTS FOR NON-CURRENT ASSETS AND PROVISION FOR DEPRECIATION

Businesses must maintain separate records of the cost and accumulated depreciation of each type of non-current asset. In the general ledger you will find the following two accounts for each type of non-current asset:

- cost account – where the historic costs of the asset are recorded
- provision for depreciation account – where the accumulated depreciation is recorded.

At the end of each financial year, the provision for depreciation account is updated with the depreciation charge for the year. The balance on the account is entered into the statement of financial position alongside the cost, and the expense is entered into the statement of profit or loss and other comprehensive income.

Depreciation is recorded in the general journal and the journal entry as:

Dr Depreciation expense: asset
Cr Provision for depreciation: asset

Depreciation of a non-current asset is shown not only in the statement of financial position but also in the statement of profit or loss and other comprehensive income. From the entry above, you can see that an expense account, titled depreciation expense, is created. Another account, provision for depreciation, is created to record the total depreciation to date.

It is worth noting that accountants do not deduct the depreciation directly from the non-current asset account because we need to provide information to users about the original cost of the non-current asset and how much depreciation has been accumulated so far.

At the end of each financial year, the provision for depreciation account is updated with the depreciation charge for the year. The balance on the account is entered into the statement of financial position alongside the cost and the expense entered into the statement of profit or loss and other comprehensive income.

The ledger accounts for our examples would look like this:

Straight line method

Machine

Date	Details	£	Date	Details	£
Year 1	Bank/trade payables	55000	Year 1	Balance c/d	55000
Year 2	Balance b/d	55000			

Provision for depreciation: machine

Date	Details	£	Date	Details	£
Year 1	Balance c/d	10000	Year 1	Depreciation: machine	10000
Year 2	Balance c/d	20000	Year 2	Balance b/d	10000
				Depreciation: machine	10000
		20000			20000
Year 3	Balance c/d	30000	Year 3	Balance b/d	20000
				Depreciation: machine	10000
		30000			30000
Year 4	Balance c/d	40000	Year 4	Balance b/d	30000
				Depreciation: machine	10000
		40000			40000
Year 5	Balance c/d	50000	Year 5	Balance b/d	40000
				Depreciation: machine	10000
		50000			50000

Depreciation expense: machine

Date	Details	£	Date	Details	£
Year 1	Provision for depreciation: machine	10 000	Year 1	Statement of comprehensive income	10 000
Year 2	Provision for depreciation: machine	10 000	Year 2	Statement of comprehensive income	10 000
Year 3	Provision for depreciation: machine	10 000	Year 3	Statement of comprehensive income	10 000
Year 4	Provision for depreciation: machine	10 000	Year 4	Statement of comprehensive income	10 000
Year 5	Provision for depreciation: machine	10 000	Year 5	Statement of comprehensive income	10 000

EXAM HINT

Note that because the depreciation expense account for the machine is equal on both sides of the account, there is no need for totals. Therefore, each figure is ruled with a double underline underneath, but no single line above.

Reducing balance method

Machine

Date	Details	£	Date	Details	£
Year 1	Bank/trade payables	55 000	Year 1	Balance c/d	55 000
Year 2	Balance b/d	55 000			

(Note that the cost accounts for both methods are the same.)

Provision for depreciation: machine

Date	Details	£	Date	Details	£
Year 1	Balance c/d	11 000	Year 1	Depreciation: machine	11 000
Year 2	Balance c/d	19 800	Year 2	Balance b/d	11 000
				Depreciation: machine	8 800
		19 800			19 800
Year 3	Balance c/d	26 840	Year 3	Balance b/d	19 800
				Depreciation: machine	7 040
		26 840			26 840
Year 4	Balance c/d	32 472	Year 4	Balance b/d	26 840
				Depreciation: machine	5 632
		32 472			32 472
Year 5	Balance c/d	36 978	Year 5	Balance b/d	32 472
				Depreciation: machine	4 506
		36 978			36 978

The reducing balance method shows the annual depreciation charge reducing each year.

Depreciation expense: machine

Date	Details	£	Date	Details	£
Year 1	Provision for depreciation: machine	11 000	Year 1	Statement of comprehensive income	11 000
Year 2	Provision for depreciation: machine	8 800	Year 2	Statement of comprehensive income	8 800
Year 3	Provision for depreciation: machine	7 040	Year 3	Statement of comprehensive income	7 040
Year 4	Provision for depreciation: machine	5 632	Year 4	Statement of comprehensive income	5 632
Year 5	Provision for depreciation: machine	4 506	Year 5	Statement of comprehensive income	4 506

WORKED EXAMPLE

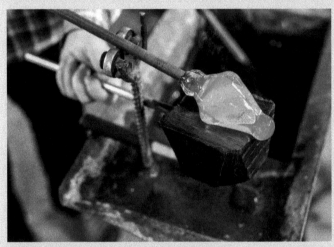

▲ Heating glass to create glass sculptures

Henri started a business making glassware. He began trading on 1 January 2015. He purchased a furnace with which to heat the glass for £50 000 by cheque on that date. He has been advised that he should depreciate the equipment by 5 per cent per annum using the straight line method. We now need to prepare the cost account and the provision account. We will do this for two years.

Furnace cost account

Date	Details	£	Date	Details	£
2015			2015		
1 Jan	Bank	50 000	31 Dec	Balance c/d	50 000
		50 000			50 000
2016			2016		
1 Jan	Balance b/d	50 000	31 Dec	Balance c/d	50 000
		50 000			50 000
2017			2017		
1 Jan	Balance b/d	50 000			

Calculation of annual depreciation charge

$$\text{Cost} \times 5\% = 50\,000 \times 5\% = £2\,500 \text{ p.a.}$$

Provision for depreciation – furnace account

Date	Details	£	Date	Details	£
2015			2015		
31 Dec	Balance c/d	2 500	31 Dec	Statement of profit or loss	2 500
		2 500			2 500
2016			2016		
31 Dec	Balance c/d	5 000	1 Jan	Balance b/d	2 500
			31 Dec	Statement of profit or loss	2 500
		5 000			5 000
			2017		
			1 Jan	Balance b/d	5 000

(NB: the format of these ledger accounts is the same as you will find in your examination mark schemes.)

All provision accounts have credit balances, this balance will remain all the time the business has that non-current asset (in this case, the furnace). The closing balance is entered into the statement of financial position and is subtracted from the cost to obtain the carrying value.

ILLUSTRATION OF DEPRECIATION METHODS

Reducing balance method

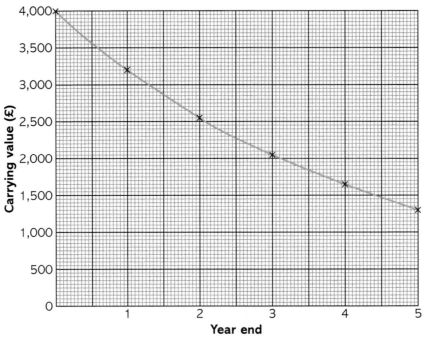

▲ Figure 1 Graph showing NBV using reducing balance method

	£	£	£
	Opening balance	20% depreciation p.a.	Year-end NBV
Year 1	4000	800	3200
Year 2	3200	640	2560
Year 3	2560	512	2048
Year 4	2048	409	1639
Year 5	1639	327	1312

Straight line method

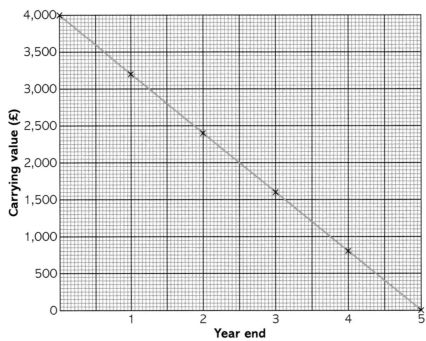

▲ Figure 2 Graph showing NBV using straight line method

	£	£	£
	Opening balance	20% depreciation p.a.	Year-end NBV
Year 1	4000	800	3200
Year 2	3200	800	2400
Year 3	2400	800	1600
Year 4	1600	800	800
Year 5	800	800	NIL

METHODS OF DEPRECIATION AND THEIR EFFECT ON PROFIT

Straight line method
- There is an identical depreciation expense over every accounting period, which reflects the use of buildings, machinery and equipment.
- Profit is reduced by the same amount in every accounting period.

Reducing balance method
- The depreciation expense will be higher in the early years, reducing over time. This may reflect the use of an asset such as motor vehicles
- This method may result in a more accurate expense, if maintenance costs are taken into consideration. These are likely to be higher in later years.
- Profit will be lower in the early years as the depreciation will be greater.

In summary, the reducing balance method tends to result in lower profits than the straight line method in the early years, while in later years it will result in higher profits than the straight line method. Over time, the same expense will be charged to profit, just at different times.

CHANGING THE METHOD OF DEPRECIATION

It is acceptable to change the method of calculating depreciation, but this should only be done after a careful review as it does not comply with the accounting concept of consistency. However, if the current method of calculating depreciation does not reflect the usage of the non-current asset then, applying the materiality concept and the prudence concept, it would be appropriate to change the method used in order that the profit and asset value is not under- or overstated. Over the lifetime of the non-current asset the cost of the deprecation will be the same, regardless of which method is used, it is just a matter of the timings of the cost over the accounting periods.

DISPOSAL OF NON-CURRENT ASSETS

When we sell a non-current asset, we receive an amount of money which may be more or less than the carrying value at the time. If it is more, then we have made a profit; if the amount received is less than the carrying value, a loss is made. The profit or loss on disposal must be recorded in the statement of profit or loss and other comprehensive income. A loss on disposal would be recorded as an expense and a profit on disposal would be recorded as other operating income. It is possible to calculate the profit or loss on disposal without the use of ledger accounts.

Using the calculations in the worked example on page 57, let us assume that we sell the machine at the end of year 3 for £20000. The carrying value (as shown in the table) using the reducing balance method is £28160. Therefore, we have made an additional loss of £8160 and this is the additional amount to be written off to the statement of profit or loss and other comprehensive income as a loss on the sale of the furnace. This can be calculated as follows:

	£
Cost of furnace sold	55000
Provision for depreciation	26840
Carrying value	28160
Revenue from the sale	20000
Loss on disposal	(8160)

In the case of the straight line method, as illustrated in the worked example on page 56 the table shows a balance of £25000 at the end of year 3. In this instance, the additional amount to be written off is £5000.

Ledger accounts for the disposal of non-current assets

To record the profit or loss, we open a disposal account to record the transactions associated with the disposal. These are:

Step 1: Remove the cost of the non-current asset sold:
   Dr Disposal
   Cr Non-current asset sold

Step 2: Remove the accumulated depreciation on the asset:
   Dr Provision for depreciation account
   Cr Disposal

Step 3: Enter the revenue from the sale:
   Dr Bank
   Cr Disposal

If the asset is sold in exchange for another asset, then:

Dr   New non-current asset
Cr   Disposal
Cr   Bank

The balance is then calculated and if it is a debit balance, it is a loss, while any credit balance reflects a profit on disposal. Whatever this balancing figure is, it is transferred to the statement of profit or loss and other comprehensive income. A loss on disposal is an expense, a profit on disposal is recorded as other income.

WORKED EXAMPLE

So far, we have illustrated the accounting entries for straight line depreciation and the reducing balance method. You will now find out how to record the sale in the example below.

On doing this, we transfer the cost of the machine sold and all the provision for depreciation on that machine to the disposal account. After entering the payment received, we then decide if there is a profit or loss. In this instance, there is an additional loss of £8 160 and this is credited to the disposal account (to balance that account to zero). This is transferred to the statement of profit or loss and other comprehensive income, as an expense.

Following the steps given above, the journal entries would be:

Step 1:

	£	£
Dr Disposal	55 000	
Cr Furnace		55 000

Step 2:

	£	£
Dr Provision for depreciation: furnace	26 840	
Cr Disposal		26 840

Step 3:

	£	£
Dr Bank	20 000	
Cr Disposal		20 000

These are entered into the disposal account. The balancing figure in this account will represent either a loss on disposal or a profit on disposal. This amount can be calculated as follows:

	£
Cost	55 000
Provision for depreciation	26 840
Carrying value	28 160
Revenue from the sale	20 000
Loss on disposal	8 160

Furnace

Date	Details	£	Date	Details	£
	Balance b/d	55 000		Disposal	55 000
		55 000			55 000

Provision for depreciation: furnace

Date	Details	£	Date	Details	£
Year 1	Balance c/d	11 000	Year 1	Depreciation: furnace	11 000
Year 2	Balance c/d	19 800	Year 2	Balance b/d	11 000
				Depreciation: furnace	8 800
		19 800			19 800
Year 3	Disposal of furnace	26 840	Year 3	Balance b/d	19 800
				Depreciation: furnace	7 040
		26 840			26 840

Disposal account: furnace

	£		£
Furnace account	55 000	Provision for depreciation	26 840
		Bank	20 000
		Statement of profit or loss	8 160
	55 000		55 000

The entry for the Statement of profit or loss and other income represents the balancing figure and shows a loss on the disposal. From this, you can see that the loss on the sale of the asset is identical to our previous calculation.

WORKED EXAMPLE

In this example, we use the information shown in the previous example but are told that the sale of the furnace in year 3 is for an amount of £32000 instead of the £20000 used in the previous example. As such, we will show a profit on the sale, as illustrated in the disposal account shown below:

Disposal account

Date	Details	£	Date	Details	£
	Furnace account	55000		Provision for depreciation	26840
	Statement of profit or loss	3840		Bank	32000
		58840			58840

ACCOUNTING FOR PART EXCHANGE OF AN ASSET

Sometimes a business will part exchange (trade in) an old asset when purchasing a new one. This requires a slightly different accounting treatment to take into account the value given to the traded-in asset.

WORKED EXAMPLE

Miray operates a taxi service in her local town. In the current year, she purchased a new vehicle at a cost of £25000. She traded in a vehicle with an original cost of £12000 and the provision for depreciation was £4000. Miray paid £20000 for the new vehicle, and paid by cheque.

The part exchange value of the old vehicle is calculated as the difference between the cost of the new vehicle and the amount paid. Therefore, the part exchange value is:

£25000 – £20000 = £5000

Profit or loss on disposal

	£
Cost of vehicle sold	12000
Provision for depreciation	4000
Carrying value	8000
Part exchange allowance	5000
Loss on disposal	3000

Ledger account entries (dates omitted)

Vehicle account

Details	£	Details	£
Balance b/d	12000	Disposal	12000
Bank	20000	Balance c/d	25000
Disposal (p-ex)	5000		
	37000		37000
Balance b/d	25000		

Disposal account

Details	£	Details	£
Vehicle a/c	12000	Provision for depreciation	4000
		Vehicle (p-ex)	5000
		Statement of profit or loss (loss)	3000
	12000		12000

ACTIVITY 1   **SKILLS**   PROBLEM SOLVING, EXECUTIVE FUNCTION

CASE STUDY: JOURNAL ENTRIES FOR PART EXCHANGE

1 Create the journal entries which would be used to complete the ledger accounts for the worked example above. (Hint: refer back to the step-by-step guide on pages 63–64.)

SCHEDULE OF NON-CURRENT ASSETS

A schedule of non-current assets is a summary of the movement of non-current assets over the year. It shows additions, disposals and revaluations. It also includes the depreciation charge for the year. It is used to calculate the carrying values which appear in the statement of financial position. An example of a schedule of non-current assets is given on page 66.

J Baxter
Schedule of non-current assets at 31 July 2017

	Property £	Equipment £	Motor vehicles £
Cost at 1 August 2016	300000	75000	30000
Additions	50000	25000	12000
Disposals		(20000)	
Cost at 31 July 2017	350000	80000	42000
Provision at 1 August 2016	(80000)	(30000)	(10000)
Depreciation on disposals		10000	
Depreciation for year ended 31 July 2017	(35000)	(15000)	(4000)
Total provision for depreciation	(115000)	(35000)	(14000)
Carrying value at 31 July 2017	235000	45000	28000

The process required to construct a schedule of non-current assets is:
- enter the cost of the non-current assets at the start of the year
- for additions – add the cost of any non-current asset which has been bought
- for disposals – subtract the cost of any non-current assets sold
- total the cost of the non-current assets at the end of the year
- enter the opening balance for the provision for depreciation
- remove the depreciation on the assets that have been sold
- calculate the depreciation charge for the current accounting period
- calculate the total provision for depreciation to be carried forward
- calculate the carrying value of the assets by subtracting the provision for depreciation from the year-end cost.

WORKED EXAMPLE

The following information has been obtained from Moosa.

Non-current assets	Balances at 1 March 2016 £	
	Cost	Provision for depreciation
Property	95000	10000
Equipment	40000	10000
Motor vehicles	30000	20000

During the year, the following transactions took place:
- additional building purchased for £30000
- additional equipment purchased for £10000, while equipment with a carrying value of £1000 was sold. (The original cost of this equipment was £5000.)
- motor vehicle additions to the value of £20000 were purchased.

Moosa applies the following with regard to depreciation:
- no depreciation is charged on land, which cost £60000
- depreciation is charged on buildings using the straight line method at the rate of 5 per cent per annum
- equipment is depreciated at the rate of 20 per cent on cost
- motor vehicles are depreciated at the rate of 20 per cent using the reducing balance method.
- no depreciation is charged in the year of disposal, a full year is charged in the year of purchase.

Moosa schedule of non-current assets at 28 February 2017

	£ Property	£ Equipment	£ Motor vehicles
Cost at 1 March 2016	95 000	40 000	30 000
Additions	30 000	10 000	20 000
Disposals		(5 000)	
Cost at 28 Feb 2017	125 000	45 000	50 000
Provision at 1 March 2016	(10 000)	(10 000)	(20 000)
Depreciation on disposals		4 000	
Dep. for year ended 28 Feb 2017	(3 250)	(9 000)	(6 000)
Total provision for depreciation	(13 250)	(15 000)	(26 000)
Carrying value at 28 Feb 2017	111 750	30 000	24 000

Workings
Property
Cost opening balance + additions = £95 000 + £30 000 = £125 000

Depreciation = Cost	£125 000
minus value of land not depreciated	£60 000
Value of buildings	£65 000
Depreciation at 5% on cost	£3 250

Equipment
Cost opening balance + additions − disposals = 40 000 + 10 000 − 5 000
Cost closing balance = £45 000
Remove the depreciation on asset which has been sold = £4 000.
Calculate depreciation for year, following policies for charging depreciation.
Cost = £45 000 at 20% on cost = £9 000

Motor vehicles
Cost closing balance = opening balance + additions = £30 000 + £20 000 = £50 000
Depreciation = cost − depreciation to date = £50 000 − £20 000 = £30 000
Annual depreciation charge = £30 000 × 20% = £6 000

ACTIVITY 2   SKILLS ▶ PROBLEM SOLVING, ANALYSIS, EXECUTIVE FUNCTION

CASE STUDY: KAY & CO.

Kay & Co. is a health food business that makes healthy snacks. A machine is purchased by Kay & Co. for £450 000 on 1 January 2019. The machine has an expected life of five years and the scrap value is expected to be £100 000.

1 Using straight line depreciation, prepare calculations to show the charge to the statement of profit or loss and other comprehensive income each year, as well as the statement of financial position during the life of the machine.

The business also purchased a new factory building for £950 000 on 1 January 2019. The business depreciates all buildings at a rate of 2 per cent p.a. using the reducing balance method.

2 Prepare calculations to show the charge to the statement of profit or loss and other comprehensive income and the statement of financial position entries for the first three years.

ACTIVITY 3   SKILLS ▶ PROBLEM SOLVING, ANALYSIS, EXECUTIVE FUNCTION

CASE STUDY: MISHA'S SOAP FACTORY

At 31 December 2018, Misha's ledger for his soap-making factory contained the following balances:

Plant and machinery	£50 000
Provision for depreciation on plant and machinery	£22 500

During the year ended 31 December 2019, the following transactions took place:

- On 31 March, Misha exchanged part of his machinery for more modern equipment.
- He received a trade-in allowance on the old plant of £7 000 and the balance of £2 000 was paid by cheque.
- The old plant cost £13 000 when it was originally purchased on 1 July 2013.
- Plant and machinery are depreciated on a strict time basis at 20 per cent p.a. using the reducing balance method.

1 Prepare the plant and machinery account and the provision for depreciation account – plant and machinery – for the year ended 31 December 2020.

2 Prepare the disposal account at 31 March 2020.

ACTIVITY 4

SKILLS ▶ PROBLEM SOLVING, EXECUTIVE FUNCTION

CASE STUDY: FATIMA

On 19 June 2018, Fatima purchased a new machine for her textiles factory. The following are the payments made by her relating to this purchase:

	£	£
Cost of machine	42 000	
Less trade discount	4 000	38 000
Delivery costs incurred		3 100
Installation charge paid		5 200
Annual maintenance charge		1 300

1 Show what amount is to be used as the total cost price of the machine.
2 What is the total cost recorded in the machine account?
3 Prepare the ledger account for the new machine for the years ending 31 December 2018 and 2019 and allow depreciation of 15 per cent per annum on a reducing balance. (Note that depreciation is charged in full for the year in which the machine is purchased.)
4 Assuming that Fatima decides to use a straight line method of depreciation of 10 per cent per annum, what would the charges be for depreciation in the years ending 31 December 2018 and 2019?

ACTIVITY 5

SKILLS ▶ PROBLEM SOLVING, EXECUTIVE FUNCTION

CASE STUDY: SINEAD

Sinead started a business on 1 March 2018.

- She purchased a printer for £1 300 and a photocopier for £870 on 1 March 2018.
- On 28 February 2019, she traded in the printer for a new one. The total price of the new printer was £1 900 and she received a credit for the trade-in of £985.
- On 1 March 2019 she also decided to purchase a second photocopier. The price was £1 200, but she received a discount of 10 per cent because she was a returning customer and a discount of 5 per cent for paying in cash.
- Depreciation is charged at 15 per cent p.a. on the printer using the straight line method and at 10 per cent p.a. on the photocopiers using the reducing balance method.

1 Show the ledger accounts for the non-current assets and the provision for depreciation accounts for the years ending 28 February 2019 and 2020.

EXAM HINT

Depreciation is an important accounting topic and will appear in many questions. When preparing a statement of profit or loss and other comprehensive income or a statement of financial position, you will probably be required to calculate depreciation on one or more non-current assets. You need to remember that depreciation appears in both financial statements.

When calculating depreciation, it is important to apply the correct method for that category of non-current asset. In addition, you must apply the stated policy for calculating depreciation on non-current assets when they have been purchased or sold during the financial year.

EVALUATE

The choice of depreciation method is a subjective decision made by a business – there is no right or wrong method, merely a series of guidelines based on accounting concepts and conventions. As a result, it is important to be able to evaluate the choice of method as it applies to the type of non-current asset and the business, and make decisions and recommendations based on your arguments.

Straight line depreciation	
Advantages	**Disadvantages**
It reflects the equal usage of an asset; each accounting period will be charged the same depreciation expense.	As assets age they become less efficient, maintenance costs would increase in later years, distorting the true cost of using the asset.
It is relatively easy to use – since the depreciation expense charge remains the same throughout its useful life. Accountants are not required to calculate the depreciation expense yearly. This is particularly useful when a business has a lot of non-current assets.	The accuracy of residual value – it is difficult to predict the amount the asset could be sold for at the end of its useful life. Furthermore, the number of years of useful life is also based on estimation, therefore it may not truly reflect the consumption of economic benefit.
It takes into account any residual value of the asset.	This method is not suitable if an asset loses a lot of value in early years as the assets would then be overstated in the early years.

Reducing balance method	
Advantages	**Disadvantages**
It reflects a higher loss in value in the early years of assets like motor vehicles, so costs of depreciation are accurately allocated to accounting periods on a diminishing scale.	It does not take into account any residual value, as reducing balance assumes the asset as an infinite life.
The total expense of using an asset will be uniform when increasing maintenance costs are considered – as the economic benefit is small at the end of its useful life, this implies that the asset needs more repairs and maintenance since it is less productive than before.	The carrying value of the asset will never reach zero – this means that the accountant may need to write off the asset when it is close to zero. However, it is difficult to determine at which value the asset should be written off.
It is useful when the benefits of using assets are high in the early years as it matches cost with the benefit.	It is difficult to determine the rate of charging the depreciation – the purpose of the reducing balance method is to reflect the fact that some assets' economic benefit may be used up at a greater rate at the beginning of their useful life. If accountants charge an incorrect rate, the pattern cannot be accurately reflected, therefore the purpose could not be achieved.

CHECKPOINT

1 State one accounting concept that applies to depreciation.

2 Give three reasons why non-current assets depreciate.

3 Depreciation is a cash transaction. True or false?

4 Explain the difference between the straight line method of depreciation and the reducing balance method.

5 Provide the formula that is used to calculate straight line depreciation.

6 What type of non-current assets would be depreciated using the revaluation method?

7 The method of depreciation must never be changed. True or false?

8 What would a credit entry to the statement of profit or loss and other comprehensive income in a disposal account represent?

9 How is the carrying value of a non-current asset calculated?

SUBJECT VOCABULARY

carrying value (net book value) the current value of a non-current asset after accumulated depreciation is deducted

depreciation the loss in value of a non-current asset over its useful economic life, which is apportioned to the accounting periods that benefit from its use

dispose to remove an asset from the books of accounts. This could involve selling the asset, or scrapping the asset if it has no resale value

other operating income (sundry income) revenue from non-trading activities

provision an expected future liability or future expectation of expenditure that is uncertain

provision for depreciation account the account where the accumulated depreciation is recorded

reducing balance method of depreciation a method of depreciation based on the carrying value of the non-current asset

residual value the value of a non-current asset at the end of its useful economic life

revaluation method a method of calculating the annual depreciation charge based on a year-end annual valuation of the assets

schedule of non-current assets a summary of the movement of non-current assets over the accounting period

straight line method of depreciation a method of calculating annual depreciation based on the cost of the non-current asset

EXAM PRACTICE

CASE STUDY: NAZMUL'S TEA COMPANY

SKILLS   PROBLEM SOLVING, EXECUTIVE FUNCTION, DECISION MAKING

Nazmul's business produces several varieties of tea. The following information has been extracted from Nazmul's books for 30 June 2016.

	£	£	£
	Cost	Provision for depreciation	Carrying value
Machinery	30 000	4 500	25 500

The following records relate to the purchase and disposal of machinery:

Machine		Date	£
A	Purchased	1 July 2015	15 000
A	Sold	31 December 2016	11 500
B	Purchased	1 January 2016	15 000
C	Purchased	30 April 2017	20 000

Nazmul's depreciation policy is:
- sales of non-current assets are recorded in a disposal account
- machinery is depreciated using the reducing balance method at a rate of 20 per cent
- depreciation is calculated on a monthly basis.

(Note: All sales and purchases were made by cheque.)

Q

1. Calculate the depreciation to be charged on each machine for the year ended 30 June 2017 and the total depreciation charge for machinery for the year.
(4 marks)

2. Prepare the journal entries for the sale of machine A on 31 December 2016. (Narrative required.) **(4 marks)**

3. Prepare the following accounts for the year ending 30 June 2017:
   (a) machinery account **(4 marks)**
   (b) disposal account. **(4 marks)**

4. Evaluate the use of the reducing balance method of depreciation for machinery. **(12 marks)**

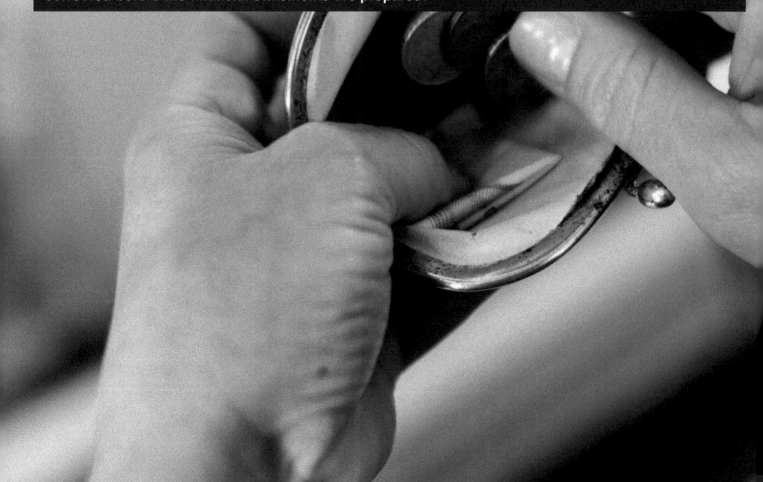

CONTROL PROCEDURES

As you will have noted from the previous chapters, the double-entry accounting system requires many transactions to be recorded over a long period of time. These entries are made in the books of prime entry and the many ledger accounts. Having processed this information, it is wise for a business to have procedures in place which will check the accuracy of the data entered.

To do this, many businesses will have formal control procedures in order to verify the entries made in the ledgers. These include the trial balance, to check the arithmetical accuracy of the general ledger, and control accounts to verify the accuracy of the trade receivables ledger and the trade payables ledger. Should any mistakes be identified, then the errors will be investigated and corrected before the financial statements are prepared.

7 TRIAL BALANCE

LEARNING OBJECTIVES

After you have studied this chapter, you should be able to:
- understand the nature and purpose of a trial balance
- prepare a trial balance from a set of ledger account balances
- understand the limitations of a trial balance.

GETTING STARTED

At the month end, the ledger accounts are all balanced. If you add up all the debit balances and then add up all the credit balances, what will you discover? Why do you think this is the case?

The trial balance is a list of balances taken from the ledger accounts at a set point in time. The trial balance is often prepared at month end using these balances. It is done in order to check the accuracy of our double entry.

The ledger accounts are balanced off, and all of the debit balances are shown in the debit column and all credit balances in the credit column. We saw in Chapter 2 how we balance off the ledger accounts; we also noted how these balances are transferred to the trial balance. It is important to realise that the trial balance is not part of the double-entry system but is simply a list of balances.

The following example shows a list of balances taken from the ledger at 31 December 2018. These balances are listed as below and then used (after any adjustment) in the relevant financial statement.

Trial balance for the year ended 31 December 2018

	£	£
	Debit (Dr)	Credit (Cr)
Trade payables		5 400
Cost of sales	11 500	
Wages	3 100	
Revenue		27 500
Rent	1 900	
Office furniture	1 800	
Capital account		4 000
Bank overdraft		1 200
Trade receivables	19 800	
Total	38 100	38 100

If the trial balance balances, it means that the postings have been made to the *correct side* of an account. It does not, however, indicate that a posting has been entered to the *correct account*. At this stage of your studies, you do not need to worry about errors; however, these are covered in Chapter 9.

PURPOSE OF A TRIAL BALANCE

The primary purpose of preparing a trial balance is to check the arithmetical accuracy of the ledger account. It is part of the checking procedure, which also includes control accounts (Chapter 8). However, it does have an additional purpose, since it acts as an intermediate step in the preparation of financial statements. The account balance from the trial balance can be used to prepare the statement of profit or loss and other comprehensive income and the statement of financial position (Chapter 10).

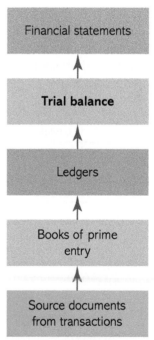

▲ Figure 1 The relationship between the trial balance, the ledger accounts used to produce it and the financial statements

PREPARING THE TRIAL BALANCE

We need a list of account balances at the end of the accounting period in order to prepare the trial balance. This list will be generated from the ledger accounts which have been balanced at the end of the period. This extracted list of balances is generally presented in your studies as a single-column list. This needs to be presented as a list of debit balances and credit balances. It is essential that you understand the rules of double entry to correctly enter an account in the trial balance. If you are unsure, go back to Chapters 2 and 3 to refresh your understanding.

Debit	Credit
Assets	Liabilities
Expenses	Other income
Drawings	Capital
Purchases	Revenue

(Note: Drawings is a debit entry in the trial balance as it is a reduction of the owner's capital.)

WORKED EXAMPLE

Eleni runs a shop selling flowers. The following balances were extracted from Eleni's books on 31 March 2018:

Account	£
Capital	155 440
Purchases	96 250
Drawings	9 450
Revenue from sales	146 390
Loan from bank	20 000
Trade receivables	10 390
Revenue returns	8 500
Trade payables	12 495
Cash	150
Admin expenses	10 240
Wages	28 980
Telephone expenses	3 020
Interest paid	2 350
Travel expenses	1 045
Bank	1 050 (Cr)
Premises	125 000
Machinery	40 000

We will now prepare a trial balance from the list of account balances at 31 March 2018:

Eleni: trial balance at 31 March 2018

	£ Dr	£ Cr
Capital		155 440
Purchases	96 250	
Drawings	9 450	
Revenue from sales		146 390
Loan from bank		20 000
Trade receivables	10 390	
Revenue returns	8 500	
Trade payables		12 495
Cash	150	
Admin expenses	10 240	
Wages	28 980	
Telephone expenses	3 020	
Interest paid	2 350	
Travel expenses	1 045	
Bank		1 050
Premises	125 000	
Machinery	40 000	
Total	**335 375**	**335 375**

(Note: the bank balance is on the credit side of the trial balance. The Cr indicates that it is an overdraft, so it is a liability, not an asset.)

If all the account balances are correct but the trial balance does not balance, then a **suspense account** needs to be added to the list of balances in order to balance the trial balance. The suspense account is a temporary account where the difference is held until errors are located and corrected. Suspense accounts are covered in detail in Chapter 9, which looks at the correction of errors.

LIMITATIONS OF A TRIAL BALANCE

The trial balance simply checks the arithmetical accuracy of the double-entry system. However, even if the trial balance totals match, it does not mean that the ledgers are free from mistakes. Below are some limitations.

- A trial balance gives only summarised information on each account, no details are available.
- It does not provide information on the profits or losses of the business.
- Some errors made in the double-entry system will not be revealed by the trial balance. There are six types of error that are not revealed by a trial balance. How these are corrected is covered in Chapter 9. Briefly, these errors are:
  - commission
  - omission
  - principle
  - reversal
  - original entry
  - compensating.

ACTIVITY 1   SKILLS   ANALYSIS, EXECUTIVE FUNCTION

CASE STUDY: SIU WAH

The following balances were extracted from Siu Wah's books at 31 December 2018:

	£
Motor vehicles at cost	5 600
Fixtures and fittings at cost	4 200
Property at cost	5 600
Loan	1 680
Advertising	280
Administration expenses	1 316
Loan interest	56
Bank overdraft	840
Trade receivables	3 150
Trade payables	2 086
Profit 1 January 2018	5 250
Allowance/provision for irrecoverable debts at 1 January 2018	210
Siu Wah – capital account	5 446
Revenue	10 850
Purchases	5 180
Opening inventory at 1 January 2018	3 500
Depreciation on motor vehicles at 1 January 2018	1 680
Depreciation on fixtures and fittings at 1 January 2018	840

1 Prepare the trial balance for Siu Wah at 31 December 2018. (Hint: for profit account – the profit belongs to the owner of the business.)

ACTIVITY 2   SKILLS   ANALYSIS, PROBLEM SOLVING, EXECUTIVE FUNCTION

CASE STUDY: RASHMI

Rashmi is the owner of an electrical repair business. After the first year of operations she presented the following trial balance, which did not balance because a number of accounts were shown in the incorrect column.

	£	£
	Dr	Cr
Cash	2 150	
Trade receivables	6 500	
Inventory at 1 January 2018		1 900
Equipment	18 900	
Trade payables		4 750
Rashmi, capital account	13 000	
Rashmi, drawings		1 800
Revenue	37 250	
Wages		9 500
Rent	8 600	
Postage and telephone	3 750	
Travel and motor expenses		1 900

1 Place the accounts in the correct column to check if the trial balance is in balance.

ACTIVITY 3   SKILLS › ANALYSIS, PROBLEM SOLVING, EXECUTIVE FUNCTION

CASE STUDY: NATHAN

Nathan prepares a trial balance from his records. In doing so, he places some debit and credit balances on the incorrect side of the trial balance. As a result, the trial balance does not balance. The following trial balance was prepared for the year ended 31 December 2017:

Trial balance for Nathan, year ended 31 December 2017

	£	£
	Dr	Cr
Revenue	21 860	
Purchases		11 180
Motor vehicles at cost		15 600
Fixtures and fittings at cost	4 200	
Advertising	980	
Bank interest paid	456	
Opening inventory at 1 Jan 2017		6 500
Provision for depreciation – Motor vehicles (at 1 Jan 2017)	4 680	
Trade receivables		9 150
Trade payables	9 086	
Allowance/provision for irrecoverable debts (at 1 Jan 2017)	1 910	
Nathan – capital account		27 446
Property at cost		19 600
Selling expenses	6 680	
Administration expenses		4 316
Bank overdraft	9 840	
Provision for depreciation – fixtures and fittings (at 1 Jan 2017)		3 840

1 Redraw the trial balance, placing the debit and credit balances in their correct columns.
2 At the end of the exercise, total the debits and credits to ensure that the trial balance now balances.

ACTIVITY 4   SKILLS › ANALYSIS, EXECUTIVE FUNCTION

CASE STUDY: THOMAS

Thomas's business sells and delivers furniture. You are given the following list of balances for Thomas at 30 September 2019:

	£
Advertising	9 600
Postage and telephone	3 280
Lighting and heating	5 104
Drawings	50 560
Bank overdraft	27 796
Insurance	15 584
Rent and rates	60 352
Salaries and wages	41 088
Motor expenses	37 172
Purchases	330 061
Returns inwards	1 440
Returns outwards	2 416
Inventory at 1 October 2018	112 448
Trade receivables	65 005
Commission received	3 200
Trade payables	51 028
Fixtures and fittings	49 280
Capital at 1 October 2018	150 432
Cash in hand	1 450
Bank interest and charges	4 928
Revenue	604 960
Motor vehicles	52 480

1 Prepare the trial balance at 30 September 2019.

ACTIVITY 5

SKILLS ANALYSIS, EXECUTIVE FUNCTION

CASE STUDY: FINAL TRADING CO.

On 30 June 2019, Final Trading Co. extracted a list of balances from their ledger.

	£
Office expenses	11 880
Postage and stationery	3 900
Rent and rates	7 500
Insurance	1 095
Lighting and heating	1 548
Motor expenses	5 880
Salaries and wages	14 550
Revenue	109 800
Purchases	61 950
Bank charges	2 418
Vans	10 500
Trade payables	9 750
Trade receivables	20 430
Property	84 000
Inventory 1 July 2018	24 060
Cash at bank	3 402
Drawings	18 834
Capital	152 397

1 Place these balances in a trial balance to check the accuracy of the ledger postings.

ACTIVITY 6

SKILLS ANALYSIS, PROBLEM SOLVING, EXECUTIVE FUNCTION

CASE STUDY: PRIYA

The following balances were extracted from Priya's books on 30 June 2018.

	£
Office expenses	3 880
Lighting and heating	2 570
Motor expenses	5 820
Salaries and wages	4 650
Revenue	79 850
Purchases	41 750
Bank charges	2 010
Delivery vehicles	23 580
Trade payables	9 150
Trade receivables	29 930
Office equipment	24 530
Inventory 1 July 2017	14 960
Cash at bank	9 450
Drawings	25 870
Capital	?

1 Prepare the trial balance at 30 June 2018, showing the value of the capital account at that date.

ACTIVITY 7

SKILLS ANALYSIS, PROBLEM SOLVING, EXECUTIVE FUNCTION

CASE STUDY: MIMI

When Mimi prepared her trial balance, she incorrectly listed the balances in the wrong columns. As a result, she was unable to balance her trial balance.

Mimi & Co. trial balance at 30 June 2019

	£	£
	Dr	Cr
Trade receivables		5 100
Purchases	24 000	
Insurance	350	
Electricity		700
Motor expenses	2 960	
Salaries and wages	5 830	
Revenue	28 891	
Drawings	8 000	
Motor vehicle		7 500
Trade payables		3 250
Fittings and fixtures	3 160	
Inventory 1 July 2018	5 020	
Cash at bank		320
Capital	30 799	

1 Redo the trial balance to ensure that it is balanced.

ACTIVITY 8

SKILLS › ANALYSIS, EXECUTIVE FUNCTION

CASE STUDY: MAX & CO.

Max owns an independent book shop. He prepared a list of balances from his ledger accounts.

Max & Co. balances at 30 June 2019

	£
Postage and stationery	1 300
Rent and rates	2 500
Drawings	11 340
Capital	80 000
Motor expenses	1 960
Salaries and wages	4 850
Revenue	63 400
Purchases	48 650
Motor vehicle	3 500
Trade payables	7 100
Trade receivables	39 540
Bank overdraft	5 120
Fittings and fixtures	23 960
Opening inventory	18 020

1 Prepare the trial balance from this list.

EVALUATE

As preparing a trial balance does not provide any additional information, it can be argued that its preparation is of no benefit to a business. You may be asked to evaluate the use of a trial balance in an exam. The table shows some advantages and disadvantages:

Advantages	Disadvantages
Checks the arithmetical accuracy of the ledger accounts before preparing financial statements.	Does not reveal all errors (COPROC) so accuracy cannot be assured.
Saves time when preparing financial statements as no need to refer back to numerous ledger accounts.	Does not provide information about financial position and financial performance.

CHECKPOINT

1 On which side of the trial balance would you find liabilities?
2 On which side of the trial balance would you find capital?
3 On which side of the trial balance would you find carriage outwards?
4 If the trial balance balances, then there are no errors. True or false?
5 State two errors not revealed by the trial balance.
6 Identify one reason for preparing a trial balance.

SUBJECT VOCABULARY

suspense account a temporary account used to balance the trial balance until errors are found and corrected. It is used to record the elimination of errors
trial balance a summary of all the balances extracted from the ledgers of a business

EXAM PRACTICE 1

CASE STUDY: RAN'S BALANCES

SKILLS ANALYSIS, EXECUTIVE FUNCTION

Ran's bookkeeper extracted the following balances from his books of account on 31 August 2017.

	£
Buildings	122 000
Cash in hand	2 469
Carriage in	500
Carriage out	400
Capital	25 000
Drawings	9 000
Discounts received	200
Equipment	30 000
Fixtures	3 000
Heating and lighting	1 000
Computer supplies	300
General expenses	20
Rent paid	2 300
Motor expenses	500
Wages	21 789
Inventory, 1 Sept 2016	3 456
Loan payable 2020	80 300
Purchases	45 000
Sales	128 870
Revenue returns	870
Purchase returns	550
Trade payables	27 684
Trade receivables	20 000

1 Prepare the trial balance for Ran at 31 August 2017.
(25 marks)

EXAM PRACTICE 2

CASE STUDY: PALAK'S TRIAL BALANCE

SKILLS ANALYSIS, EXECUTIVE FUNCTION, DECISION MAKING

Palak's bookkeeper extracted the following trial balance on 30 September 2017:

	£ Dr	£ Cr
Cash in hand	10 500	
Capital		130 000
Discount allowable		2 000
Discount receivable	3 500	
Drawings		22 000
Electricity	23 000	
General expenses	5 000	
Inventory at 1 October 2016		22 000
Non-current assets at cost		
Premises	80 000	
Machinery	30 000	
Motor vehicles	29 000	
Provisions for depreciation		
Premises		18 000
Machinery		3 000
Motor vehicles		12 500
Purchases		100 000
Rent and rates	5 500	
Returns inwards	4 000	
Revenue	185 000	
Trade receivables	19 000	
Trade payables	22 000	
Wages	22 000	
Suspense account		129 000
Total	438 500	438 500

Palak was aware that the trial balance contained errors and would need to be corrected before completing the financial statements.

1 Complete a trial balance, correcting all errors, and eliminate the suspense account. **(9 marks)**
2 State three errors not revealed by a trial balance. **(3 marks)**
3 Evaluate the use of a trial balance. **(6 marks)**

8 CONTROL ACCOUNTS

LEARNING OBJECTIVES

After you have studied this chapter, you should be able to:
- prepare control accounts for trade receivables and trade payables
- evaluate the use of control accounts.

GETTING STARTED

You work for a business that has over 1 000 customers and over 500 suppliers. Each of these has an individual account in the trade receivables and trade payables ledgers. If you wanted to know how much was owed to you by customers, would this be easy to calculate? If you were asked by your manager to provide a total for monies owed to suppliers, could you quickly provide this information?

The accuracy of the double-entry system for recording transactions is checked through the trial balance (see Chapter 7). There are many entries made from the revenue and purchase day books to the trade receivables and trade payables accounts. Because of this, we use control accounts to check the accuracy of the entries made in these ledgers. Control accounts record the totals from the books of original entries. We have a control account for each ledger, so we can identify arithmetical errors when they occur. This process is known as reconciliation, where two separate records are used to confirm that the account balances are correct.

The control accounts consist of summaries of the totals taken from books of prime entry (Chapter 3). All individual entries are summarised; that is, an entry made in the ledger account is also made in the control account, thus acting as a check on the accuracy. A debit entry made in the ledger account is a debit entry in the control account. A credit entry in the ledger account is a credit entry in the control account.

Control accounts can be either memorandum (totals) or actually part of the double-entry system with the individual trade payables/receivables accounts memorandum. The approach used in IAL is to treat control accounts as memorandum (totals) accounts and therefore they are not part of the double-entry system. We are able to use the balances of the control accounts in a trial balance instead of the individual balances.

Using the total, we then add entries that increase the individual trade receivables balances and deduct totals that decrease the balances. The closing balance must equal the total of the individual trade receivables balances and, if not, then it proves that there are errors in posting to the trade receivables accounts. This, of course, also applies to the trade payables ledger and control.

ADVANTAGES OF CONTROL ACCOUNTS

There are several benefits for a business in using control accounts:

Accuracy

Control accounts can be used to eliminate errors that occur in posting entries in the personal accounts. It proves the arithmetical accuracy of the ledger accounts. The control account total should agree with the sum of the individual personal accounts. A reconciliation would be carried out to check and calculate the totals of the individual balances and see that they agreed with the control balances.

Improve the speed of decision making

By employing control accounts we can produce a trial balance without having to add up each individual trade receivables account or trade payables account in order to include those balances into our trial balance. The advantage of this is that accountants can provide trade receivables and trade payables balances immediately, so management can make their decisions faster. It also speeds up the process of preparing the financial statements.

Internal control (prevention of fraud)

The control account provides some protection against fraud. In many businesses, control accounts are prepared by a different employee. When a transaction occurs, an employee is responsible for entering the transactions in the day book and subsidiary accounts (i.e. individual accounts). A copy of the source document will be sent to another staff member for preparing the control account.

This control also applies to all purchases and sales transactions. It ensures that all payments made by trade receivables are accounted for, and that no individual trade receivables account is credited without a payment having been made or a credit note having been issued. Similarly, it ensures that all payments to trade payables are accounted for and any discounts given by trade payables are recorded.

Therefore, we can say that the main function of a control account is to make the process of finding errors

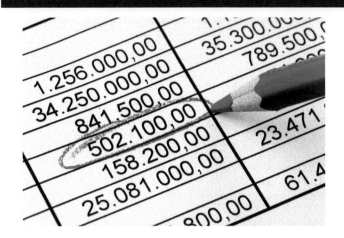

easier by drawing attention to the ledger in which those errors are likely. This ensures that errors are kept to a minimum and opportunities for fraud or theft of cash are very small. This is achieved by a system of internal control that is set up within the business.

Control accounts are of great value as they allow for the splitting of duties between staff members. Figures entered into the control account should be calculated by a number of different staff and this means the control accounts also act as a check on their work.

LIMITATIONS OF CONTROL ACCOUNTS

Not all errors can be detected
Even though a control account aims to prevent fraud and facilitate finding errors, it does not mean all errors can be identified. There are errors that cannot

be revealed in a trial balance, particularly when a business has a poor internal control system; for example, error of omission. Errors are covered in more detail in Chapter 9.

The control account may contain errors
If the quality of the workers preparing the control account is not good, then the control account may contain errors, such as transposition error. This affects the accuracy of the control account and could affect the management's decision making.

Cost
Additional time and effort is required to maintain control accounts. They contain no new information, and they act as a check on the accuracy of other postings. As such, it could be argued that it is an additional expense which would not be required if all entries were made accurately in the first place. This additional cost might reduce the profit made by the business.

TRANSFER OF TRANSACTIONS TO THE CONTROL ACCOUNT
Figure 1 illustrates the use of the control account. You will note that, in this illustration, the revenue day book and returns day book have been posted to the various trade receivables accounts. Entries from the cash book are also shown. At the same time, the totals from all subsidiary books are posted to the trade receivables

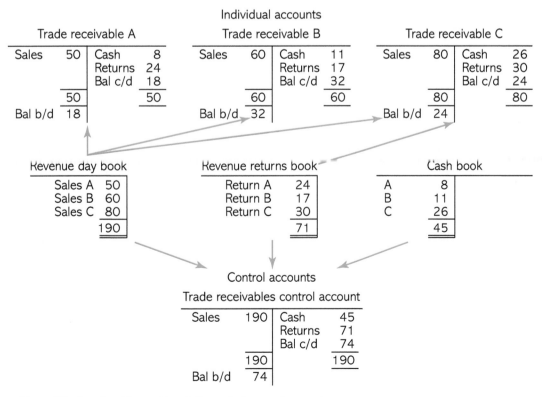

▲ Figure 1 The transfer of transactions to the control account

control account. From there, a balance (in this case £74) is calculated. This balance can be used as the trade receivables balance in the trial balance without reference to individual trade receivables accounts; this speeds up the preparation of a trial balance and financial statements.

You will also see that the individual balances on each trade receivables account will – and must – total the £74 shown as the control account balance. This is the arithmetical check on the accuracy of our trade receivables postings.

The balance of £74 is made up of the balances of:

- Trade receivable A = £18
- Trade receivable B = £32
- Trade receivable C = £24

TRADE RECEIVABLES CONTROL ACCOUNT

This account is used to 'control' the trade receivables accounts and contains the accounts of customers who have bought inventory on credit – that is, credit sales. This control account duplicates all entries made in the individual trade receivable ledger accounts. Remember that it is a memorandum account and so the entries are on the same side as the individual ledger accounts. The entries made to the control account must *not* be reversed. All too often, this is a common mistake made during examinations!

The following table is a summary of transactions/ entries found in the trade receivables control account, together with their related books of prime entry and the related source document:

Transaction	Debit or credit	Book of prime entry	Source documents
Opening balance	Dr or Cr (or both*)		
Credit sales	Dr	Revenue day book	Invoice
Receipts from trade receivables	Cr	Cash book	Receipts
Discount allowed	Cr	Cash book	Invoice
Dishonoured cheque by a customer	Dr	Cash book	Bank statement and letter from the bank
Irrecoverable debts	Cr	General journal	Note from customers

Transaction	Debit or credit	Book of prime entry	Source documents
Interest charged to customers	Dr	General journal	Statement of account
Credit sales returns	Cr	Revenue returns day book	Credit note issued
Transfer of debit balances in the trade receivables account to trade payables account (contra entry or set-off)	Cr	General journal	Invoices

*The opening balance of the account should have a debit balance as it represents money owed to the business. It can also have an opening credit balance. See section later in the chapter.

When we use the revenue day book, each sale is entered into that subsidiary book and posted to the individual ledger account. The total would be credited to sales. Rather than entering each sales transaction again to the control account (remember – the same side as the ledger!) we enter the total, thus saving time.

Trade receivables control account

Date	Details	£	Date	Details	£
1 Apr	Balance b/d	2 300	30 Apr	Bank	3 200
	Revenue day book	5 650		Discounts allowed	120
				Returns inwards day book	350
				Irrecoverable debts	600
				Balance c/d	3 680
		7 950			7 950
1 May	Balance b/d	3 680			

The above example shows the items that are normally found in the trade receivables control account.

At the month end, the business would extract a list of trade receivables balances. The balance on the control account (£3 680) would equal the total of balances in the trade receivables accounts in the trade receivables ledger.

WORKED EXAMPLE

The following is a list of transactions in Melody's books for May 2018:

		£
1 May	Opening balance	6 035
31 May	Revenue day book	29 549
31 May	Cheques from trade receivables	13 800
31 May	Discount allowed	1 003
31 May	Dishonoured cheque – cash book	622
31 May	Returns inwards	1 176
31 May	Irrecoverable debts written off	974

We will write up the trade receivables control account and show the closing balance at 31 May 2018.

Trade receivables control account

Date	Details	£	Date	Details	£
2018			2018		
1 May	Balance b/d	6 035			
31 May	Sales	29 549	31 May	Revenue returns	1 176
	Dishonoured cheque (bank)	622		Irrecoverable debts	974
				Bank	13 800
				Discount allowed	1 003
				Balance c/d	19 253
		36 206			36 206
1 June	Balance b/d	19 253			

TRADE PAYABLES CONTROL ACCOUNT

This control account checks the accuracy of the individual trade payables ledger accounts. It contains information obtained from individual suppliers' accounts for inventory purchased on credit – that is, credit purchases. The following is a summary of transactions/entries found in a control account:

Transaction	Debit or credit	Book of original entry	Source documents
Opening balance	Dr or Cr or both*		
Credit purchases	Cr	Purchases day book	Invoice
Payments to trade payables	Dr	Cash book	Cheque counterfoil
Discount received	Dr	Cash book	Invoice
Dishonoured cheque to a supplier	Cr	Cash book	Bank statement and letter from the bank
Interest charged by suppliers	Cr	General journal	Statement of account
Credit purchase returns	Dr	Purchases returns day book	Credit note received
Transfer of debit balances in the trade receivables account to trade payables account (contra entry or set-off)	Dr	General journal	Invoices

*The opening balance may contain a debit entry as well as the expected credit entry, see the next section.

CONTRA ACCOUNTS (SET-OFFS)

There is one additional item that is recorded in a control account and that is a contra entry (or set-off). This comes about when a business deals with another business both as a supplier of goods (and therefore a trade payable) and a purchaser of goods (a trade receivable).

For example, suppose Ace Trading sells goods to Joe & Co. for £3 200 and also purchases goods from Joe & Co. for £4 500. Ace Trading has a situation where Joe & Co. is owed £4 500, but it also owes £3 200 for the goods purchased from Ace Trading. Instead of paying the amount due to Joe & Co., Ace Trading sets off the amount owing of £3 200 and issues a cheque to Joe & Co. for £1 300. We always use the smaller amount for the contra entry.

The entries needed for such a transaction with Ace Trading are shown below as individual ledger accounts:

Joe & Co. – trade receivable account

Date	Details	£	Date	Details	£
	Sales	3 200		Joe & Co. trade payable (contra)	3 200

Joe & Co. – trade payable account

Date	Details	£	Date	Details	£
	Joe & Co. trade receivable (contra)	3 200		Purchases	4 500
	Bank	1 300			

To do the contra entry, we would need to record it in the journal as follows:

	£	£
	Dr	Cr
Joe & Co. (trade payable)	3 200	
Joe & Co. (trade receivable)		3 200

The amount owing by Joe & Co. for goods is set off against an amount due to Joe & Co. The entry is also posted to the trade receivables and trade payables control accounts. This means that the debit entry to the trade payables account is also posted to the debit side of the trade payables control account:

Trade payables control account

Trade receivable control	3 200	

Similarly, the credit entry is posted to the credit in the trade receivables control account:

Trade receivables control account

	Trade payable control	3 200

WORKED EXAMPLE

	£
Trade payables at 1 January 2019	15 430
Credit purchases	21 000
Cash paid to trade payables	16 570
Discounts received	6 020
Returns outwards	1 000
Set-off of trade receivables balance	100

We will prepare the trade payables ledger control account, showing the balance outstanding at the month end:

Trade payables control account

Date	Details	£	Date	Details	£
31 Jan	Bank	16 570	1 Jan	Balance b/d	15 430
	Returns outwards	1 000	31 Jan	Purchases	21 000
	Set-off – trade receivable	100			
	Discounts received	6 020			
	Balance c/d	12 740			
		36 430			36 430
			1 Feb	Balance b/d	12 740

BALANCES ON BOTH SIDES

Finally, we should note that there may be balances brought down on both sides of the ledger account. Therefore, in the trade receivables control account there may be a credit balance brought down in addition to the normal debit balance. This means that:

- certain trade receivables accounts are in credit because they have overpaid the account and so become a liability for the business
- they have returned goods after they paid their account
- a customer may make a deposit payment before sales have taken place. This means the business owes the customer goods, therefore the balance becomes credit (Cr)
- the business may discover having overcharged a customer after he settled his account.

In a similar way, the trade payables control account may also show a debit balance in addition to the normal credit balance. The reason for this could be a return of goods after the account was paid or an overpayment of the account.

For example, we use Joe & Co.'s trade payables account, as in the previous section. After payment of £1 300 is made, goods to the value of £430 are returned to Ace Trading. This will be shown as follows:

Joe & Co. – trade payables account

Details	£	Details	£
Contra entry	3 200	Purchases	4 500
Bank	1 300		
	4 500		4 500
Returns	430		

This will result in a debit balance in the trade payables account of £430. Similarly, the trade payables control account will also show this debit balance.

It is important to note that all balances must be shown and not deducted from each other.

ACTIVITY 1

SKILLS   ANALYSIS, PROBLEM SOLVING, EXECUTIVE FUNCTION

CASE STUDY: NICOLAS

The following information is available to allow you to prepare a trade payables control account for Nicolas at 30 June 2019:

		£
1 June	Opening balance	8 512
30 June	Purchases day book	7 190
30 June	Payments to trade payables	4 996
30 June	Discount received	711
30 June	Returns outward	657
30 June	Contra	755
30 June	Cash sales	200
30 June	Allowance/provision for irrecoverable debts	50
30 June	Dishonoured cheque received from customer	80

1 Show the ledger account and the closing balance at 30 June 2019.

ACTIVITY 2

SKILLS   ANALYSIS, EXECUTIVE FUNCTION

CASE STUDY: HELLENCO TRADING

The following is an extract from the books of Hellenco Trading for the year ended 31 March 2019:

	£
Trade receivables ledger control account balance on 1 April 2018 (debit)	22 060
Sales	153 900
Cheques received from trade receivables	92 282
Discounts allowed	4 160
Discounts received	3 021
Returns inwards	2 050
Returns outwards	1 604
Irrecoverable debts written off	1 901
Set-off to trade receivable of a credit balance	196
Amounts due from customers transferred to trade payables ledger	904
Interest charged on trade receivables overdue account	68
Total of balances ledger on 31 March 2019 (debit)	81 034
Total of balances in trade receivables' ledger on 31 March 2019 (credit)	6 107

1 Prepare the trade receivables ledger control account for the year ended 31 March 2019, using the relevant figures selected from the data shown.

ACTIVITY 3

SKILLS   ANALYSIS, PROBLEM SOLVING, EXECUTIVE FUNCTION

CASE STUDY: SHAYLA

Shayla's company manages vending machines in public spaces. They sell snacks through their vending machines. This is Shayla's ledger account for June 2019:

		£
1 June	Trade payables ledger balance	9 843
1 June	Trade receivables ledger balance	6 488
30 June	Purchases for month	12 992
30 June	Sales for month	19 745
30 June	Paid to suppliers	10 622
30 June	Discounts received	255
30 June	Returns inwards	790
30 June	Returns outwards	681
30 June	Discount allowed	1 003
30 June	Irrecoverable debts written off	780
30 June	Unpaid cheque of customer	147
30 June	Cheques received from customers	5 933

1 From the balances in Shayla's ledger account, prepare both the control accounts at 30 June 2019.

ACTIVITY 4   SKILLS   ANALYSIS, PROBLEM SOLVING, EXECUTIVE FUNCTION

CASE STUDY: KATIE

Katie's books include three ledgers comprising the nominal (general) ledger, trade receivables ledger and trade payables ledger.

The following information relates to the year ended 30 June 2020:

	£
Trade receivables ledger control account balance on 1 July 2019 (debit)	23 105
Trade payables ledger control account balance on 1 July 2019 (credit)	19 714
Cheques received	42 033
Cheques paid	41 206
Sales	104 500
Purchases	77 390
Returns outwards	12 120
Returns inwards	16 430
Discount received	5 619
Discount allowed	6 230
Irrecoverable debts	5 910
Cash received in respect of a debit balance from trade payable	3 104
Amount due from trade receivables transferred to trade payable ledger	3 021
Total balances in trade payables ledger on 30 June 2020 (credit)	38 295

1 Prepare the trade receivables ledger and trade payables ledger control accounts at 30 June 2020. The balances for trade receivables and any debit balances on trade payables accounts must be calculated at 30 June 2020.

ACTIVITY 5   SKILLS   ANALYSIS, PROBLEM SOLVING, EXECUTIVE FUNCTION

CASE STUDY: HILMAR & CO.

Hilmar & Co. build virtual reality headsets. Their books include three ledgers comprising the general ledger, trade receivables ledger and trade payables ledger. The general ledger contains the trade receivables ledger and trade payables ledger control accounts.

The following information relates to the month of March 2019:

	£
Trade receivables control account balance on 1 March 2019 (Dr)	5 900
Trade receivables control account balance on 1 March 2019 (Cr)	425
Trade payables control account balance on 1 March 2019 (Dr)	370
Trade payables control account balance on 1 March 2019 (Cr)	7 290
Credit sales for the month	41 800
Credit purchases for the month	30 433
Trade receivables balances set against accounts in the trade payables ledger	1 011
Returns inwards	884
Returns outwards	470
Cheques received from trade receivables	17 470
Interest charged on trade receivables overdue accounts	185
Discount allowed	706
Discount received	471
Irrecoverable debts	902
Dishonoured (unpaid) cheques from trade receivables	1 940
Irrecoverable debts recovered	217
Cheques paid to trade payables	20 084
Cash received from trade receivables	6 130
Cash paid to trade payables	4 020
Trade payables control account balance on 31 March 2019 (Dr)	816
Trade receivables control account balance on 31 March 2019 (Cr)	413

1 Prepare the trade receivables and trade payables ledger control accounts for March 2019 and find the balances at the month end.

EXAM HINT

Control accounts have very long names and many entries, but remember, they are essentially the same as an individual account of a credit customer (trade receivable) and a credit supplier (trade payable). One way to remember which entry goes where is to think of the effect the transaction has on the amount of money owed.

Trade receivables control account

Asset account

Money owed **to** us increases ↑	Money owed **to** us decreases ↓

Trade payables control account

Liability account

Money owed **by** us decreases ↓	Money owed **by** us increases ↑

▲ Figure 2 The effect of transactions on the trade receivables and trade payables control accounts

Contra entries appear in both the control accounts. The entry is always to:
- debit the trade payable control account
- credit the trade receivable control account.

CHECKPOINT

1 State two entries on the debit side of the trade receivables control account.

2 Give two entries on the debit side of the trade payables control account.

3 Name the contra entries made in the control accounts.

4 What does a credit opening balance represent in the trade receivables control account?

5 Explain two reasons why a credit balance might exist in the trade receivables control account.

6 Purchase returns are put in on the debit side of the trade payables control account. True or false?

7 Explain one advantage of maintaining control accounts.

8 Explain one disadvantage of maintaining control accounts.

SUBJECT VOCABULARY

contra entry (or set-off) an entry in the control accounts which cancels a debit balance with a credit balance
reconciliation the process of comparing two different accounting records to ensure that they agree with each other
subsidiary book another term for the books of prime entry or day books

EVALUATE

Control accounts are prepared primarily to prove the accuracy of the entries made in the trade receivables and trade payables ledgers. They are generally not part of the double-entry system and so are effectively memorandum accounts. As they provide little more information, it is often debated whether a business should prepare them. It is a popular examination question.

Advantages	Disadvantages
Checks the accuracy of double-entry system	Not all errors are detected (see Chapter 9)
Allows for the preparation of financial statements	Requires a skilled bookkeeper to prepare control accounts – expense implications
Shows the value of assets and liabilities relating to credit sales and credit purchases	The control accounts themselves may contain errors
Helps reduce fraud	

EXAM PRACTICE

CASE STUDY: OFURE

SKILLS EXECUTIVE FUNCTION, CRITICAL THINKING, DECISION MAKING

Ofure is a retailer who buys and sells shoes. She has extracted the following information from her books on 31 October 2016:

Balances of the trade receivables control account on 1 October 2016:

£
5 550 Dr
150 Cr

Balances of the trade payables control account on 1 October 2016:

£
100 Dr
2 410 Cr

Summary of transactions for October 2016:

	£
Sales: credit	32 450
Sales: cash	15 320
Revenue returns	2 250
Irrecoverable debts	350
Purchases: credit	13 500
Purchase: cash	2 500
Purchase returns	755
Discounts allowed	355
Discounts received	265
Cheques received from trade receivables	26 350
Payments by cheque to trade payables	8 010
Contra entry	250
Interest charged on overdue account	25

1 Prepare the trade receivables ledger control account and the trade payables ledger control account for October 2016. **(18 marks)**

2 State one error not revealed by control accounts. **(1 mark)**

3 Explain the difference between the trade payables ledger control account and the purchase day book. **(4 marks)**

4 Ofure has decided that this will be the last month she prepares control accounts. Evaluate her decision to stop preparing control accounts. **(12 marks)**

9 CORRECTION OF ERRORS

LEARNING OBJECTIVES

After you have studied this chapter, you should be able to:
- identify the errors that do not affect the trial balance
- identify and explain the nature of the additional errors affecting a trial balance
- prepare journal entries to correct errors and prepare a suspense account
- prepare statements of revised profits
- correct errors in control accounts.

GETTING STARTED

During your studies, how many accounting errors have you made? Have you been able to locate these errors and correct them? The answer to these is probably 'many' and 'not always'. Do not worry, fully trained accountants sometimes make mistakes. Because of this, techniques and procedures have been developed to help minimise errors or locate and correct them. As you develop your accounting skills your answers to the two questions will be 'not as many' and 'yes'.

It is important you are aware that, even if the trial balance balances, there can still be errors. Below is a list of the types of errors you are likely to come across and their explanations (see Exam hint for a mnemonic to help you remember them).

Errors of commission

This is where the correct amount is entered in the correct class but to the wrong account in that class. For example, sales on credit to J Smith are debited to S Smith's account. The error does not affect the statement of profit or loss and other comprehensive income or the statement of financial position, as the class of account (i.e. asset, liability, income or expenditure) is correct.

Errors of omission

Here, the transaction has not been entered into the ledger. This error does have an effect on the statement of profit or loss and/or the statement of financial position.

Errors of principle

The transaction is posted to an incorrect class of account, e.g. an asset is entered as an expense, or the purchase of a motor vehicle is entered as an expense. This affects both financial statements.

Complete reversal of entries

A debit is posted as a credit and vice versa. This could be where, for example, the revenue account is debited and the trade receivables account is credited with a sale. Both the financial statements may be affected.

Errors of original entry

This is where the wrong amount is entered. For example, an amount of £93 is entered as £39 in both the debit and credit entry. This affects both financial statements.

Compensating errors

Such errors occur where two mistakes, for the same amount, in two separate transactions, have the effect of cancelling each other. For example, the ledger account for interest paid is overcast by £100. In addition, the ledger account for discount receivable is also overcast by £100. As a result, both accounts will be overstated in the trial balance. As interest is debited by £100 in excess and discount is credited by £100 excess, the trial balance will still balance. It must be noted that the one account could be an expense item while the other could be an asset or liability. As such, the statement of profit or loss and/or statement of financial position may be affected.

In the examination, you will need to be able to recognise those errors that do not affect the trial balance and correctly identify the name of the errors. Without looking back, how many can you remember?

EXAM HINT

Do not forget that not all errors affect the trial balance. Remember the mnemonic COPROC for errors that *do not* affect the trial balance:

        Commission
        Omission
        Principle
        Reversal
        Original entry
        Compensating

Before the financial statements are prepared, these errors must be corrected in the journal and the appropriate ledger accounts. They are corrected in the journal day book so that a suitable description can be included which explains the correction of the error.

WORKED EXAMPLE

Saburo extracted a trial balance from his books of account on 30 April 2018 and discovered that it did balance. However, he did discover other errors in the accounts:

1 A credit sale to Uday of £120 was wrongly debited to Udom's account.
2 Credit sales of £330 to Nanda were not included in the accounts.
3 Motor vehicle expenses of £55 had been debited to the motor vehicle account.
4 A payment of £75, by cheque, to Demir, a trade payable, was entered on the debit side of the bank account and was credited to Demir's account.
5 A cheque for £45, paid for general expenses, was incorrectly entered as £54 into both accounts.
6 The account for heating and lighting was overcast by £120, as was the revenue account.

We will prepare the journal entries to record the correction of all errors (narratives are required).

Journal

	£	£
	Dr	Cr
Uday	120	
Udom		120
Correction of error of commission in personal accounts		
Nanda	330	
Sales		330
Correction of error of omission on credit sales		
Motor vehicle expenses	55	
Motor vehicles		55
Correction of error of principle, expenses entered as assets in error		
Demir	150	
Bank		150
Correction of error of reversal of entries on payment to trade payable		
Bank	9	
General expenses		9
Correction of an error of original entry of £9		
Sales	120	
Heating and lighting		120
Correction of compensating error, both accounts overcast by £120		

Explanation of journal entry errors

1 Error of commission – Udom's account, a trade receivable, will be overstated by £120. To correct this, we need to make a credit entry into the account. Uday's account now needs to have the £120 posted to the account. This entry will be on the debit side to reflect the amount owed to the business.
2 Error of omission – both the debit and credit entries are missing from the ledgers. The transaction must be entered, we must debit Nanda, a trade receivable, and then credit sales.
3 Error of principle – motor vehicle expenses of £55 have not been entered into the expense account so, to correct this, we must debit the account. The motor vehicle account, a non-current asset, has to have this amount removed as this is a capital expenditure account, therefore it needs to be credited with the £55.
4 Error of reversal – a payment of £75 from the bank was incorrectly posted to the debit side of the bank account. This increases the bank balance by £75, instead of reducing the balance by £75. To correct the error we must credit the account by £150 – in effect, we credit the account by £75 to eliminate the error, then we credit it again by £75 to enter the correct transaction. The same logic applies to the debit entry, we must debit the account (2 × £75) to correctly reflect that the amount outstanding to Demir has reduced by £75, not increased by £75.
5 Error of original entry – an additional £9 has been incorrectly posted to the two ledger accounts. We need to correct this by entering £9 into the opposite side of the ledger to that of the original transaction. In this example, general expenses, an expense account, is overstated by £9, so we need to credit the account with £9. The bank account will be debited with £9, as the original incorrect transaction credited the account with £9 too much.
6 Compensating error – two different accounts have been overstated by the same amount but on different sides of the ledger. In this example, heating and lighting, an expense account, has been overcast on the debit side by £120. To correct it, we must credit the account by £120. The revenue account has been overcast on the credit side by the same amount, so must be debited by £120 to correct the account.

It is important to remember that if a business uses control accounts then the transactions must be entered into the relevant control accounts, as well as the trade receivables ledger and trade payables ledger. The treatment of errors in control accounts is covered later in this chapter.

WORKED EXAMPLE

Shamma Al-Farsi sells handbags by offering them to people after she knocks on their door. She prepared a trial balance on 31 December 2018, but the totals did not agree. After investigation, the following errors were revealed:

1 Shamma had taken inventory costing £900 from the business for her own use. No entries had been made for this. This error is one of omission, as the entry charging Shamma for the goods has not been made.

2 Sales on credit to D Alexander for £800 were debited to the account of J Alexander. This is an example of an error of commission. The trade receivables' account of J Alexander was incorrectly charged with goods purchased.

3 A sales invoice for A Marquez had been incorrectly totalled as £378, instead of £478. This error is one of original entry. The trial balance remains unaffected as both revenue and trade receivables have been similarly posted with £378. As a result, debits and credits are in balance but the sales are understated

by £100 and the trade receivables in the statement of financial position are undervalued by £100.

4 A cash refund of £110 was given to D Alexander. Shamma entered the refund on the debit side of her cash book and credited the account of D Alexander. As there is a double entry, there is no error shown in the trial balance. The refund should, however, have been shown on the credit side of the cash book and debited to D Alexander. This error is a complete reversal of entries.

5 A motor vehicle had been purchased during the year at a cost of £12 000. This amount had been debited to motor expenses in the accounts. This is a non-current asset and should not show as an expense item. As such, this error is one of principle as the posting was to an incorrect class of account.

The journal entries to correct the errors would be:

	£	£
	Dr	Cr
Drawings	900	
Purchases		900
Correction of error of omission		
D Alexander	800	
J Alexander		800
Correction of error of commission		
A Marquez	100	
Sales		100
Correction of invoice no.111 – should be £478 instead of £378		
D Alexander	220	
Cash book		220
Correction of entry reversal*		
Motor vehicle	12 000	
Motor expenses		12 000
Correction of error of principle		

*Note that the amount is double.

The above worked example shows the journal entries required to correct the various errors. As these types of error lead to incorrect accounting information, it is important that you:

- understand how they arise
- realise what their effect is on the statement of profit or loss and other comprehensive income, as well as on the statement of financial position
- know what steps you need to take to rectify them.

Errors must be found and corrected before any accounts can be prepared. Additions of the trial balance should be checked and then the individual balances on every account must be checked to see that the accounts are correctly added up and balanced off. Then the balances should be checked against the trial balance to make sure that the debits and credits are in the correct columns. Often this latter exercise can show the errors without having to check all the additions.

ERRORS AFFECTING THE TRIAL BALANCE AND SUSPENSE ACCOUNT

If the trial balance does not balance, the difference is placed in a temporary account called a **suspense account**. If the debit column is smaller than the credit column then the suspense account is said to be in debit, and vice versa.

Errors that affect the trial balance include:
- a single entry, omitting either the debit entry or the credit entry
- entering two debits or two credits for a transaction
- entering different amounts for the debit and credit entries.

The balance may be shown in the statement of financial position until it is sorted out. Naturally, this must be done before finalising the financial statements for the period. (In an exam, do not leave a suspense account in the statement of financial position as you would lose marks for this.)

When the errors are found, the accounts are corrected. To do this, we need a journal entry to effect the correction. The entry will be to the suspense account and also to another account to maintain the double-entry system.

All errors must be investigated, and the corrections recorded in the journal with a proper description.

Errors that affect the trial balance are often the result of making a single-entry transaction rather than a double-entry transaction. This is why the entry goes into the suspense account, one account is correct and does not need to be adjusted, the other account is corrected, with the suspense used to enter the contra entry from the double entry.

WORKED EXAMPLE

We have prepared a trial balance that does not balance, so we need to create a suspense account to allow for the difference. The trial balance therefore appears as follows:

	£	£
	Dr	Cr
Subtotal	59 875	61 960
Suspense account	2 085	
Totals	61 960	61 960

This suspense account is a temporary account and would be closed off after finding the errors.

We now need to find the difference and correct the trial balance. Once this is done, we would use journal entries to make the adjustments. On investigation, we find the errors are as follows:
- The total of the purchases account is understated by £2 200 (that is, the total is £2 200 less than it should be).
- A cheque received from trade receivables of £115 is not entered in the trade receivables account.

We show you the journal entries below so that you understand how they will eventually help us to close off the suspense account and balance the trial balance:

Purchases Dr	2 200
Suspense Cr	2 200

Because the purchases were undercast, the account must now be increased by that shortfall. As this is an expense account, we need to debit it with the £2 200. The remainder of the entry (i.e. the credit entry) is not affected so we merely credit the suspense account.

Suspense Dr	115
Trade receivable Cr	115

In a similar situation we find that we have not credited our trade receivables with the amount paid. The bank account has been entered correctly and does not need to be adjusted, so we must use the suspense account to maintain the double entry.

These journal entries are then posted to the suspense account, as shown below:

Suspense account

Date	Details	£	Date	Details	£
Date	Trial balance	2 085	Date	Purchases	2 200
	Trade receivables	115			
		2 200			2 200

WORKED EXAMPLE

We extracted a trial balance at 30 June 2018 but, as it does not balance, it is vital that we investigate the causes of this imbalance. We find the following:

- The rates are overcast by £20.
- Sales are undercast by £100.
- A credit to William (a trade receivable) of £35 has not been posted into his account.
- The sale of goods to John for £45 has been entered as £54 in both accounts.

The journal entries to correct the above are:

Account	£ Dr	£ Cr
Suspense	20	
Rates		20

The expense account has been overcast by £20, this needs to be reduced, so the account is credited with £20. When we have completed this entry, all accounts are now correct. The opposite entry, the bank account, did not contain an error. Therefore, to maintain the double entry we must debit the suspense account with £20.

	£ Dr	£ Cr
Suspense	100	
Sales		100

The revenue account has been undercast, so we must add £100 to the account. Sales are recorded on the credit side, so we credit sales £100. No other account is incorrect, so we must debit the suspense account.

	£ Dr	£ Cr
Suspense	35	
William		35

William, a trade receivable account, has paid an amount which has been correctly entered into the bank account as a debit entry, but the credit entry to his account has been omitted. To correct the error, we must credit William £35 and then debit the suspense account with £35 to maintain the double entry.

	£ Dr	£ Cr
Sales	9	
John		9

This is an error of original entry and does not affect the trial balance, so no suspense account entry is required.

Make sure that you understand why the above entries have been made. See which one has not been debited or credited. Remember that half of the double entry has been made. It is the other half that we have to make to balance the trial balance.

After writing up the entries in the journal, we must then post them to the ledger and close the suspense account.

Suspense account

Date	Details	£	Date	Details	£
30 June 2009	Rates	20	30 June 2009	Balance b/d	155
	Sales	100			
	William	35			
		155			155

STATEMENTS OF REVISED PROFIT

The correction of errors will often have an effect on any profit figure that has been calculated prior to the correction of the errors. Therefore, it is necessary to recalculate the profit figure. This recalculation is often referred to as a statement of revised profit. Profit may be affected by errors that do not affect the trial balance *and* errors that do affect the trial balance.

WORKED EXAMPLE

The bookkeeper for Dorothy's Denim has produced a draft statement of profit or loss and other comprehensive income of £25 640 for the year ended 31 May 2018. On further inspection, the following errors were discovered:

1 There was a transaction for £8 500, which related to drawings by Dorothy, in the wages account.
2 Wages of £1 200 paid to employees had not been included in the books.
3 The purchases day book was undercast by £320.
4 Received discounts of £95 had been debited to the discounts allowed account.
5 A cash drawing of £250 had been omitted from the accounts.

We will prepare a statement of revised profit for the year after the correction of all the errors.

Statement of revised profit

	Increase £	Decrease £	No effect (☑)
Draft profit for year		25 640	
Error 1	8 500		
Error 2		1 200	
Error 3		320	
Error 4	190		
Error 5			☑
Revised profit for the year		32 810	

Approach to correcting the errors and calculating the effect on profit

Error 1 – wages, an expense, is overstated as the debit entry should be in the drawings account, which is a statement of financial position account. This will reduce expenses and so increase profit.

Error 2 – wages, an expense, will be increased when the error is corrected, so profit will be reduced.

Error 3 – the purchases account is undercast by £320, so the total will be increased when corrected. This will increase the cost of sales and reduce profit.

Error 4 – the discounts allowed account has been wrongly overstated by £95, correcting this will increase the profit by £95. In addition, the discounts received account needs to be credited with £95 to correct the error, thus increasing profit by £95. Therefore, the profit for the year will increase by £190 (twice the value of the error).

Error 5 – in this case, there will be no effect on the profit as both entries will affect the statement of financial position, drawings will increase while the bank and cash will decrease.

It is important to remember that not all errors will affect the profit for the year.

CORRECTION OF ERRORS IN THE CONTROL ACCOUNTS

Control accounts are used to check the accuracy of the personal ledgers. The entries for the control accounts come from information in the trade payables ledger and the trade receivables ledger. If errors have been made in the books of prime entry, then probably these errors would have been transferred to the control accounts at the time of entry. Therefore, it is essential that any errors identified be corrected in the control accounts. When a reconciliation takes place and the balances do not agree, it will be necessary to investigate the accounts to identify and correct the errors in the control accounts. Once the errors have been identified and corrected, the totals in the ledgers and the control accounts should balance.

WORKED EXAMPLE

Baba Perera is a wholesaler who buys and sells kitchen appliances. On 31 May 2018 he extracted the following from his books of account:

	£
Trade payables balances (Cr) 1 May 2018	12 450
Credit purchases	6 500
Returns out	350
Discounts received	255
Cheque payments to suppliers	9 250
Interest paid on overdue accounts	35

On inspection of the books, Baba discovered the following additional information:

1 A cheque for £150 which had been paid to a credit supplier had been incorrectly posted to the debit side of the motor vehicle account.

2 A cheque for £285, paid to a supplier, was returned unpaid by his bank. The cheque was in full payment for an invoice after deducting a cash discount of 5 per cent.

3 A contra entry for £210 was omitted from the accounts.

We shall prepare a trade payables control account for 31 May 2018, taking additional information into account.

Approach

1 The bank account credit entry is correct. However, the individual trade payables account will be incorrect, as will the control account. We need to

debit the control account and credit the motor vehicle account. The journal entry is:

	£	£
	Dr	Cr
Trade payables control	150	
Motor vehicle account		150

2 The bank account was credited when the cheque was written out; as it has been returned, the bank account must be debited. The trade payables ledger account was debited at the same time, so we must credit the individual trade payables account and the control account. In addition, we must account for the cash discount which was applied to the transaction. The value of the discount is £15, and we must credit the control account to recognise that the amount owing has increased by a total of £300 = £285 bank plus £15 discount received. The journal entry is:

	£	£
	Dr	Cr
Bank	285	
Discount received	15	
Trade payable control		285
Trade payable control		15

3 The contra entry must be entered into the control account on the debit side:

	£	£
	Dr	Cr
Trade payable control	210	
Trade receivables control		210

Trade payables control account

Date	Details	£	Date	Details	£
31 May	Bank	9 250	1 May	Balance b/d	12 450
	Returns outward	350	31 May	Purchases	6 500
	Trade receivables control (contra)	210		Interest	35
	Discount received	255		Bank	285
	Motor vehicles	150		Discount rec'd	15
	Balance c/d	9 070			
		19 285			19 285
			1 June	Balance b/d	9 070

ACTIVITY 1   SKILLS   ANALYSIS, EXECUTIVE FUNCTION
CASE STUDY: L GREEN

L Green cannot balance her trial balance at 31 December 2018 and opens a suspense account for the difference. This account shows a debit of £140. After checking the books, she discovers the following errors:

- A credit note for £18 was entered twice in a trade receivables account.
- An invoice for £96 which was entered correctly in the revenue day book was incorrectly entered to a trade receivables account as £69.
- A payment of £110 to a trade payable was entered in the cash book but not posted to the trade payables account.
- The returns inwards day book total has been overcast by £90.
- Two payments of £75 each were made to a trade payable but only one was entered to the trade payables account.

1 Show the journal entries needed to adjust the suspense account and balance the trial balance.

ACTIVITY 2   SKILLS   ANALYSIS, EXECUTIVE FUNCTION
CASE STUDY: MERLE

Merle's books show the following:

2019

20 May	Machine repairs for £111 were posted to the plant and machinery account.
22 May	Discount allowed of £49 was posted to the debit of discount received.
24 May	A printer costing £820 was purchased for the office on credit from BB Stores, but the transaction had not yet been entered.
25 May	Goods valued at £90 were returned to A Brown, but the return had been posted to the account of D Brown.
27 May	A delivery van had been sold for £5 400 but the receipt was posted to sales.
30 May	Rent received of £100 was posted to commission received.

1 Draw up the necessary journal entries in Merle's books to correct the errors.

ACTIVITY 3
SKILLS ▸ ANALYSIS, EXECUTIVE FUNCTION, PROBLEM SOLVING

CASE STUDY: HINDES

During the year, the following events occurred:

- On 1 January 2018, Hindes bought parts for £8 600 on credit from Joe.
- On 31 March he sold the old parts to Fritz for £600, the full amount payable in July.
- Steve owes Joe £500. As the debt is outstanding for more than a year it is treated as irrecoverable.
- Goods purchased on credit from A Bryan for £400 were incorrectly posted to L Bryan.
- On 30 June, Hindes sold the old delivery van for £200 to Chantelle.

1 Show the journal entries, including the narrations and dates, for all the above transactions.

ACTIVITY 4
SKILLS ▸ ANALYSIS, EXECUTIVE FUNCTION, PROBLEM SOLVING

CASE STUDY: C WHYTE

At 31 December 2018, C Whyte prepared his trial balance for the year. It did not balance, and he entered the difference into a suspense account. Thereafter, he prepared his accounts and the profit for the year shown was £9 720.

It was subsequently discovered that the following errors had been made in the trial balance:

- Salaries of £4 200 had been debited to the office equipment account in error.
- Purchases of £962 were correctly entered in the purchases day book, but were incorrectly credited to the trade payables account as £926.
- The revenue day book total of £6 280 was posted to the revenue account as £6 820.
- A received discount of £192 was posted to the wrong side of the discount received account.

1 State how, and by how much, each of the errors above would affect the trial balance. Show the adjusted profit for the year.

ACTIVITY 5
SKILLS ▸ ANALYSIS, EXECUTIVE FUNCTION, REASONING

CASE STUDY: JAY & CO.

Jay & Co. manufacture jewellery and sell it to retailers. In preparing the trial balance for Jay & Co., a difference of £222 was entered as a credit to a suspense account in order to balance the trial balance. Some time later, after examining the books, the following errors were discovered:

- The total of the returns inward book was overcast by £600.
- When writing off an irrecoverable debt of £720, the irrecoverable debt account was incorrectly debited with £72.
- A cheque for £110 received from a trade receivable was not paid, but no entry reflecting this has been made in the books.
- A receipt of £320 from Justin was credited to the account of Austin.
- A credit note from I Buy for £360, for goods returned, was not entered in the books.
- On 31 December 2019 the quarterly rent of £600, for the period 1 December 2019 to 28 February 2020 was paid. No adjustment has yet been made for the prepayment.
- The total of the discount received column in the cash book of £135 was posted to the debit side of the discount allowed account.

1 Prepare journal entries for the above adjustments and show the adjustments to the suspense account.
2 You are required to show the effect of the above errors on the profit for the year of £12 380 for the year ended 31 December 2019.

ACTIVITY 6   SKILLS   ANALYSIS, EXECUTIVE FUNCTION, PROBLEM SOLVING

CASE STUDY: ELIJAH

Elijah prepares a trial balance on 30 June 2019. As it does not balance, he opens a suspense account with a credit balance of £101. He then checks his books and discovers the following errors:

- Two payments of £90 each have been made to Thomas but only one has been entered in the trade payables account.
- An invoice for £98 has been entered correctly in the revenue day book but the entry to Smythe (trade receivable) is shown as £89.
- A payment of £14 to Vashi has been entered in the cash book but no double entry has been made.
- The returns inward day book has been overcast by £200.
- A credit note for £14 received from Hilife (trade payable) has been entered twice in their account.

1 Show the suspense account as it would appear after the correction of errors.

ACTIVITY 7   SKILLS   ANALYSIS, EXECUTIVE FUNCTION

CASE STUDY: ROGER

Roger extracts a list of balances and presents the following trial balance at 31 July 2019.

	£	£
	Dr	Cr
Capital		22 350
Drawings	9 000	
Inventory 1 August 2018	7 500	
Trade receivables	8 850	
Trade payables		8 052
Shop fittings	4 590	
Purchases	15 420	
Revenue		22 380
General expenses	2 580	
Discount received		120
Cash and bank	4 980	
Returns outwards		120
Suspense account	102	
	53 022	53 022

The following errors and omissions were subsequently discovered:

- A credit balance of £48 in the trade payables ledger had been omitted from the trial balance.
- A credit note for £39 issued by Roger to a customer had been omitted from the books.
- Sales invoices for £450 entered in the revenue day book had not been entered to a customer's personal account.
- A purchase of shop fittings totalling £1 320 had been debited to purchases.
- The revenue day book was undercast by £300 in March 2019.

1 Show the journal entries for the above errors and also write up the suspense ledger account.
2 Draw up an amended trial balance.

ACTIVITY 8   SKILLS   ANALYSIS, EXECUTIVE FUNCTION

CASE STUDY: RAHMAN

The following information has been extracted from Rahman's books of account for the month of November 2017:

	£
Trade receivables balances at 1 November 2017	23 500
Cash purchases	13 900
Credit sales	16 450
Returns in	350
Discounts allowed	750
Receipts from credit customers	17 700

On further investigation, the following additional information became available:

- Begum, a credit customer, has ceased trading. The full balance of £530 must be written off as an irrecoverable debt.
- A return of goods, £80, from Mujeeb, a credit customer, had not been recorded in the books.
- Hasan is both a supplier and a customer. A set-off needs to be entered into the accounts to clear the balance owing of £250.

1 Prepare the trade receivables account for 30 November 2017, taking into account the additional information provided.

EXAM HINT

All errors will require a debit and a credit entry in order to be corrected. When correcting errors in the suspense account, only one side of the journal entry is entered into the suspense account. The other entry goes into the account affected by the error.

When adjusting profit for the year, it is best not to use minus signs or brackets but use the term 'add' or 'less'. If you are provided with a table for entries, make sure you put the addition to profit in the increase column and vice versa.

EVALUATE

Given the volume of accounting data that is processed it could be argued that errors are inevitable. Locating errors and correcting them is often very difficult. A common exam question is to evaluate whether draft financial statements should be prepared when it is known that errors still exist.

Arguments for	Arguments against
Some errors may not be important	Some errors may have an important effect on the level of profit or value of assets
Gives a reasonable estimate of profit	Difficult to rely on the information knowing that errors exist
Provides information for managers to make decisions	Can lead to poor decisions being made by management
Allows timely draft figures for use by stakeholders	Work preparing the statements has to be repeated, this has time and cost implications
Easier to adjust draft statements and so save some time if deadlines are close	

CHECKPOINT

1 State six types of error that will not affect the trial balance.

2 Debiting the motor vehicle expenses account instead of the motor vehicle cost account would affect the trial balance. True or false?

3 Explain why the suspense account is a temporary account.

4 State the journal entry that is required if a receipt from a customer was posted to the wrong side of the customer's personal account.

5 State the effect on profit if carriage inwards had been overcast by £200.

SUBJECT VOCABULARY

overcast entering an amount greater than the correct amount into an account

set-off a contra entry between control accounts

suspense account a temporary account used to balance the trial balance until errors are found and corrected. It is used to record the elimination of errors

undercast entering an amount lower than the correct amount into an account

EXAM PRACTICE

CASE STUDY: NUAN'S PARCEL DELIVERY SERVICE

SKILLS CRITICAL THINKING, EXECUTIVE FUNCTION, DECISION MAKING

Nuan extracted a trial balance for his parcel delivery business on 31 August 2018. The books of account contained errors and the trial balance failed to agree. On inspection of the books, Nuan discovered the following:

1 The revenue day book had been undercast by £3 500.
2 Discounts received of £500 had been debited to the discounts allowed account.
3 Nuan had withdrawn £200 cash for his own use. No entries had been made.
4 Purchases of £530 on credit from Shui had been recorded in the ledger account for Shun.
5 General expenses of £552 had been correctly recorded in the bank account but had been recorded as £225 in the general expenses account.
6 The purchase of a new motor vehicle for £18 000 had been recorded in the motor vehicle expenses account. Depreciation is charged at the rate of 20 per cent per annum using the straight line method.

Q

1 Prepare the journal entries to record the correction of all the errors. Narratives are not required.
(15 marks)
2 Prepare the suspense account after the correction of all errors, clearly showing the opening balance. Dates are not required. **(6 marks)**
3 State the type of error in points 3, 4 and 6 in Nuan's list of discoveries. **(3 marks)**
4 Evaluate the use of the suspense account. **(6 marks)**

FINANCIAL STATEMENTS OF ORGANISATIONS

So far in your studies you have learned about the fundamental principles of accounting and how to ensure that accounting records are consistent and free from errors. In this section, you will learn how the books you have previously prepared are presented to the different users of accounting information.

Organisations produce a range of financial statements, each having a different purpose. Sole traders, partnerships and non-profit-making organisations will produce financial statements that show how much profit/surplus they have made during a financial period and the value of the business assets and liabilities they have at the end of the period.

Some business organisations will consist of different departments and you will learn how to present their financial statements. In addition, you will learn how to present the financial statements of businesses that manufacture their products rather than purchase inventory for resale.

Finally, you will study how to prepare financial statements from organisations who do not maintain a formal set of accounting books.

10 FINANCIAL STATEMENTS OF SOLE TRADERS

LEARNING OBJECTIVES

After you have studied this chapter, you should be able to:
- prepare a statement of profit or loss and other comprehensive income
- prepare a statement of financial position.

GETTING STARTED

You have maintained a formal set of books for a complete financial period, but do you know how much profit has been made by the business? You have followed the correct accounting concepts and conventions, you have correctly accounted for capital and revenue expenditure and have depreciated the non-current assets, but do you know the value of the business?

INTRODUCTION

An important reason for recording financial transactions is to prepare **financial statements** for the users of accounting information, as discussed in Chapter 1. Financial statements are prepared in order to provide information about the performance and financial position of a business to a wide range of users who are making economic decisions. A complete set of financial statements is usually prepared by a business at the end of the financial period. The two primary financial statements for sole traders are:
- the statement of profit or loss and other comprehensive income
- the statement of financial position.

These two financial documents allow the business owner to see if the business has generated a profit or loss in the previous year and details for the owner the assets and liabilities of the business.

Once the double-entry accounts have been balanced off at the year end and the trial balance has been prepared and verified as being correct, the business is able to prepare the financial statements for the financial year just ended.

THE STATEMENT OF PROFIT OR LOSS AND OTHER COMPREHENSIVE INCOME

This financial statement includes the revenue and expenses of the business for the financial year, and therefore the profit or loss. It can be divided into two clear sections.

The first section relates to the trading activities of the business. You might still see '**trading account**' used to refer to this section, and you will see it used below, but it is no longer used in the financial statement itself. The final entry in this section of the statement of profit or loss and other comprehensive income is the gross profit earned by the business.

The second section includes other income earned by the business and all the expenses of the business for that year. The statement ends with profit for the year. These two profits are important indicators of business performance and will be used later in Chapter 21 when analysing business performance.

The trading account

The trading account records the amount of profit earned from selling the goods the business 'trades' in. It contains two pieces of accounting information – the revenue earned from the sales and the cost of those sales. The difference between the two items is gross profit. This is the profit from selling goods before deducting expenses.

All accounts that relate to the purchase and sale of goods and services are transferred from the related ledger accounts and shown in the trading account section of the statement of profit or loss and other comprehensive income. Remember that other income still has to be added and business expenses still have to be deducted from the gross profit and that the trading account only shows the gross profit from the buying and selling of goods.

Revenue

There are two items in the revenue section: revenue (from sales) and returns inwards (revenue returns).

Revenue is the monies received from selling goods and services to customers. Returns inwards, sometimes also called revenue returns, are created when previously sold goods or services are returned to the business by customers. These are shown as a separate entry in the trading account and are deducted from the revenue figure to arrive at a net revenue figure.

Cost of sales

This section of the trading account shows the direct items that are required to calculate the cost of the sales made to the customers. The cost of sales is calculated following the accrual concept, and the cost of the sales made is matched to the revenue for the period:

- opening inventory – this is the inventory that is brought forward from the previous accounting period and is assumed to be sold in the current accounting period
- plus purchases – this is the cost of goods purchased for resale from supplies
- less returns outwards (purchase returns) – these are the purchases that have been returned

to suppliers. As with returns inwards, these are recorded separately and not netted off the purchases figure

- plus carriage inwards – this is the cost incurred by the business in receiving the goods from the suppliers. It includes amounts paid for freight, postage and packing of goods. It is a cost of sales, as without paying for the delivery the business would not have the goods to sell
- less inventory drawings – this represents the value of inventory which has been taken from the business by the owner for their own personal use. As such, the value of the inventory should not be regarded as a cost of sales, this follows the business entity concept
- less closing inventory – this is the value of the inventory at the end of the accounting period. This is deducted when calculating cost of sales, since the goods have not been sold. The closing inventory is usually found as a note to the trial balance. The inventory figure in the trial balance is the opening inventory. We always add the opening figure and deduct the closing figure of inventory.

WORKED EXAMPLE

Karen provides the following information. From this we will prepare an extract of statement of profit or loss and other comprehensive income for the year ended 31 March 2018 to show the trading section.

	£	£
	Dr	Cr
Revenue		45 000
Purchases	20 000	
Returns inwards	1 000	
Return outwards		3 000
Carriage inwards	4 500	
Inventory – 1 April 2017	8 000	

Additional Information:
- Inventory at 31 March 2018 was valued at cost = £7 000.
- During the year, Karen had taken £300 of goods for her own use. This had not been recorded in the books.

The statement will appear as follows:

Karen: extract of statement of profit or loss and other comprehensive income for the year ended 31 March 2018

	£	£
Revenue		45 000
Less: Returns inwards		(1 000)
		44 000
Less: Cost of sales		
Opening inventory	8 000	
Plus: Purchases	20 000	
Less: Returns outwards	(3 000)	
Plus: Carriage inwards	4 500	
	29 500	
Less: Inventory drawings	(300)	
Less: Closing inventory	(7 000)	
Cost of sales		22 200
Gross profit		21 800

Explanatory notes:
- Revenue – the business received £45 000 from selling goods to customers. During the year, some customers are not satisfied with the products and returned goods worth £1 000 to the business. Therefore, the business only received revenue of £44 000 from selling the goods.
- Cost of sales:
  (i) At the beginning of the accounting year, 1 April 2017, the business had inventory in hand of £8 000.
  (ii) Since the goods in hand were not sufficient for the whole year, the business purchased goods costing £20 000 from suppliers. This is what 'purchases' represents.
  (iii) Some of the goods purchased were defective and the business returned goods costing £3 000 to suppliers. These are 'returns outwards'.
  (iv) Some suppliers charged delivery fees when sending goods to the business, this is called 'carriage inwards', in this case, £4 500 delivery charges occurred.
  (v) During the year, Karen withdrew inventory worth £300 from the business for her own personal use. This amount needs to be deducted from the cost of sales as it was not a cost of the sales made by the business – this follows the business entity concept.
  (vi) It is very common to have some inventory items unsold at the end of an accounting year. This is called 'closing inventory'. Since the goods were unsold, then this cannot be a cost of the goods sold and so is deducted from the cost of sales.
- Gross profit – the difference between the income the business received from selling the goods (revenue) and the cost of sales is called gross profit. It is the profit before paying expenses, for example, electricity or wages.

EXAM HINT

Carriage in is a cost of sale; carriage out is an expense. Always label the cost of sales figure.

It is important to learn and remember the six items that potentially make up the cost of sales. These are:
- add opening inventory
- add purchases
- less returns out
- add carriage in
- less inventory drawings
- less closing inventory.

ACTIVITY 1 SKILLS ANALYSIS, EXECUTIVE FUNCTION
CASE STUDY: J ANTHONY

	£
Inventory, 1 January 2019	12 500
Inventory, 31 December 2019	16 400
Purchases	32 345
Revenue	87 213
Returns inwards	1 106
Returns outwards	2 348
Carriage inwards	1 984

1 Prepare a trading account section of the statement of profit or loss and other comprehensive income, showing the gross profit, for J Anthony from the above information.

ACTIVITY 2 SKILLS ANALYSIS, EXECUTIVE FUNCTION
CASE STUDY: CHRISTINA

Christina presents you with an extract from her ledger for the year ended 30 June 2019:

	£
Revenue	211 980
Opening inventory	43 650
Returns by customers	35 800
Closing inventory	65 780
Purchases	98 650
Inventory drawings	5 650
Carriage inwards	76 500
Delivery charges	51 900
Depreciation van	5 870
Discount allowed	6 997
Advertising	9 946

1 The accounts she lists are not all needed for the trading account, but she asks you to use those required to prepare a trading account.

ACTIVITY 3 — SKILLS: ANALYSIS, PROBLEM SOLVING, EXECUTIVE FUNCTION

CASE STUDY: HOPE

Hope buys and sells second-hand electronic equipment, such as games consoles and tablets. She presents you with a summary of certain transactions for the year ended 30 June 2019. She asks you to prepare the trading account for her first year of trading, so that she can work out the gross profit.

The following are the accounts given to you:

	£
Revenue	421 000
Purchases	214 000
Returns inwards	40 108
Carriage inwards	2 790

Hope also tells you that her closing inventory amounts to £37 890.

1 Prepare the trading account so that the gross profit is shown.

ACTIVITY 4 — SKILLS: ANALYSIS, EXECUTIVE FUNCTION

CASE STUDY: HASSAN

The following items are extracted from Hassan's books – he sells sweets and chocolate – for the year ended 30 June 2019:

	£
Revenue	43 988
Closing inventory	8 967
Purchases	11 870
Opening inventory	9 876
Returns to suppliers	1 245

1 Prepare the trading account for the year.

LINKING TRADING AND PROFIT AND LOSS

Once we have worked out the gross profit, we move to the next stage, which is the completed statement of profit or loss and other comprehensive income. In effect, there are two parts to the statement of profit or loss and other comprehensive income:

- the trading account section (shown above) is used to arrive at the gross profit
- the profit and loss account, which contains all other revenue expenses. These are then deducted from the gross profit to calculate the profit for the year. This account also includes any revenue items from non-trading sources, for example, interest or discounts received.

STATEMENT OF PROFIT AND LOSS AND OTHER COMPREHENSIVE INCOME (PROFIT AND LOSS SECTION)

Earlier in the chapter we saw how the gross profit was calculated. While that figure is extremely important, we still need to establish if the business is making an overall profit. To do this, we take the gross profit from the trading account and add any revenue receipts. From that we deduct all the remaining costs incurred in creating the revenue. There are no fixed names for the individual items of expenditure and different businesses may use different headings to describe the expenses. The important thing to note is that all these expenses must be of a revenue nature (refer back to Chapter 5 for an explanation of revenue expenditure). Once all the expenses are deducted, we are left with the profit (or loss) for the year.

FORMAT OF THE PROFIT AND LOSS ACCOUNT

Although the format is similar for both sole trader and companies, there are certain variations. At this stage we should note that a sole trader would want far more detail in the profit and loss account than that shown in the company's profit and loss account. In the accounts of a sole trader, each expense account heading is shown in the profit and loss.

The classification of expenses is dependent on how useful it is to identify such an expense. For example, we could group telephone, postage and stationery as one item. However, if postage was a material item (that is, of considerable size and importance) then it may be sensible to show it as a separate one from the others.

The section of the statement of profit or loss and other comprehensive income lists all the income (other than from sales, which is shown in the trading section) immediately after the gross profit. From this total, all expenses including provisions for depreciation and allowances/provisions for irrecoverable debts are deducted. The final figure is the profit for the year – in this case, for the year ended 31 December 2019.

Prima Trading: statement of profit or loss account for the year ended 31 December 2019

	£	£
Gross profit		104 000
Add: Interest received		2 000
Add: Commission received		5 000
		111 000
Less: Expenses		
Salaries and wages	31 500	
Rent and rates	10 000	
Heat and light	2 500	
Telephone and postage	1 400	
Insurance	1 200	
Motor expenses	2 400	
Interest paid	3 100	
Depreciation of non-current assets	4 000	
Allowance/provision for irrecoverable debts	900	57 000
Profit for the year		54 000

ACTIVITY 5

 SKILLS   ANALYSIS, PROBLEM SOLVING, EXECUTIVE FUNCTION

CASE STUDY: ELLA

Ella has prepared a trading account showing a gross profit of £56 900:

Ella: extract of balances at 30 June 2019

	£	£
	Dr	Cr
Motor expenses	3 140	
Finance income		2 980
Bank charges	720	
Wages	1 360	
Rent payable	5 870	
Discount received		1 040
Insurance	3 800	
Postage	1 010	

1 Prepare a statement of profit or loss and other comprehensive income for Ella, as she is not sure what has to be shown in that account. The above is an extract of balances that she thinks are relevant.

WORKED EXAMPLE

The first part of the statement is concerned with calculating gross profit for the period. This first part is referred to as the trading account or trading section. We will now examine the second part of the statement – the profit and loss section. Note the title of the financial statement.

Ying Trading: statement of profit or loss and other comprehensive income for the year ended 31 October 2019

	£	£
Revenue		232 000
Less: cost of sales		154 000
Gross profit		78 000
Interest received		2 000
		80 000
Less		
Salaries and wages	24 500	
Rent and rates	14 200	
Heat and light	7 500	
Telephone and postage	1 200	
Insurance	1 000	
Motor vehicle expenses	3 400	
Loan interest	1 100	
Depreciation of fixtures and fittings	1 000	
Depreciation of motor van	600	(54 500)
Profit for the year		25 500

In the above example, we see that the gross profit calculated (£78 000) has had other income (interest) added to it before the various expenses are deducted. The net amount arrived at is the profit for the year.

ACTIVITY 6

SKILLS ANALYSIS, PROBLEM SOLVING, EXECUTIVE FUNCTION

CASE STUDY: JACQUES

The following is the trial balance for Jacques at 31 December 2019:

Jacques: trial balance at 31 December 2019

	£	£
	Dr	Cr
Advertising	3000	
Bank	700	
Trade payables		6900
Bank loan		7000
Trade receivables	30000	
Electricity	2800	
Insurance	1700	
Investments	2800	
Investment income		400
Machinery:		
At cost	42000	
Provision for depreciation at 1 January 2019		15200
Office expenses	4900	
Owner's capital		25000
Interest paid	400	
Profit and loss account at 1 January 2019		13200
Allowance/provision for irrecoverable debts		800
Rent and rates	7500	
Inventory at 31 December 2019	15500	
Vehicles:		
At cost	8000	
Provision for depreciation at 1 January 2019		4000
Wages and salaries	41300	
Gross profit		88100
	160600	160600

Depreciation for the year is £4 200 for machinery and £1 600 for vehicles.

1 Prepare the statement of profit or loss and other comprehensive income, having been given the gross profit for the year.

(Note: although you are given the complete trial balance, you must be aware that there are certain account balances that are not required for answering the above question because they are statement of financial position items. We will deal with these later in the chapter.)

EXAM HINT

Always label the different sections of the statement of profit or loss and other comprehensive income.

CHANGES TO PROFIT FOR THE YEAR

We saw in Chapter 9 that errors may be found after we have prepared the profit and loss account. You will need to be able to work out the adjusted profit for the year caused by several errors or adjustments. All you need to do is consider which account would be debited and which credited with these adjustments.

WORKED EXAMPLE

How do each of the following errors affect the profit for the year of £29 000 as shown in the profit and loss account?

- Opening inventory was undervalued by £858.
- Interest on a business investment of £289 was treated as interest charged.
- A loan of £900 made to the business was credited to the statement of profit or loss and other comprehensive income.
- Discounts received of £340 were debited to the statement of profit or loss and other comprehensive income.
- Credit purchases of £540 were omitted from the purchases day book.

	£
Original profit for the year	29000
Less: Inventory adjustment	(858)
Add: Interest received	578
Less: Loan	(900)
Add: Discounts received	680
Less: Purchases	(540)
Adjusted profit for the year	27960

Calculating the effect of errors on profit is complicated, you will need to refresh your understanding of the correction of errors as detailed in Chapter 9.

STATEMENT OF FINANCIAL POSITION

Having prepared the statement of profit or loss and other comprehensive income, our next stage in the preparation of financial statements is the statement of financial position.

The statement of financial position, which consists of assets and liabilities, shows the financial position of the firm at a specific time. For this reason, it is important that we label the statement of financial position correctly. We must always state the name of the firm, the fact that it is the statement of financial position and end with the important words 'at [date]'. The assets of the business are shown in the first section of the statement of financial position, while capital and liabilities are shown in the second section. The two sections must always balance.

Do you remember the following accounting equation?

$$\text{Assets} - \text{Liabilities} = \text{Capital}$$

Therefore:

$$\text{Assets} = \text{Capital} + \text{Liabilities}$$

You will note from this equation that there are really three sections:
- the assets (A)
- the capital (C)
- the liabilities (L).

We have said that the statement of financial position consists of assets and liabilities, so before we go on with our study of the statement of financial position, we need to examine the definitions of these items.

Assets

Assets are resources owned by a business which have a future economic value. Once an asset is acquired, it remains in the business until it is used up, its benefits have run out (e.g. motor car less annual depreciation) or until it is sold. The two subsections are:
- non-current assets
- current assets.

Non-current assets

A non-current asset is one that is bought for ongoing use within a business and is likely to be held and used for more than one accounting period. Examples are property, machinery, office equipment and motor vehicles. All these are tangible non-current assets – in other words, they are physical assets which have a real existence.

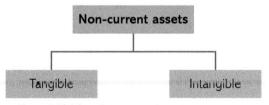

▲ Figure 1 Division of non-current assets

In addition, there are also non-current assets such as goodwill and brand names (e.g. Coca-Cola®, Nike®, Microsoft®). These are intangible non-current assets, which are often more valuable than the tangible assets.

Typically, intangible assets have no physical substance – they cannot be touched – although they do provide future benefits. The most common, and often the most valuable of all intangible assets, is goodwill. As such, we will spend a little time discussing this important intangible asset.

One important point is that we never show goodwill that is internally generated in a statement of financial position. Goodwill is only shown where it comes from a purchase of a business. At that stage, goodwill (and other purchased intangible assets) are capitalised and disclosed as intangible assets non-current.

Once the asset is created (capitalised), it is depreciated (impaired) over its useful economic life (as covered in Chapter 6). This becomes difficult in the case of most goodwill amounts as the question that will arise is, what is its useful economic life?

Current assets

Current assets are those assets that are expected to be realised during the normal trading activities of the business. The usual intention is to turn the current asset into cash within one year. They exist primarily for the purpose of trading. The most common current assets are inventory, trade receivables, other receivables, as well as bank and cash.

We have discussed inventory earlier and therefore only need to say a few things about the remaining current assets:
- Trade receivables arise where money is owed to the business as a result of sales made on credit.
- Other receivables (prepayments) are where goods and/or services are paid for at the end of the accounting period but will only be used in a future period.

In the case of current assets, there is a listing order. This order is worked out by answering the question: how quickly can the current asset be turned into cash? This allows us to prepare a list in descending order of liquidity – that is, the time it takes to convert an asset into cash. Using this order, we would place inventory first, then trade receivables, other receivables and lastly bank and cash.

Liabilities

Liabilities are amounts owed by the business to another entity. These arise from the purchase of goods and services on credit or taking out a loan. Liabilities are either long-term (non-current) or current. Here again, these types of liabilities are separately defined.

Non-current liabilities

A non-current liability is a debt where the amount due is payable in more than one year. Examples are long-term loans.

Current liabilities

A current liability is a debt where the amount is to be paid within the business's normal operating cycle – usually within one year of the statement of financial position date. They arise from the day-to-day operating activities of the business.

Remember that not all liabilities are shown as current liabilities, and the date they are due for repayment plays a vital part in determining where they are shown in the statement of financial position. This seems self-evident, but it is all too often forgotten or ignored in an examination. The following list is of payables that we would expect to see listed as current liabilities:

- Trade payables are amounts owed by the business to suppliers for goods or services received in the accounting period but paid for in the subsequent one.
- Short-term loans and other trade payables are also shown in this group and consist of all amounts due for repayment within 12 months. We would expect to find items such as a bank overdraft in this section.
- Other payables (accruals) are for expenses incurred during the accounting period, but which are still to be paid. This includes interest owed but as yet unpaid.

Although each business would have its own unique types of assets and liabilities, they would fall into the main groupings as described above.

Capital

The third section of the accounting equation is the capital section. This is the amount put into the business by the owner(s). It is of fundamental importance, because without capital no business can exist.

Capital is an equity term. It represents the amount of owner's interest in the business; that is, the owner's share in the business's assets. Capital varies depending on the nature of the entity. In the case of a sole trader, the capital is the amount introduced by the owner. To this is added the accumulated profits earned during the past years, less any drawings made by the owner(s).

Capital will be increased if the business has made a profit for the year, and decreased if it has made a loss for the year. This figure will come from the statement of profit or loss and other comprehensive income.

The capital will also be affected by the drawings taken during the period. The drawings will be shown as a deduction in the capital section of the statement of financial position.

> **EXAM HINT**
>
> Drawings are a reduction in the capital of a business not an expense – always show these separately in the capital section of the statement of financial position.

ACTIVITY 7   SKILLS CRITICAL THINKING, REASONING

CASE STUDY: ASSET OR LIABILITY

Description	Non-current asset	Current asset	Current liability
Motor vehicle			
Cash			
Goods for resale			
Amount due to supplier			
Amount due by customers			
Rent outstanding			
Bank overdraft			
Office furniture			

1 Using the information in the preceding paragraphs, complete the table.

ACTIVITY 8   SKILLS CRITICAL THINKING, REASONING

CASE STUDY: CURRENT OR NON-CURRENT ASSETS

1 Identify the assets from the list below. State if the asset is a current or a non-current asset:
   (a) inventory
   (b) money owed to supplier
   (c) computer equipment
   (d) money outstanding for goods sold.

2 Identify the liabilities from the following list. Give the nature of each liability, i.e. whether it is current or non-current:
(a) a loan due to be repaid to Loans Inc in four months' time
(b) money owed to a supplier
(c) fixtures and fittings
(d) money outstanding for goods sold by us
(e) a loan due to be repaid to National Bank in three years' time
(f) VAT due to be paid to HMRC
(g) a bank overdraft.

ACTIVITY 9 SKILLS CRITICAL THINKING, REASONING

CASE STUDY: ALLOCATING ACCOUNTS

Details	Asset	Liability	Income	Expense	Statement of financial position	Statement of profit or loss
Bank overdraft						
Rent paid quarterly in advance						
Motor vehicle						
Factory premises						
Sale of goods						
Purchase of stationery						
Bank interest received						
Insurance premium						
Amount owed to stationery supplier						
Inventory held for resale						
Loan interest paid						
Computer equipment						

1 Identify the nature of each item in the list and where each would appear in the financial statements.
(Remember that all the items must appear in one of the first four columns and also in either column 5 or 6.)

ACTIVITY 10 SKILLS ANALYSIS, EXECUTIVE FUNCTION

CASE STUDY: JULIET

Juliet runs a business delivering lunches at people's places of work. She borrowed £30 000 for her business on 1 January 2019. The loan is repayable in full in four years' time, but interest at the rate of 8 per cent is payable annually.

She has also financed the purchase of a delivery vehicle by a loan of £8 000, which is repayable in full over four years as from 1 January 2020. Interest of 7 per cent annually is payable on the loan.

The business has purchased goods for resale totalling £2 100. This amount is to be paid on 15 January 2020.

1 Show the total amount of current liabilities at 31 December 2019 (show your workings). Assume that no payments have been made during 2019 for interest.

STATEMENT OF FINANCIAL POSITION LAYOUT

Statement of financial position of J Jones at 31 December 2019

	£ Cost	£ Provision for depreciation	£ Carrying value
Non-current assets			
Land & buildings	130000	10000	120000
Plant & equipment	23000	13000	10000
	153000	23000	130000
Current assets			
Inventory		15000	
Trade receivables		6000	
Cash at bank		4000	
			25000
Total assets			155000
Capital and liabilities			
Opening capital			
Plus: Capital introduced		90000	
Plus: Profit		50000	
Less: Drawings		(15000)	
Closing capital			125000
***Add:* Non-current liabilities**			
8% Bank loan			10000
***Add:* Current liabilities**			
Trade payables	18500		
Other payables	1500		20000
Total capital and liabilities			155000

Having defined the various types of assets and liabilities, we now need to see where they are placed in the statement of financial position.

> Assets = Capital + Liabilities

Above is an example of a statement of financial position, showing the format required.

From the above, you can see that the statement of financial position starts with the non-current assets and ends with current liabilities.

> Non-current assets + Current assets =
> Capital + Non-current liabilities + Current liabilities

The groups are in the reverse order of liquidity for the statement of financial position. Non-current assets appear first and then current assets. Within the current asset heading, the least liquid current asset (inventory) appears first and the list descends to cash (the most liquid current asset).

WORKED EXAMPLE

The above format is illustrated when we look at the following example.

At 31 December 2019 we are given the following information as it relates to statement of financial position items:

	£
Premises	80000
Inventory	5000
Trade receivables	2000
Cash at bank	2500
Trade payables	4500

We will prepare the statement of financial position using the above information.

The problem we have is that the statement of financial position must balance – but there is an amount of £85 000 missing. We know this because we can see that the accounting equation does not balance. We know that:

$$\text{Assets} - \text{Liabilities} = \text{Capital}$$

This can also be shown as:

$$\text{Assets} = \text{Capital} + \text{Liabilities}$$

In the details above, we have assets of £89 500 and liabilities of £4 500. This means that capital must be equal to the difference (£89 500 – £4 500) of £85 000. Once we have worked out the missing number, we are able to draw up the statement of financial position.

Statement of financial position at 31 December 2019

	£	£
	Dr	Cr
Non-current assets		
Premises		80 000
Current assets		
Inventory	5 000	
Trade receivables	2 000	
Cash at bank	2 500	9 500
Total assets		89 500
Capital		85 000
Current liabilities		
Trade payables		4 500
Total capital and liabilities		89 500

PREPARING FINANCIAL STATEMENTS FROM THE TRIAL BALANCE

Often in examinations you are asked to prepare a statement of profit or loss and other comprehensive income and a statement of financial position from a trial balance, after accounting for additional post-trial balance events such as the calculation of depreciation. In the following worked example, we will prepare the financial statements straight from the information in the trial balance, and in the next chapter we will incorporate further adjustments in preparation of the financial accounts.

WORKED EXAMPLE

Ellis has extracted the following trial balance on 31 March 2018.

Ellis: trial balance at 31 March 2018

	£	£
	Dr	Cr
Capital		30 700
Revenue		210 000
Purchases	120 000	
Returns inwards	1 000	
Inventory at 1 April 2017	31 000	
Buildings	70 000	
Provision for depreciation – building		35 000
Motor vehicles – cost	23 000	
Provision for depreciation – motor vehicles		10 000
Wages	27 000	
Discount allowed	1 600	
Discount received		3 100
Allowance/provision for irrecoverable debts		500
Rent and rates	8 500	
Electricity	4 600	
Interest paid	3 500	
Bank and cash	3 200	
Drawings	11 900	
Carriage inwards	3 000	
Carriage out	1 000	
Returns out		2 000
Loan – repayable 2025		20 000
Trade payables		30 000
Trade receivables	32 000	
	341 300	341 300

Additional information:
- inventory at 31 March 2018 was valued at £21 000
- depreciation of buildings to be included of £2 000 and motor vehicles of £1 000.

You are asked to prepare a statement of profit or loss and other comprehensive income for the year ended 31 March 2018 and a statement of financial position at 31 March 2018.

Ellis: statement of profit or loss and other comprehensive income for the year ended 31 March 2018

	£	£	£
Revenue			210000
Less: Returns in			1000
			209000
Less: Cost of sales			
Opening inventory		31000	
Purchases	120000		
Less: Returns outwards	2000		
	118000		
Add: Carriage inwards	3000	121000	
		152000	
Less: Closing inventory		21000	
Cost of sales			131000
Gross Profit			78000
Other Income			
Discounts received			3100
			81100
Less: Expenses			
Wages	27000		
Carriage out	1000		
Discount allowed	1600		
Rent and rates	8500		
Electricity	4600		
Interest paid	3500		
Depreciation – building	2000		
Depreciation – motor vehicles	1000		48200
Profit for the year			31900

Ellis: statement of financial position at 31 March 2018

	£ Cost	£ Provision for depreciation	£ Carrying value
Non-current assets			
Buildings	70000	37000	33000
Motor vehicles	23000	11000	12000
	93000	48000	45000
Current assets			
Inventory		21000	
Trade receivables	32000		
Less: Allowance/ provision for irrecoverable debts	500	31500	
Bank and cash		3200	
			55700
Total assets			100700
Capital and liabilities			
Opening capital		30700	
Profit for year		31900	
		63600	
Less: drawings		11900	
Closing capital			50700
Non-current liabilities			
Loan			20000
Current liabilities			
Trade payables		30000	30000
Total capital and liabilities			100700

We can see from the statement of financial position that:

Total assets = total capital + liabilities.

ACTIVITY 11   SKILLS ▷ CRITICAL THINKING, ANALYSIS, PROBLEM SOLVING

CASE STUDY: MISSING FIGURE

Non-current assets	Current assets	Non-current liabilities	Current liabilities	Capital
48000	22000	14000	6000	
	17500	3100	6000	35000
102000		30000	25000	65000
102000	46000		28000	110000
48000	22000	Nil		65000

You will note that we can always find the missing part of the statement of financial position if we remember the accounting equation:

Assets = Capital + Liabilities.

1 Supply the missing figures in the table.

ACTIVITY 12 SKILLS ⟩ ANALYSIS, PROBLEM SOLVING, EXECUTIVE FUNCTION

CASE STUDY: DINAH

The following is an extract of Dinah's trial balance at 31 December 2019:

Dinah: trial balance at 31 December 2019

	£	£
	Dr	Cr
Bank	700	
Trade payables		6 900
Bank loan due 2025		7 000
Trade receivables	30 000	
Investments	2 800	
Machinery: at cost	42 000	
Provision for depreciation – machinery, at 31 December 2019		19 400
Owner's capital		38 200
Allowance/provision for irrecoverable debts		800
Vehicles: at cost	8 000	
Provision for depreciation – vehicles, at 31 December 2019		5 600
Closing inventory	15 500	
Profit for the year		21 100
	£99 000	£99 000

1 Prepare the statement of financial position, having already worked out that the profit for the year amounted to £21 100.

VALUATION IN THE STATEMENT OF FINANCIAL POSITION

Valuation of items appearing in the statement of financial position is usually at historic cost. In current assets, however, if the net realisable value is less than the cost then the asset is shown at the former value (using the prudence concept, see Chapter 17).

In the case of a non-current asset, it has a limited life and is, therefore, depreciated. But, in some cases, a non-current asset can appreciate in value, for example, property. In this case, it can be revalued to the current market value and this increase in value is shown in the statement of financial position.

ACTIVITY 13 SKILLS ⟩ ANALYSIS, PROBLEM SOLVING, EXECUTIVE FUNCTION

CASE STUDY: MICHAEL ENTERPRISES

You are given the following trial balance and a list of additional adjustments to be made:

Michael Enterprises: trial balance at 1 November 2018

	£	£
	Dr	Cr
Trade payables		71 190
Returns inwards	1 400	
Electricity and gas	16 912	
Insurance	1 435	
Capital		204 792
Rates	6 342	
Salaries and wages	109 823	
Motor expenses	9 912	
Sales		618 100
Purchases	358 050	
Cash in hand	1 050	
Returns outwards		2 450
Inventory 31 October 2018	109 830	
Trade receivables	114 198	
Rent	24 500	
Fixtures and fittings	44 100	
Drawings	76 650	
Delivery expenses	7 105	
Cash at bank	15 225	
	896 532	896 532

Closing inventory was valued at £188 870

1 Prepare the statement of profit or loss and other comprehensive income and statement of financial position at 31 October 2019, incorporating the above adjustments.

ACTIVITY 14 SKILLS ANALYSIS, EXECUTIVE FUNCTION

CASE STUDY: SEDRA

	£
Closing inventory	9 500
Commission received	300
Heating and lighting	2 550
Marketing expenses	3 750
Purchases	35 510
Rent paid	600
Revenue	65 555
Wages and salaries	21 000

1 From the above information, produce a statement of profit or loss and other comprehensive income for Sedra for the year ended December 2018.

ACTIVITY 15 SKILLS ANALYSIS, EXECUTIVE FUNCTION

CASE STUDY: YANI

Yani provided the following balance on 31 December 2018:

	£
Bank overdraft	2 200
Capital	65 000
Drawings	12 000
Equipment	10 000
Provision for depreciation (equipment)	2 500
Inventory	8 550
Profit for the year	
Property	60 000
Provision for depreciation (property)	2 000
Trade payables	15 250
Trade receivables	18 200

1 From the information, prepare a statement of financial position at that date. You will need to calculate the profit as a balancing number.

EXAM HINT

Returns in are deducted from revenue, as they are sales being returned; returns out are deducted in cost of sales, as they are purchases the business has sent back.

A bank overdraft is a current liability.

Loans repayable within the next financial period will be current liabilities rather than non-current liabilities.

Always label the total assets calculation.

CHECKPOINT

1 What are the financial statements?

2 How is gross profit calculated?

3 How is the cost of sales calculated?

4 How is carriage treated in the statement of profit or loss and other comprehensive income?

5 Other income is entered immediately after revenue. True or false?

6 How is profit for the year different to gross profit?

7 Accumulated depreciation is added to the cost of a non-current asset to find the carrying value. True or false?

8 State three types of current asset.

9 The bank is always a current asset. True or false?

10 Explain how the allowance/provision for irrecoverable debts is treated in the financial statements.

11 Complete the following equation:

Total assets =

Capital + _____ – Drawings + _____ Liabilities + Current _____

12 Explain why total assets should always = Capital + Liabilities.

SUBJECT VOCABULARY

cost of sales (cost of goods sold) the direct costs related to the manufacture or purchase of a product that is sold to a customer

financial statements (final accounts) produced by the business to provide a summary of the performance of the business (the statement of profit or loss and other comprehensive income) and the financial position of the business (the statement of financial position)

goodwill an intangible non-current asset reflecting the value given to the reputation of the business

intangible asset a non-physical asset that cannot be touched or seen, such as goodwill or a brand name

liquidity the ability to convert assets into sufficient cash to meet everyday commitments

net realisable value (NRV) inventory valuation based on the selling price less any additional costs required to affect the sale

other payables (accruals) amounts owed at the end of the financial period which match to the revenue for that period

other receivables (prepayments) amounts paid in one financial period that will match with revenue earned in the next financial period

total assets non-current assets plus current assets

trading account the part of the statement of profit or loss and other comprehensive income that calculates the gross profit from trading activities

EXAM PRACTICE

CASE STUDY: ALFREDO

SKILLS   ANALYSIS, PROBLEM SOLVING, EXECUTIVE FUNCTION

Alfredo makes and fits windows. He does most of his business with builders, who he sometimes gives discounts to. The following information has been extracted from Alfredo's books at 31 May 2017:

	£	£
	Dr	Cr
Capital		59 800
Drawings	11 900	
Revenue		205 000
Purchases	125 000	
Inventory at 1 June 2016	31 000	
Returns inwards	800	
Returns out		1 000
Discounts received		3 100
Discounts allowed	1 680	
Wages	27 000	
Rent and rate	8 500	
Electricity	4 600	
General expense	23 500	
Carriage inwards	800	
Trade payables		15 650
Trade receivables	19 000	
Allowance/provision for irrecoverable debts		400
Bank and cash	3 170	
Equipment at cost	64 000	
Provision for depreciation (equipment)		36 000
	320 950	320 950

Additional information at 31 May 2017:
- inventory £32 000
- depreciation on non-current assets is to be provided, at the rate of 25 per cent p.a., reducing balance method
- an irrecoverable debt of £600 is to be written off and the allowance/provision for irrecoverable debts maintained at 2.5 per cent
- drawings of £1 000 have been omitted from the books.

1 Prepare the statement of profit or loss and other comprehensive income for the year ended 31 May 2017. **(20 marks)**
2 Prepare the statement of financial position at 31 May 2017. **(10 marks)**

11 YEAR-END ADJUSTMENTS

LEARNING OBJECTIVES

After you have studied this chapter you should be able to:
- account for accruals and prepayment of expenses and revenue
- understand the nature and purpose of provisions
- understand provisions for depreciation
- account for irrecoverable debts and use allowance/ provision for irrecoverable debts.

GETTING STARTED

At the start of the year, your business purchased a new delivery vehicle for £25 000. It has been used all year and has covered 70 000 miles. Should the vehicle still be valued at the original cost in the books?

The business has paid for building insurance for a whole year. The payment was made, by cheque, one week before the end of the financial year. Should this amount be included in the expenses for the current year?

There are several reasons why a business may need to make adjustments to their accounts at the end of the year. The expenses and income items shown in the cash book may not be the amount of income and expenses to be reported in the statement of profit or loss and other comprehensive income. The adjustments are necessary as financial statements are prepared following the **accruals** concept. This requires that revenues and costs are recorded in the period they are incurred, not in the period they are paid.

The adjustments can be categorised into three classes:
- income or expenses owing in this accounting year – accruals
- income or expenses in advance for next accounting year – **prepayments**
- non-cash expenses, such as irrecoverable debts, an increase/decrease in allowance/provision for irrecoverable debts and depreciation – provisions.

Accruals and prepayments are adjustments made at the year end to make sure that the expenses and income are recognised in the correct accounting period. By following the accruals concept, the expenses will be recorded in the accounting period they are incurred not the period when they are recorded or paid. In the same way, income should be recognised in the accounting period it was earned not the accounting period it is recorded or received.

ACCRUALS

This concept covers both the expenses, revenue and other income that is recorded in the statement of profit or loss and other comprehensive income and the other receivables and other payables that are recorded in the statement of financial position. An accrual is an expense or income which is outstanding at the end of the financial period and needs to be included in the financial statements for that period.

ACCRUED EXPENSES

Expenses that have been incurred but not yet recorded are called accrued expenses. As such, the amounts unpaid must be recorded in the books of account prior to preparing the financial statements.

WORKED EXAMPLE

At the year end, the amount to be included for an expense is transferred from the expense account to the statement of profit or loss and other comprehensive income account. For example, the telephone and postage expense for the year is £2 414. However, the business has only paid £2 100 of this amount, so the difference (£314) is shown as the balance in the telephone and postage account. This credit balance is called an accrual.

Telephone and postage

Date	Details	£	Date	Details	£
31 Dec 2019	Bank	2 100	31 Dec 2019	Statement of profit or loss	2 414
	Accrual c/d*	314			
		2 414			2 414
			1 Jan 2020	Balance b/d	314

Motor expenses

Date	Details	£	Date	Details	£
31 Dec 2019	Bank	1 987	31 Dec 2019	Statement of profit or loss	2 587
	Accrual c/d*	600			
		2 587			2 587
			1 Jan 2020	Balance b/d	600

*Here again, we accrue £600 for motor expenses that were unpaid at 31 December 2019.

Commission paid

Date	Details	£	Date	Details	£
31 Dec 2019	Bank	11 880	31 Dec 2019	Statement of profit or loss	16 200
	Accrual c/d*	4 320			
		16 200			16 200
			1 Jan 2020	Balance b/d	4 320

*This shows an accrual of £4 320 for commission payable. NB – in the examination you *should not* use accrual c/d, but balance c/d, the above is for illustrative purposes only, so you understand that the balance c/d represents a liability.

All three accruals from above are transferred, together with the amounts paid during the year, to the statement of profit or loss and other comprehensive income as shown below.

Statement of profit or loss and other comprehensive income for the year ended 31 December 2019 (extract)

	£
Telephone and postage	2 414
Motor expenses	2 587
Commission on sales	16 200

In some cases accruals must be estimated, as no invoice has been issued before the year end. For example, we received our last phone bill on 10 December and our financial year end is 31 December. At the year end, there are 21 days of calls made but not yet billed. In the event that the amount is material (this means that it is important enough to be shown in the financial statements), we must estimate the accrued amount.

There are also instances of accrued income, for example, rent receivable, and this would be treated in the same way as an accrued expense, except that the balance brought down would be on the debit side.

ACCRUED INCOME

Sometimes accruals refer to accrued income. In this instance, the income is due to the business but has not yet been recorded in the accounts. This may, for example, be in the case of interest on a deposit account or rent receivable by the business.

Accrued income is any that belongs to a current accounting year but not yet received. For example, a business has received £22 100 rent from tenants for the year ended 31 December 2019. The owner noticed that rent of £1 900 was due but had not yet been received:

Rent receivable

Date	Details	£	Date	Details	£
31 Dec 2019	Statement of profit or loss	24 000	31 Dec 2019	Bank	22 100
				Accrued income*	1 900
		24 000			24 000
1 Jan 2020	Balance b/d	1 900			

*NB – in the examination, this should be written as Balance c/d, it is shown here as accrued income to show that the value is a current asset.

In this case, since the £1 900 rent belongs to the year ended 31 December 2019, the accountant should include this in the rent receivable income for the year ended 31 December 2019. Meanwhile, since the £1 900 will be collectible later, an asset account – namely other receivable (or accrued income) – would be entered into the current assets section of the statement of financial position. As a result, the double entry for the accrued income is:

	£	£
	Dr	Cr
Other receivables (accrued income) Statement of financial position	1 900	
Rent receivable (income) Statement of profit or loss		1 900

In terms of the financial statements:

Statement of profit or loss and other comprehensive income (extract) for the year ended 31 December 2019

	£	£
Other income		
Rent receivable		24 000

Statement of financial position (extract) at 31 December 2019

	£	£
Current assets		
Other receivables – rent received		1 900

PREPAYMENTS

Just like accruals, prepayments are required in order to follow the accruals concept. A prepayment is a payment in the current period for goods or services to be received in the next accounting period. Prepayments apply to both revenues and expenses.

PREPAID EXPENSES

With an expense prepayment, for example insurance, the amount that is not related to the period of the statement of profit or loss and other comprehensive income account must be 'taken out' (credited) to the insurance expense account with a relevant debit to other payables in the current liabilities section of the statement of financial position.

Prepaid expenses are future expenses that have been paid in advance. They relate wholly or partly to a later accounting period than when recorded. They are sometimes referred to as payments in advance. The following example illustrates prepayments.

Our business year end is 31 December 2019. On 1 October we pay one year's insurance of £1 200. This payment is for the period 1 October 2019 to 30 September 2020. That means that only a quarter of £1 200 (£300), covering the months of 1 October 2019 to 31 December 2019, is relevant to this financial year. The remaining three-quarters of £1 200 (£900) is prepaid and must be brought into account in the following year.

As is the case with accruals, adjustment for prepaid expenses can also be made in the one account. This is shown in the example below.

Insurance

Date	Details	£	Date	Details	£
1 Oct 2019	Bank	1 200	31 Dec 2019	Statement of profit or loss	300
				Balance c/d	900
		1 200			1 200
1 Jan 2020	Balance b/d	900			

Referring to the ledger entries above, we can deduce that the double entry for prepayment of an expense is:

		£	£
Dr	Prepaid insurance (asset +)	900	
Cr	Insurance (expense −)		900

In the statement of financial position, the prepayment is shown as a current asset.

Statement of financial position (extract) at 31 December 2019

	£	£
Current assets		
Other receivables – insurance	900	

In the statement of profit or loss and other comprehensive income account we show revenues for that accounting period exactly matched by the expenses that resulted in earning those sales. As such, we deduct the prepaid amount of insurance from the expenses in the statement of profit or loss and other comprehensive income account, as it is a payment made against next year's trading.

Statement of profit or loss and other comprehensive income (extract) for the year ended 31 December 2019

	£	£
Expenses		
Insurance	300	

WORKED EXAMPLE

A business has a monthly rent expense of £200. It paid an additional amount of £800 in December 2019 for rent which relates to the following year. We need to take this amount and move it into the next year, so that the statement of profit or loss and other comprehensive income account reflects the correct figure for 2019.

Rent

Date	Details	£	Date	Details	£
11 Jan 2019	Bank	600	31 Dec 2019	Statement of profit or loss	2 400
3 Apr	Bank	600		Balance c/d	800
1 July	Bank	600			
1 Oct	Bank	600			
29 Dec	Bank	800			
		3 200			3 200
1 Jan 2020	Balance b/d	800			

The payments made in the year amounted to £3 200 and the rent for the year is £2 400 (£200 × 12). The difference of £800 represents the prepaid rent which is for the next accounting period. The £800 which has been prepaid is carried down to the next accounting period and is transferred to the statement of financial position at the year end as a current asset (other receivables).

PREPAID INCOME

Prepaid income is revenue which has been received for goods or services that are going to be provided by the business in a future accounting period. Prepaid income has the effect of reducing the income in the current accounting period and creates a current liability in the statement of financial position.

WORKED EXAMPLE

Although prepaid expenditure is the most common of prepayments, there are also instances of prepaid income, such as where we receive rent for premises rented out. The accounting term for prepaid income is 'other payables'.

A business rents part of its premises to another business for £100 per month. During the year it received three payments of £600. The ledger account would be:

Rent receivable

Date	Details	£	Date	Details	£
31 Dec 2019	Statement of profit or loss	1 200	1 Jan 2019	Bank	600
			1 July 2019	Bank	600
			29 Dec 2019	Bank	600
31 Dec 2019	Balance c/d	600			
		1 800			1 800
			1 Jan 2020	Balance b/d	600

In this case, you can see that the business received an extra £600 rent for the next accounting year. Since the rent income does not belong to this year, it is necessary to deduct it from this year's income. On the other hand, the business has an obligation to provide shop space for its tenant, and therefore there is a liability – namely other payables.

The double entry for prepaid income is as follows:

		£	£
Dr	Rent received (income –)	600	
Cr	Other payables – rent received (liabilities +)		600

The presentation of the rent received and prepaid income is as follows:

Statement of profit or loss and comprehensive income (extract) for the year ended 31 December 2019

	£	£
Other income		
Rent received		1 200

Statement of financial position (extract) at 31 December 2019

	£	£
Current liabilities		
Other payables (prepaid rent receivable)	600	

EXAM HINT

When accounting for year-end adjustment for accruals and prepayments you must remember that there is an entry in *both* the financial statements. Often students will correctly account for them in the statement of profit or loss and other comprehensive income but forget to enter them as assets or liabilities in the statement of financial position.

NATURE AND USE OF PROVISIONS

The IAS definition of a provision is a liability of uncertain timing or amount. We know that a liability is an amount owed by a business, so a provision is an estimate of the amount owed by a business when it cannot, for certain, state the exact value of the transaction, or the exact timing.

An example of this is the provision for depreciation on non-current assets. The exact cost of using the asset in any financial year is purely an estimate based on past experiences. It cannot be valued with any certainty. Therefore, a provision is created to transfer the cost of using that asset to the expense section of the statement of profit or loss and other comprehensive income, while at the same time reducing the value of the asset in the statement of financial position.

In your studies, you need to account for the allowance/provision for irrecoverable debts (Chapter 3), the provision for depreciation (Chapter 6) and the provision for unrealised profit (Chapter 16).

Provisions will appear in the statement of financial position next to the asset to which it is related. While a provision will always be a credit entry, it is possible that the amount in the provision account for a financial year is reduced. The allowance/provision for irrecoverable debts might be reduced by improved collection procedures – in this case, the reduction for that year would represent other operating income in the statement of profit or loss and other comprehensive income, rather than an expense.

PROVISIONS FOR DEPRECIATION

The methods of calculating depreciation were covered in Chapter 6 and you should ensure you are fully familiar with these and the double entry required. The trial balance is produced before the annual depreciation charges have been calculated. As a result, there has to be a year-end adjustment for the provision for depreciation and the related expense for the year. The figures used to calculate the depreciation expense for the year are often those that appear in the trial balance.

IRRECOVERABLE DEBTS AND ALLOWANCE/PROVISION FOR IRRECOVERABLE DEBTS

These two transactions are often accounted for at the year end in examinations. Irrecoverable debts are certain and therefore they are not a provision. The double entry for them will be:

Dr	Irrecoverable debts
Cr	Trade receivables

The allowance/provision for irrecoverable debts is a provision because a business cannot be certain that all the outstanding value for trade receivables will be received from customers. The double entry for this will depend on whether the allowance has increased or decreased from the previous year.

An increase would represent an expense, so the double entry would be:

Dr	Increase in allowance/provision for irrecoverable debts (statement of profit or loss)
Cr	Allowance/provision for irrecoverable debts (statement of financial position)

If the new allowance was a decrease on the previous year, it would represent other operating income and the double entry would be:

Dr   Allowance/provision for irrecoverable debts (statement of financial position)

Cr   Decrease in allowance/provision for irrecoverable debts (statement of profit or loss)

The treatment of irrecoverable debts and allowance/ provision for irrecoverable debts was covered in detail in Chapter 3. The important point to remember is that the calculation of the allowance/provision for irrecoverable debts will be a year-end adjustment based on the trial balance figure for trade receivables, less any year-end adjustment for irrecoverable debts.

EXAM HINT

When calculating the year-end adjustment for irrecoverable debts and the allowance/provision for irrecoverable debts, an existing irrecoverable debt in the trial balance will be an expense and the amount will already be deducted from the trade receivables amount.

Any irrecoverable debts given in the additional information must be deducted from the trade receivables before calculating the new allowance/ provision for irrecoverable debts.

ACTIVITY 1

SKILLS   ANALYSIS, PROBLEM SOLVING, EXECUTIVE FUNCTION

CASE STUDY: JAY

Jay has taken out a four-year loan of £20 000 at 7 per cent interest. The following is the ledger account for the finance costs on the loan.

Finance costs

Date	Details	£	Date	Details	£
15 Mar 2018	Bank	350			
30 July 2018	Bank	350			
5 Nov 2018	Bank	350			

1 Complete the finance costs ledger account to correctly reflect the amount to be charged to the statement of profit or loss and other comprehensive income account for the year ending 31 December 2018. Show the balance at the start of the next financial year.

ACTIVITY 2

SKILLS   PROBLEM SOLVING, ANALYSIS, EXECUTIVE FUNCTION

CASE STUDY: NISSA

Nissa pays the rent on her café quarterly, in arrears, at the end of March, June, September and December. Her financial year end is 31 May 2019. The rent for the year is £84 000 p.a. She pays the rent from the business bank account.

1 Calculate the charge that is to be made to the statement of profit or loss and other comprehensive income account, the accrual in the statement of financial position and show the ledger account for rent.

From 1 October 2019, Nissa's rent increases to £96 000 p.a.

2 Calculate the charge in the statement of profit or loss and other comprehensive income account for the year ended 31 May 2020, the liability at that date and show the ledger account for rent.

Nissa pays insurance one year in advance. For the calendar year ended 31 December 2019, the payment is £18 000 and for the year ended 31 December 2020 it is £24 000.

3 Calculate the charge in the statement of profit or loss and other comprehensive income account for the financial year ended 31 May 2020 and the prepayment at that date. Show the insurance ledger account.

ACTIVITY 3   SKILLS   ANALYSIS, PROBLEM SOLVING, EXECUTIVE FUNCTION

CASE STUDY: ELECTRICITY EXPENSE

The electricity account for the year ending 31 December 2018 is as follows:

Electricity

Date	Details	£	Date	Details	£
15 Feb 2018	Bank	550	1 Jan 2018	Balance b/d	430
30 July 2018	Bank	280			
31 Oct 2018	Bank	310			

An amount of £425 due for charges to 31 December 2018 has not yet been paid.

1 Prepare the electricity account to correctly reflect the amount to be charged to the statement of profit or loss and other comprehensive income for the year ending 31 December 2018, showing the balance at the start of the next financial year.

ACTIVITY 4   SKILLS   ANALYSIS, PROBLEM SOLVING, EXECUTIVE FUNCTION

CASE STUDY: BB TRADING

Insurance is paid by BB Trading in a single payment. This is due on 1 August each year. BB Trading has its year end on 31 December. The following is the ledger account for insurance:

Insurance

Date	Details	£	Date	Details	£
1 Jan 2018	Balance b/d	700			
1 Aug 2018	Bank	1 800			

1 Prepare adjustments to the insurance account to correctly reflect the amount for the year ending 31 December 2018.

CHECKPOINT

1 Accrued other income is a current asset in the statement of financial position. True or false?

2 Prepaid expenses are a current asset in the statement of financial position. True or false?

3 Explain why the prepayment of motor vehicle insurance would be a current asset.

4 Explain why the balance of outstanding wages would be an accrual at the year end.

5 What would be the effect on profit if accrued expenses were ignored?

6 The allowance/provision for irrecoverable debts will always increase at the end of the year. True or false?

7 Explain what is meant by the term 'provision'.

8 Where would the provision for depreciation appear in the financial statements?

SUBJECT VOCABULARY

accruals the concept that income and expenditure for goods and services is matched to the same accounting period when calculating profit

prepayments revenues or expenses relating to the next accounting period

provision an expected future liability or future expectation of expenditure that is uncertain

EXAM PRACTICE

CASE STUDY: NAN'S SOFA SHOP

SKILLS ANALYSIS, EXECUTIVE FUNCTION, CRITICAL THINKING

Nan's shop sells and delivers sofas to its customers. The following balance has been extracted from the books on 31 July 2017:

	£
Allowance/provision for irrecoverable debts	2 300
Irrecoverable debts	1 500
Motor vehicles (cost)	120 000
Motor vehicles (provision for depreciation)	50 000
Rent of premises	25 000
Trade payables	30 000
Trade receivables	45 000
Wages	42 000

The bookkeeper has provided the following additional information at 31 July 2017:

- A trade receivable owing £1 000 has been declared bankrupt and the amount owing is to be written off.
- The allowance/provision for irrecoverable debts is to be maintained at 5 per cent.
- Rent on premises of £10 000 has been prepaid.
- Wages of £7 000 remain outstanding.
- Depreciation of motor vehicles is at the rate of 25 per cent per annum, using the reducing balance method.

Q

1 Complete the journal entries required to take into account the additional information. **(10 marks)**
2 State the accounting concepts relating to:
  (a) the adjustment for rent on premises **(1 mark)**
  (b) the adjustment for the allowance/provision for irrecoverable debts. **(1 mark)**

12 DEPARTMENTAL RECORDS

LEARNING OBJECTIVES

After you have studied this chapter, you should be able to:

■ prepare statements of profit or loss and other comprehensive income in columnar format

■ evaluate and recommend decisions relating to the expansion or closure of a department.

GETTING STARTED

A food retailer with several different sections, including fresh vegetables, fresh fish, fresh meat, a frozen food section, clothing, a pharmacy and a café, has noticed that profits have been falling over recent months, despite some sections of the business appearing to be very busy. It is concerned about this. How might it identify where problems exist? How would it identify the successful departments and the less successful department? What actions might it take with this information?

Many businesses have multiple departments within their overall operations. In these cases, it would be sensible to prepare accounting records to establish the performance of each department in terms of the profit they contribute to the business. This information can help the decision-making process of the business.

Departmental records show the contribution that each department is making to the overall results of the business. As a result, decisions can be made regarding the expansion of successful profit-making departments or the contraction or closure of less successful departments. Additionally, departmental records can be used as a part of the employee remuneration system (Chapter 18), where workers could earn a bonus based on the profit earned by a department.

PREPARING DEPARTMENTAL RECORDS – THE TRADING ACCOUNT

It is useful to split the preparation of departmental records into two clear stages. The first of these calls on your previous knowledge of the statement of profit or loss and other comprehensive income and requires you to prepare this in order to calculate the gross profit of each department. This section requires information on revenues and cost of sales for each department.

The only difference between this process and the one relating to the process for sole traders is the possible treatment of transfers of inventory between departments. Essentially, we need to remove the inventory from the department that originally purchased it, effectively reducing the cost of sales. We then transfer this cost to the department into which the inventory was transferred, increasing the cost of sales for that department. The journal entry would be:

Dr Transfer of inventory (receiving department)
Cr Transfer of inventory (original department)

This transaction should be shown in the cost of sales and **not** netted off the inventory values.

It is usual to present departmental records in columnar format as shown at the bottom of the following worked example.

WORKED EXAMPLE

Eastern Retailers operates a large retail store which has three departments, selling electrical goods, household goods and clothing directly to the public. The following information has been extracted from the books at 30 November 2017:

	£
Revenue:	
Electrical goods	500000
Household goods	400000
Clothing	100000
Purchases:	
Electrical goods	210000
Household goods	200000
Clothing	60000
Inventory 1 December 2016:	
Electrical goods	190000
Household goods	150000
Clothing	25000

Additional information at 30 November 2017:

Inventory	£
Electrical goods	210000
Household goods	180000
Clothing	10000

- During the year £10000 of household goods were taken and used in the electrical goods department.

The extract statement of profit or loss and other comprehensive income can now be prepared to show the gross profit for each department.

Eastern Retailers: statement of profit or loss and other comprehensive income (extract) for the year ended 30 November 2017

	Electrical goods £	Household goods £	Clothing £
Revenue	500000	400000	100000
Opening inventory	190000	150000	25000
Purchases	210000	200000	60000
Transfer	**10000**	**(10000)**	
Closing inventory	210000	180000	10000
Less cost of sales	200000	160000	75000
Gross profit	300000	240000	25000

The transfer entry has been highlighted to show the effect of transferring inventory between departments, the other entries are identical to those for sole traders. (NB – Normally a business would add a total column, but this is rarely asked for in examinations.)

CASE STUDY: AUTO PARTZ

Auto Partz has two departments, a new car sales department and a service workshop. The following were in the books at 30 November 2017:

	£
Revenue:	
New car sales	870000
Service department	120000
Purchases:	
New car sales	420000
Service department	80000
Inventory 1 December 2016:	
New car sales	130000
Service department	20000

At the end of the year, the following information was available:

- closing inventory for new car sales was £125000
- closing inventory for the service department was £20000
- during the year, inventory to the value of £5000 was transferred for use in the new car sales department.

1 Prepare a statement of profit or loss and other comprehensive income for the year ended 30 November 2017, to show the gross profit.

PREPARING DEPARTMENTAL RECORDS – ALLOCATING EXPENSES

One of the problems of preparing departmental accounts in the format of a statement of profit or loss and other comprehensive income is that it is often very difficult to decide which department incurs the expense and how much of an expense it incurs. Some expenses may be easily identifiable as belonging to a specific department, for example, the wages of employees working in a department. However, how should you allocate the salaries of managers who do not directly work in a particular department? Similarly, the cost of rent and rates may not be easily identifiable as being incurred by a certain department.

The solution to these problems is a process known as **apportionment**. This is simply the process whereby expenses are shared out between departments on a rational basis decided by the business, which accurately reflects how the overheads were incurred. The more common methods of apportionment include:

- wages – actual employee cost for each department
- management salaries – the number of employees in each department divided by wages costs
- rent and rates, heating – the floor space occupied by each department
- insurance – the floor space occupied by each department
- marketing expenses – the revenue generated by each department
- general expenses – the revenue generated by each department
- depreciation – the cost of non-current assets used by each department.

By apportioning expenses, the business is attempting to share out the overheads on a fair and reasonable basis to the department which benefits from its use. This is not a precise calculation, but if appropriate bases are used then it should produce accounting information which is beneficial to the business and the decision-making process. Departmental records are often used to make decisions about whether to expand a department or contract, or even close, an unprofitable one.

WORKED EXAMPLE

Having completed the trading section of the statement of profit or loss and other comprehensive income, Eastern Retailers have now provided the following additional information relating to the expenses of the business for the year ending 30 November 2017.

	£
Wages:	
Electrical goods	60 000
Household goods	30 000
Clothing	10 000
Management salaries	120 000
Heating and lighting	14 400
General expenses	6 000
Insurance	18 000
Delivery vehicles	9 000
Depreciation	12 000

Costs are apportioned on the following bases:

- management salaries – in proportion to the wage costs of each department
- heating and lighting – floor space
- general expenses – revenue
- insurance – floor space

- delivery vehicles – 90 per cent household goods, 10 per cent electrical goods
- depreciation – cost of non-current assets used by each department.

Department data:

Floor space	m²
Electrical	300
Household goods	500
Clothing	100

Non-current assets at cost	£
Electrical	40 000
Household goods	40 000
Clothing	20 000

We will start the statement of profit or loss and other comprehensive income from the gross profit, having previously calculated this. In the examination, you would just carry on the statement for the gross profit, there is no need for two titles:

- wages allocated as per cost per department
- management salaries shared out in the ratios of wages = 6 : 3 : 1
- heating and lighting by floor space ratio = 3 : 5 : 1
- general expenses by revenue = 5 : 4 : 1
- insurance by floor space = 3 : 5 : 1
- delivery vehicle expenses = 10 per cent electrical goods and 90 per cent household goods (given)
- depreciation by value of non-current assets = 2 : 2 : 1.

Eastern Retailers: Statement of profit or loss (extract) for the year ended 30 November 2017

	£	£	£
	Electrical goods	Household goods	Clothing
Gross profit	300 000	240 000	25 000
Less expenses			
Wages	60 000	30 000	10 000
Management salaries	72 000	36 000	12 000
Heating and lighting	4 800	8 000	1 600
General expenses	3 000	2 400	600
Insurance	6 000	10 000	2 000
Delivery vehicle expenses	900	8 100	
Depreciation	4 800	4 800	2 400
Total expenses	151 500	99 300	28 600
Departmental profit or loss for the year	**148 500**	**140 700**	**(3 600)**

Note the change in heading from 'profit for the year' to 'departmental profit for the year' to reflect that we are now preparing departmental records.

EXPANDING OR CLOSING DEPARTMENTS

One of the main benefits of preparing departmental records is to separate the financial performance of different departments. This allows a business to assess the performance of individual departments and therefore make decisions about the future expansion of a successful department or the closure of an unprofitable department.

In our example for Eastern Retailers, the preparation of departmental records highlighted that the clothing department was making a loss and could be considered for closure. Closing the clothing department would eliminate the loss and so should improve the level of profit at Eastern Retailers.

However, the decision is not always straightforward. Many other factors, both financial and non-financial, need to be taken into consideration if an informed decision is to be made.

- Overheads would still need to be paid and would now be apportioned between fewer departments, so the overall effect on profit might be minimal.
- The overhead costs may not have been apportioned on a fair and reasonable basis. The method of apportioning costs can be very difficult to do with any degree of accuracy.
- If the loss-making department is making a gross profit, then it is providing a positive contribution towards the **fixed costs** of the business. If the department is closed this contribution will be lost.
- Departments often complement each other and closing one department might affect the sales of the remaining departments. In the case of Eastern Retailers, it could be argued that the electrical goods and household goods departments complement each other, as would the two departments in Activity 1. Customers buying household goods may also buy electrical goods and customers buying a new car would probably like to have it serviced at the same business. The clothing department at Eastern Retailers does not appear to complement the other departments – as it is making a loss, this supports any decision to close the department.
- Other profitable departments could possibly expand into any space left behind by the closure of a department, or the space could be leased to another business. Both of these actions might improve the profit.
- The sale of non-current assets from the closure may release capital.
- The closure of a department might affect customer confidence in the business and therefore might reduce sales in the remaining departments.

- The cost of redundancy might be high, seriously affecting profit levels. In addition, staff morale might decrease, affecting the level of productivity in the business.
- There will be social accounting consequences of closing a department (see Chapter 22).

ACTIVITY 2   SKILLS   ANALYSIS, INTERPRETATION

CASE STUDY: EXPANDING OR CLOSING A DEPARTMENT

1 From the list of factors above, draw up an evaluation table showing the possible advantages and disadvantages of closing a department.
2 Draw up an evaluation table showing the possible advantages and disadvantages of expanding a department.

ACTIVITY 3   SKILLS   CRITICAL THINKING, REASONING

CASE STUDY: APPORTIONMENT

1 How might the following overhead costs be apportioned:
 (a) depreciation
 (b) rates for a building
 (c) management salaries
 (d) general expenses
 (e) property insurance
 (f) equipment insurance
 (g) marketing expenses?

ACTIVITY 4   SKILLS   ANALYSIS, EXECUTIVE FUNCTION, PROBLEM SOLVING

CASE STUDY: MILL ANTIQUES

Mill Antiques has three separate departments:
- sales of antiques to customers
- restoration of antiques for customers
- café.

The following balances were extracted from the books of account for the year ending 31 August 2017:

	£
Revenue:	
Sales of antiques	135000
Restoration of antiques	45000
Café	30000
Cost of sales:	
Sales of antiques	59500
Restoration of antiques	10000
Café	6000
Wages:	
Sales of antiques	15000
Restoration of antiques	20000
Café	10000
Management salaries	24000
Heating and lighting	4500
Rent and rates	9000
Advertising expenses	5600
Delivery expenses	2000
Insurance	3600
Non-current assets (Cost)	67000
Provision for depreciation of non-current assets	40000

Additional information:

- Non-current assets are depreciated at the rate of 20 per cent per annum using the reducing balance method.
- Depreciation of non-current assets is apportioned as follows: antiques 20 per cent, restoration 50 per cent and café 30 per cent.
- Wages accrued at the year end: antique sales, £1 000, restoration sales, £2 000.
- Rent and rates, heating and lighting, and insurance are apportioned based on floor space.
- Delivery expenses are apportioned to sales and restoration, based on revenue.
- Advertising is apportioned to all departments, based on revenue.
- Management salaries are apportioned by the wages of each department.
- Floor space = antique sales 1 400 m², restoration 200 m² and café 200 m².

1 Prepare a statement of profit or loss and other comprehensive income for the year ended 31 August 2017, showing the profit or loss for each department.

CHECKPOINT

1 Identify one reason why a business might produce departmental records.

2 What is meant by the term 'apportionment'?

3 Departmental records do not include the cost of sales for each department. True or false?

4 State three ways that expenses could be apportioned.

5 Explain why heating and lighting would be apportioned on the basis of floor space.

6 Fill in the missing words. 'For apportionment to be useful it must be both f.......... and r..............'

7 Identify two non-financial factors that must be considered before closing a department.

8 Identify two financial factors that must be considered when deciding whether to close a department.

SUBJECT VOCABULARY

apportionment the process by which overhead expenses are shared between departments
departmental records financial statements that show the profits made by different sections of a business
fixed costs costs that do not vary with output or activity levels
overheads expenditure on labour, materials and services which cannot be identified with a specific cost unit/product

EXAM PRACTICE

CASE STUDY: PC SUPPORT

SKILLS REASONING, EXECUTIVE FUNCTION, DECISION MAKING

PC Support has two departments, a shop selling computer accessories and a workshop for repairing computers. The following information relates to the year ended 31 December 2017:

	£
Revenue:	
Shop sales	75000
Repairs	45000
Purchases:	
Shop	28000
Repairs	6400
Inventory at 1 January 2017:	
Shop	25500
Repairs workshop	1800
Wages	65000
Rent and rates	12000
General expenses	5100
Marketing expenses	600
Irrecoverable debts to be written off – repairs	500
Allowance/provision for irrecoverable debts:	
Shop sales	50
Repairs workshop	90
Fixtures and equipment at cost	7000
Trade receivables:	
Shop sales	6400
Repairs	4000

Additional information at 31 December 2017:
- Inventory: shop accessories £29000, parts for repairs £2000.
- During the year, computer accessories valued at £3400 were taken from the shop to be used in repairs.
- Wages of £2500 were accrued.
- Five staff were employed, three in the shop and two in the repairs workshop.
- The floor area occupied: shop 150 m² and repair workshop 90 m².
- General expenses allocated: £1950 workshop, and the balance to shop.
- The allowance/provision for irrecoverable debts is to be maintained at 2 per cent for the shop and 4 per cent for the workshop.
- Depreciation is to be charged at 10 per cent per year on cost. The charge will be apportioned to the shop and workshop in the ratio 4:3.

Q

1 Recommend, with a reason, the basis of apportionment for the following expenses:
   (a) rent and rates
   (b) marketing expenses. **(4 marks)**
2 Prepare the statement of profit or loss and other comprehensive income for the year ended 31 December 2017, showing the profit or loss for each department. A totals column is **not** required. **(20 marks)**

The owner has been advised by his accountant that he should specialise by expanding one of his departments.

3 Evaluate whether the owner should expand one of the departments. **(12 marks)**

13 INCOMPLETE RECORDS

LEARNING OBJECTIVES

After you have studied this chapter, you should be able to:
- prepare statements of profit or loss and other comprehensive income from incomplete records
- prepare statements of financial position from incomplete records.

GETTING STARTED

Imagine you have just started a small business. Would you have the knowledge and skills to record and prepare all your transactions into a formal accounts system? If you made all sales and purchases by cash, would you need to prepare the purchase day books and associated ledgers? Would you have the time and resources to prepare a full set of books? The answer to these is probably 'no'!

Not all businesses maintain complete accounting records. This may be because the owner has neither the desire nor the skills to keep a complete set of accounting records. In some cases, many of the figures used are estimates, resulting in the trading profit being found by approximation.

Some accounting records may be more complete than others. In some cases, a firm may have little or no information, while others may have a cash book and even a trade receivables and trade payables ledger. In the latter case, this becomes a good starting point. This is obviously not a complete set of books and the accountant may have to write up the rest of the books at year end. This will involve completing all double-entry work and preparing the financial statements.

In cases where the business has no books at all, the accountant may have to prepare the accounts from the original source documents.

PREPARING ACCOUNTING RECORDS FROM INCOMPLETE RECORDS

There are many ways to build accounting records from incomplete information. In doing this, we will come across unidentified payments and drawings which must be dealt with in some logical manner. We need to apply all our accounting knowledge in order to identify the information needed to complete the accounts. In order to do this, there are a number of techniques that can be used to complete the financial statements. The approach used will vary, depending on the information provided. These techniques include:
- preparing a **statement of affairs** to find opening and closing capital
- using ratios to determine revenue and cost of sales and gross profit
- using control accounts to determine revenues and purchases
- using ledger accounts to find bank and cash balances and expenses.

STATEMENT OF AFFAIRS

Using the accounting equation, it is possible to calculate missing information relating to assets, capital and liabilities:

$$\text{Assets} = \text{Capital} + \text{Liabilities}$$

If a business has a record of its assets and liabilities at the start and end of the financial period, it is possible to calculate the opening and closing capital values.

WORKED EXAMPLE

Bilal designs and sells handmade jewellery. He does not keep a set of books, but the following information was available at the start of the financial period:

	£
Assets:	
Equipment	20 000
Inventory	7 500
Trade receivables	3 500
Bank	2 000
Liabilities:	
Trade payables	2 900
Other payables	900
Loan (repayable in 5 years)	16 000

To find the opening capital, we need to rearrange the accounting equation:

Capital = Assets – Liabilities
= £33 000 – £19 800
= £13 200

If we have the information for the end of the period, we can calculate the retained profit by subtracting the opening capital from the closing capital. Let us assume that Bilal was able to calculate his closing capital and that it was £15 400:

Retained profit = Closing capital – Opening capital
= £15 400 – £13 200
= £2 200

Bilal now informs us that during the year he made drawings of £2 500. What affect would this have on his profit?

Closing capital = Opening capital + Profit – Drawings

So, putting in the figures we have:

£15 400 = £13 200 + Profit – £2 500

Bilal's profit, therefore = £4 700

ACTIVITY 1   SKILLS ▷ ANALYSIS, PROBLEM SOLVING

CASE STUDY: LASITH

Lasith has provided the following list of balances:

Lasith: assets and liabilities at 1 January 2019 and 31 December 2019

	£	£
	1 January 2019	31 December 2019
Office fixtures at cost	3 500	3 500
Inventory (as valued)	1 060	1 300
Trade receivables	6 580	7 345
Bank balance (from bank statement) (DR balances)	8 195	210
Trade payables	9 300	6 135

1 Calculate the opening and closing capital balances.
2 Calculate the profit for the year; assume Lasith made no drawings.

ACTIVITY 2   SKILLS ▷ ANALYSIS, PROBLEM SOLVING

CASE STUDY: EVE

Eve started a business with £18 000 of her own money. In addition, she made use of a loan of £5 000 given by her uncle. This loan was deposited into the business bank account. Using the money available, she purchased office equipment for the business. The total cost of the equipment was £10 000.

1 What is the amount of her capital in the business?

ACTIVITY 3   SKILLS ▷ ANALYSIS, PROBLEM SOLVING

CASE STUDY: ROSHAN

The following is a summary of Roshan's net assets:
- At 1 January 2019, he had assets of £65 000 and liabilities of £11 000.
- On 31 December 2019, the assets amounted to £83 000 and the liabilities to £14 000.
- During the year, Roshan withdrew £10 000.

1 What is the profit for the year?

CALCULATING THE TRADING RESULTS USING RATIOS

Many small businesses do not have specialist accounting staff or the time to prepare accurate costings or pricing policies. Many sole traders will determine the price they charge by adding a set percentage mark-up to their goods, based on the cost, or a margin, based on the selling price. These ratios can be used to calculate revenue, cost of sales and gross profit. Ratios are covered in depth in Chapter 21. The formula for mark-up is:

$$\frac{\text{Gross profit}}{\text{Cost of sales}} \times 100$$

The formula for margin is:

$$\frac{\text{Gross profit}}{\text{Revenue}} \times 100$$

WORKED EXAMPLE

Bebi has calculated her revenue for the year to be £630 000 and has marked up the goods she sells by 40 per cent. We will calculate the cost of sales and gross profit.

Using the mark-up formula, we can determine that the revenue is 140 per cent. Therefore, we divide £630 000 by 140 to obtain 1 per cent, then simply multiply by 100 per cent for the cost of sales and by 40 per cent for the profit.

Revenue:	140%	£630 000
Gross profit:	40%	£180 000
Cost of sales:	100%	£450 000

If Bebi had stated that she used a margin of 40 per cent, then the calculation would be as follows. Revenue is 100 per cent, the cost of sales is 60 per cent and the profit margin is 40 per cent:

Revenue:	100%	£630 000
Gross profit:	40%	£252 000
Cost of sales:	60%	£378 000

EXAM HINT

The mark-**up** goes **up** from 100 per cent by the value of the percentage profit given.

The margin goes **down** from 100 per cent by the value of the percentage profit given.

Using mark-up and margin, together with other information from the trading account, allows missing information to be found.

WORKED EXAMPLE

Sudesh has provided the following information from which we are asked to work out the value of purchases:
- revenue for the year was £200 000
- gross profit margin was 25 per cent
- the opening inventory was £15 000 and the closing inventory was valued at £18 000.

To calculate the purchases, we need to know the cost of sales, since:

Cost of sales = opening inventory + purchases – closing inventory

Using the margin:
- Revenue = £200 000 and cost of sales is 100% less 25% = 75% of revenue.
- Therefore, cost of sales = £200 000 × 75/100 = £150 000.
- Substituting this into our cost of sales equation we get: £150 000 = £15 000 + purchases – £18 000
- Therefore, purchases = £153 000

ACTIVITY 4 — SKILLS ANALYSIS, PROBLEM SOLVING

CASE STUDY: NITA

Nita runs a small business providing packaging supplies. She does not keep a formal set of books. She has a gross profit mark-up of 20 per cent. She has provided the following information for the year ended 31 January 2019:
- opening inventory was £36 500
- closing inventory was £32 300
- revenue was £150 000.

1 Prepare an extract of the statement of profit or loss and other comprehensive income to show the gross profit.

PURCHASES AND SALES FROM CONTROL ACCOUNT INFORMATION

Even with incomplete records, we may still need to calculate our purchases and sales so that we are able to assess the gross profit of the business. To do these calculations we need a list of receipts and payments. These can usually be obtained from the cash book or bank statement. Once the lists are established, we then need to identify receipts that relate to sales and payments in connection with purchases. Naturally, any payments for other expenses and capital expenditure must be excluded.

WORKED EXAMPLE

In this example, we want to calculate the sales for the year. Even with incomplete records we can establish the following:

	£
Trade receivables balances at 1 January 2019	6 580
Trade receivables balances at 31 December 2019	7 345
Receipts from trade receivables during the year	47 200

To calculate sales, we do the following:

	£
Receipts	47 200
Less balances 1 January	6 580
	40 620
Plus balances 31 December	7 345
Credit sales for the year	47 965

We looked at missing figures in Chapter 8, Control accounts, and it would be useful if you reread that chapter at this stage. A control account could be constructed to find the sales for the year:

Trade receivables control account at 31 December 2019

Date	Details	£	Date	Details	£
1 Jan 2019	Balance b/d	6 580	31 Dec 2019	Bank	47 200
	Credit sales **balancing figure**	47 965		Balance c/d	7 345
		54 545			54 545
1 Jan 2019	Balance b/d	7 345			

A similar method of calculation is used to work out purchases. The following example illustrates this:

	£
Trade payables balances at 1 January 2019	9 300
Trade payables balances at 31 December 2019	6 135
Payments to trade payables during the year	51 320

To calculate purchases, we do the following:

	£
Payments	51 320
Less balances 1 January	9 300
	42 020
Plus balances 31 December	6 135
Purchases for the year	48 155

Using a control account format, the following would calculate the credit purchases:

Trade payables control account at 31 December 2019

Date	Details	£	Date	Details	£
31 Jan 2019	Bank	51 320	1 Jan 2019	Balance b/d	9 300
	Balance c/d	6 135	31 Jan 2019	Purchases **balancing figure**	48 155
		57 455			57 455
			1 Feb 2019	Balance b/d	6 135

In addition to calculating credit sales and credit purchases, you must add any cash sales and cash purchases to the figures you calculate in order to calculate the total sales and total purchases required to complete a trading account.

EXAM HINT

In the exam there may be other entries in the control account that affect the sales and purchases – good knowledge of control accounts is required for dealing with incomplete records.

CALCULATING EXPENSES AND BANK USING LEDGER ACCOUNTS

A cash book summary will allow the bank and cash balances to be calculated at the year end. From the following information, we can construct a cash book to calculate the closing balance:

At the start of the year, a business had a bank overdraft of £2 000. During the course of the year, cheque receipts of £105 000 were banked, as well as £5 000 banked from cash sales. The business paid £6 750 in motor vehicle repairs by cheque. Credit purchases of £98 000 were paid by cheque.

Cash book summary

Date	Details	£	Date	Details	£
31 Dec	Receipts	105 000	1 Jan	Balance b/d	2 000
	Cash sales	5 000	31 Dec	Motor vehicle repairs	6 750
				Payments	98 000
				Balance c/d	3 250
		110 000			110 000
1 Jan	**Balance b/d**	3 250			

By completing the ledger account, we find the bank balance at the end of the year is £3 250. In a similar way, we find missing figures for expense accounts, using the formula:

> Expenses for the year = Bank/cash paid
> Add   other receivables at the beginning of the year
> Less other payables at the beginning of the year
> Add   other payables at the end of the year
> Less other receivables at the end of the year.

WORKED EXAMPLE

Bharti operates a small knitting business but does not keep formal records. She has provided the following information relating to rent and rates and has asked for the expense figure that needs to be recorded in the financial statements for the year ending 31 December 2018:

- payments for rent and rates made during the year were £5 000
- at 31 December 2017 rent prepaid was £2 400 and rates owing were £30
- at 31 December 2018 rent prepaid was £1 200 and rates prepaid were £50.

To calculate the expenses, we use the above formula to arrive at:

	£
Bank/cash paid	5 000
Add other receivables at the beginning of the year	2 400
Less other payables at the beginning of the year	(30)
Less other receivables at the end of the year (1 200 + 50)	(1 250)
Expenses for the year	5 850

Alternatively, this information could be recorded in a ledger account to find the missing figure to balance the account – this would be the figure transferred to the statement of profit or loss and other comprehensive income.

The depreciation expense for the year can be calculated by use of the opening and closing balances for the carrying value of the non-current asset. If no assets are purchased or sold during the year, then the depreciation expense is the difference between the opening and closing balances given. In this case, the closing balance must be less than the opening balance to reflect the fall in value of the asset. The difference is entered into the expense section of the statement of profit or loss and other comprehensive income.

Where there have been purchases and disposals, the calculations are more complicated, but if you follow a logical approach, the correct expense can be determined.

The method required is:

> Opening balance of non-current asset (carrying value)
> Add   purchases of non-current asset during the year at cost (cash and credit)
> Less disposal of non-current asset during the year (at carrying value)
> Less closing balance of non-current asset (at carrying value).

ACTIVITY 5   SKILLS ANALYSIS, PROBLEM SOLVING
CASE STUDY: BHARTI

1 Using the information for Bharti given in the worked example, prepare the rent and rates account, showing the transfer to the statement of profit or loss and other comprehensive income.

FINANCIAL STATEMENTS

In order to prepare the financial statements for a business, we normally require a trial balance setting out all the balances at year end. However, when we have incomplete records, we often have very limited data from which to build our financial statements. In the following worked example we will examine such a case.

WORKED EXAMPLE

We have been provided with the following information:

Statement of assets and liabilities at 1 January 2019 and 31 December 2019

	1 January 2019 £	31 December 2019 £
Office fixtures at cost	3 500	3 500
Inventory (as valued)	1 060	1 300
Trade receivables	6 580	7 345
Bank balance (from bank statement)	8 195	210
Total assets	19 335	12 355
Trade payables	9 300	6 135
Net worth = Capital balance	£10 035	£6 220

We have been given details of the receipts from trade receivables and payments to trade payables:

	£
Trade receivables balances at 1 January 2019	6 580
Trade receivables balances at 31 December 2019	7 345
Receipts from trade receivables during the year	47 200
Trade payables balances at 1 January 2019	9 300
Trade payables balances at 31 December 2019	6 135
Payments to trade payables during the year	£51 320

From these details, we have already established the purchases and sales figures (see above). Additional information provided:

- payments for expenses during the year totalled £1 765 and drawings by the owner were £2 100
- we are told that the owner wants to depreciate his office fixtures by 10 per cent p.a.

From what seems to be very little information, we are now able to construct the financial statements:

Statement of profit or loss and other comprehensive income for the year ended 31 December 2019

	£	£
Sales		47 965
Opening inventory	1 060	
Purchases	48 155	
	49 215	
Less closing inventory	1 300	
Cost of sales		47 915
Gross profit		50
Expenses	1 765	
Depreciation	350	2 115
Net loss for the year		2 065

We can now prepare the statement of financial position. We know from the opening statement that the capital account at 1 January is £10 035:

Statement of financial position (extract) at 31 December 2019

	£	£
Non-current assets at cost	3 500	
Less depreciation	350	
		3 150
Inventory	1 300	
Trade receivables	7 345	
Bank	210	8 855
Total assets		12 005
Capital at 1 January	10 035	
Less net loss	2 065	
Less drawings	2 100	5 870
Add trade payables		6 135
Total capital and liabilities		12 005

ACTIVITY 6 SKILLS ANALYSIS, PROBLEM SOLVING

CASE STUDY: CHAN

On 1 January 2019 Chan had trade receivables owing him £17 400. During the year, he received payments totalling £89 300. Chan gave discounts of £4 940 to the trade receivables. At 31 December 2019 the balance on the trade receivables ledger was £19 740.

1 Calculate the sales for the year.

ACTIVITY 7   SKILLS ANALYSIS, PROBLEM SOLVING

CASE STUDY: NATALYA

Natalya presented you with the following information:
- at 1 January 2019 she had assets of £70 000 and liabilities of £7 300
- at 31 December 2019 assets were £90 000 and trade payables for goods purchased amounted to £8 700.

During the year, Natalya was given a bank overdraft fixed for two years. At 31 December 2019 the balance was £17 000.

Natalya had drawings of £11 300 during the year.

1 Calculate the profit for the year.

ACTIVITY 8   SKILLS ANALYSIS, PROBLEM SOLVING, EXECUTIVE FUNCTION

CASE STUDY: J JONES

You are given the following information relating to the assets and liabilities of J Jones for 2019.

Assets and liabilities	1 January 2019 £	31 December 2019 £
Equipment at cost	3 000	3 000
Inventory	2 550	3 600
Trade receivables	2 130	2 490
Trade payables	1 620	1 680
Bank balance	480	420

During the year, there were a number of transactions, all of which were entered into the bank account. A summary of these is as follows:

	£
Receipts from trade receivables	20 670
Payments to trade payables	9 600
Payments for trade expenses	5 430
Drawings	5 700

The equipment is depreciated annually at 10 per cent of its cost.

1 Calculate the capital account of J Jones at 1 January 2019 and prepare the statement of profit or loss and other comprehensive income and statement of financial position for the year to 31 December 2019.

ACTIVITY 9   SKILLS ANALYSIS, PROBLEM SOLVING, EXECUTIVE FUNCTION

CASE STUDY: ALICIA

Alicia maintains limited records. At 31 December 2018 her statement of financial position was as follows:

Alicia: statement of financial position at 31 December 2018

	Cost £	Provision for depreciation £	Carrying value £
Delivery vehicles	47 000	17 530	29 470
Office equipment	30 000	3 260	26 740
			56 210
Inventory	11 250		
Trade receivables	29 390		
Prepaid insurance	1 033		
Bank	7 840	49 513	
Total assets			105 723
Capital – Alicia			97 000
Trade payables	7 320		
Wages accrued	1 403	8 723	105 723
Capital and liabilities			

The following is a record of bank transactions for the year:

	£
Cash sales	32 380
Trade receivables payments	41 906
Additional capital paid in	5 800
Loan from Fry on 1 July 2019	10 000
Payment to trade payables	49 320
Cash purchases	20 006
Wages	11 310
Motor expenses	8 670
Insurance	8 931
Bank charges	1 004

In addition, Alicia has taken cash from her sales before depositing it into the bank. She prepared a summary of those takings.

	£
Drawings	21 010
Motor repairs	4 031
Cash purchases	1 610

The following additional information is also available at 31 December 2019:
- closing inventory was £13 210
- trade receivables were £31 047

- trade payables were £8 240
- insurance prepaid was £924
- wages not yet paid were £643
- the loan bears interest at 10 per cent per annum
- depreciation is calculated as follows:
  - vehicles = 10 per cent on reducing balance
  - office equipment = 5 per cent straight line.

1 Prepare the statement of profit or loss and other comprehensive income, as well as statement of financial position for the year ending 31 December 2019.

ACTIVITY 10   SKILLS   ANALYSIS, PROBLEM SOLVING, EXECUTIVE FUNCTION

CASE STUDY: MIRO

Miro's shop sells rugs imported from India. His statement of financial position is as follows:

Miro: statement of financial position at 31 July 2019

	Cost £	Provision for depreciation £	Carrying value £
Property (at cost)	45 000		45 000
Fixtures and fittings (cost £20 000)	20 000	5 200	14 800
			59 800
Inventory		6 300	
Trade receivables		8 120	
Telephone prepaid		416	
Bank		6 000	20 836
Total assets			80 636
Capital			74 000
Trade payables		6 140	
Electricity accrued		496	6 636
Total capital and liabilities			80 636

The only record kept by Miro is a cash book in which all transactions that pass through the bank account are recorded. A summary of the cash book for the year ended 31 July 2020 is as follows:

Cash book summary

Details	£	Details	£
Balance b/d	6 000	Wages	7 301
Cash sales	14 310	Telephone	420
Payments from trade receivables	40 014	Electricity	680
Additional capital	4 000	Motor expenses	1 904
		Payments to trade payables	32 061
		Printing	600
		Purchases	5 314
		Balance c/d	16 044
	64 324		64 324
Balance b/d	16 044		

From the supporting documents, we can see the following amounts were paid from the cash takings before they were banked:

	£
Drawings	6 000
Purchases	1 803
Car repairs	1 002
Printing	210
Total	9 015

Additional information:
- inventory at 31 July 2020 was valued at £4 130
- at 31 July 2020 there are prepaid telephone charges of £240 and accrued electricity charges of £490
- the trade receivables and trade payables outstanding at the end of the year are £6 840 and £5 930 respectively
- Miro has taken goods that cost £710 from the business for his own use
- fixtures and fittings are to be depreciated at 20 per cent per annum using the reducing balance method.

1 Prepare a statement of profit or loss and other comprehensive income for the year ended 31 July 2020 and a statement of financial position at that date.

ACTIVITY 11

SKILLS ANALYSIS, PROBLEM SOLVING, EXECUTIVE FUNCTION

CASE STUDY: NADIA

Nadia owns a retail shop selling handknitted garments. The statement of profit or loss and other comprehensive income and statement of financial position are prepared annually by you from records consisting of a bank statement and a file of unpaid suppliers and outstanding trade receivables.

The following balances were shown on her statement of financial position at 1 January 2019:

	£
Trade payables	937
Shop fittings (cost £1 800) at written-down value	490
Inventory in hand	535
Trade receivables	107
Cash at bank	192

The following is a summary of her bank statement for the year ended 31 December 2019:

	£
Trade receivables payments banked	7 430
Payments to suppliers	6 024
Rent of premises to 31 December 2019	800
Other operating expenses	44
Advertising	72
Repairs	94

You obtain the following additional information:
- inventory at 31 December 2019 was valued at £1 021
- trade receivables payments are banked daily. Nadia withdraws £100 per week for herself and pays her assistant £52 per week prior to banking any payments from trade receivables.
- amounts outstanding are: £630 due to suppliers, £24 due in respect of sundry (various) expenses, and £103 outstanding trade receivables
- Nadia took £130 worth of goods for her own use without payment
- depreciation on shop fittings is provided at 10 per cent of cost.

1 Prepare Nadia's statement of profit or loss and other comprehensive income for the year ended 31 December 2019, and her statement of financial position at that date. (Note: All weekly amounts are paid for 52 weeks.)

ACTIVITY 12

SKILLS ANALYSIS, PROBLEM SOLVING, EXECUTIVE FUNCTION

CASE STUDY: MONICA

Monica keeps some basic records of her business activities. The statement of financial position information at 1 April 2019 was as follows:

	£
Trade payables	2 901
Shop fittings (cost £6 200) at written-down value	3 800
Inventory in hand	4 090
Trade receivables	3 021
Cash at bank	1 064

The following is a summary of her bank statement transactions for the year ended 31 March 2020:

	£
Bank charges	102
Repairs	194
Salaries to staff	3 040
Payments to suppliers	5 094
Rent for the year	1 021
Cash sales banked	4 920
Trade receivables payments	9 874
9% loan from Ali	4 000

- All the receipts are banked, although Monica takes £400 per month from the cash sales before banking.
- At the year end the inventory was valued at £5 260 and amounts due to Monica totalled £4 063. Monica also owed suppliers £2 830.
- She depreciated the shop fittings at 10 per cent p.a. using the straight line method of depreciation.
- The loan from Ali was given on 1 June 2019.

1 Prepare a statement of financial position for Monica at the year end.
2 Calculate what her profit was for the year.

EXAM HINT

When calculating total sales and purchases do not forget to include any cash sales or cash purchases in your totals.

Make the most of your accounting expertise – construct control accounts in order to find the relevant information for your answer.

EVALUATE

Many small firms do not keep full accounting records via a double-entry system, but still manage to provide the required information for the different users of accounting information. So, what are the advantages and disadvantages of maintaining incomplete records?

Advantages of incomplete records	Disadvantages of incomplete records
Time-saving	More difficult to check arithmetical accuracy of the accounts
Cost-effective – does not need expensive software	If information is missing, the figures for profit may be inaccurate
Requires little accounting knowledge – no need to hire a qualified accountant	May not reflect a true and fair view
Convenient and flexible	More difficult to detect errors and fraud

CHECKPOINT

1 All businesses must maintain a full set of accounts. True or false?

2 How can the accounting equation be used to calculate profit for the year?

3 A business had an opening capital balance of £45 000. During the year, the owner withdrew £10 000 as drawings and had a closing capital balance of £59 000. How much profit did the business make?

4 State what is included in a statement of affairs.

5 State two reasons why a business might only maintain incomplete records.

6 State two disadvantages of maintaining incomplete records.

SUBJECT VOCABULARY

margin gross profit in relation to revenue
mark-up gross profit in relation to the cost of sales
statement of affairs a basic statement of financial position used to find missing values in the accounting equation

EXAM PRACTICE

CASE STUDY: MAI'S FLOWER BUSINESS

SKILLS ANALYSIS, PROBLEM SOLVING, EXECUTIVE FUNCTION

Mai began her first business venture on 1 April 2016 delivering flowers to customers in her local neighbourhood. As she had no accounting experience, she did not maintain a formal set of books. However, she has provided the following incomplete records for the year ending 31 March 2018, her second year of trading.

Mai: statement of assets and liabilities at 31 March 2018

	£	£
	31 March 2017	31 March 2018
Motor vehicles (carrying value)	25 000	22 000
Inventory	9 500	8 500
Trade receivables	6 000	6 500
Commission receivable (accrued)		800
Trade payables	8 500	6 500
Wages (accrued)	400	500

Mai: cash book summary at 31 March 2018

Details	£	Details	£
Balance b/d	4 500	Payments for credit purchases	19 500
Receipts from credit sales	18 500	Wages	6 000
Cash sales	6 000	Drawings	2 000
Commission received	400	Motor vehicles expenses	2 300

Before banking the cash sales, Mai paid the following in cash: drawings £2 000, wages £200 and cash purchases of £1 000.

1. Calculate the balance on the cash book at 1 April 2018. **(2 marks)**
2. Calculate, for the year ended 31 March 2018:
   (a) total purchases **(5 marks)**
   (b) total revenue. **(5 marks)**
3. Prepare the statement of profit or loss and other comprehensive income for the year ended 31 March 2018. **(12 marks)**
4. Mai has been concerned about the performance of the business over the last year. A bookkeeper friend has advised that she keep a formal set of books in the future. Evaluate whether Mai should keep a formal set of books for her business. **(12 marks)**

EXAM HINT

When calculating missing figures from a list of given values, it is important that you label each number to show what it represents. You need to remember that this is an accounting examination and not a mathematics exam. Communicating what each number represents is important.

Show all your workings on the answer paper not the question paper.

14 PARTNERSHIPS

LEARNING OBJECTIVES

After you have studied this chapter, you should be able to:
- prepare appropriation accounts
- prepare capital and current accounts for partnerships
- explain the use of partnership agreements and the application of the Partnership Act of 1890 to partnerships
- account for the introduction or retirement of partners.

GETTING STARTED

Your business is growing but you are finding it difficult to raise additional funds to expand the business. Would you consider inviting somebody else to become a partner in the business? If you did, what agreements would you need to make to ensure the business continued to run smoothly? What share of the profit would your new partner take? How could you attempt to limit the amount of money the new partner took out? Are there any other things you might need to agree before they became a partner?

INTRODUCTION

Businesses are classified according to their form of ownership. We have discussed in earlier chapters the sole trader. In this chapter, we will focus on businesses owned by a partnership. In so doing, we will see if any differences arise in the preparation of financial statements.

However, before we move to that area, it is useful to remind ourselves of the ownership of a business by a sole trader.

SOLE TRADER

In all the earlier chapters we have dealt with a single (sole) trader, where a business is owned by one person. Under this form of ownership, the following points apply:
- a single owner provides capital and has total control
- the owner has the rights to all profits earned
- the owner is personally responsible for income tax
- the owner is personally responsible for all debts of the business and is said to have unlimited liability
- the owner can take legal action or can have legal action taken against them.

We can see that legally the owner and the business are one and the same, i.e. the owner is the legal entity. The business can be set up with very few legal restrictions and there are no legal requirements to publish financial statements, although the business must produce annual financial statements for the tax authorities.

The big problem of a sole trader is that it is difficult for a business to grow beyond a certain size. This is because of the difficulties of control, finance and supervision. Ownership needs to be divided and from this we can conclude that a team of owners can expand a business.

We move, then, to the simplest form of 'combined' ownership, which is the partnership.

PARTNERSHIP

This is when two or more people own a business together. It is quite common, especially in professional practices. It is important to note that not all partnerships are small in size and it must not be thought that a partnership indicates a small business.

It is quite a simple process to set up a partnership and, unlike a company, where there are fixed regulations, little formality exists. Under this form of ownership certain points apply.
- No formal agreement is required, although it is usual to have a written partnership agreement as set out below. It should be noted that in the absence of such an agreement, the Partnership Act of 1890 applies.

- Partners are entitled to a share of the profits, in proportion to an agreed ratio.
- Each partner is an agent for the partnership, which means that each partner can enter contracts and otherwise commit the partnership.
- Risk is shared, so that each partner is 'jointly and severally liable' for all the debts of the partnership – i.e. if one partner is unable to pay his or her share of the debt, the other partner will have to pay this, as well as their own share.
- There are no legal requirements to disclose financial information to the public, but specific accounting records must be maintained.
- The death of a partner effectively means the dissolution (end) of the partnership.

PARTNERSHIP AGREEMENT

All partnerships enter into an agreement which is designed to regulate the way in which the business affairs are conducted. The agreement usually states the amount of capital that each partner will contribute. In addition, it states whether interest is given on the capital amount and at what rate.

During the year, partners are allowed to draw out money in anticipation of their share of profits. The agreement would state the limits on such drawings, whether interest is charged on these drawings and at what rate. Certain partners are entitled to **partnership salaries** and this is also covered in the agreement. Finally, the agreement states the way in which profits (or losses) are shared amongst the partners.

If no partnership agreement exists then the Provisions of Section 24 of the Partnership Act 1890 apply. These state that:
- profits and losses will be shared equally
- no partners' salaries will be paid
- partners should not receive **interest on capital invested**

- partner loans to the partnership are entitled to interest at the rate of 5 per cent per annum
- no interest is charged to partners on the drawings they make.

ACCOUNTING FOR PARTNERSHIPS

One of the major differences between accounting for sole traders and accounting for partnerships is the way in which the owners' capital, profit and drawings are recorded. For a sole trader, the capital account shows the capital introduced by the owner, plus profit, less any drawings made by the owner. In a partnership, each partner will contribute capital to the partnership. This is also recorded in a capital account. Each partner will have their own capital account, and there will be also **current accounts** for partners to record the distribution of profit to partners and their drawings. Normally, individual partners' capital will be presented in a single ledger account, as will their current accounts, as shown in the next section.

CAPITAL ACCOUNTS

The capital account is normally fixed, and only alters when there is a permanent increase or decrease in the capital contributed by a partner. For example, Partners A and B respectively contributed £23 000 and £18 000 cash into the business. The cash had been paid into the bank. Furthermore, Partner A contributed a motor vehicle with a valuation of £28 000 into the business.

The journal entry for this capital contribution transaction is shown as:

Journal

Details	£ Dr	£ Cr
Bank	23 000	
Motor vehicle	28 000	
Capital – A		51 000
(for capital contribution by A)		
Bank	18 000	
Capital – B		18 000
(for contribution by B)		

Capital account

Details	A £	B £	Details	A £	B £
			Bank	23 000	18 000
			Motor Vehicles	28 000	

Capital accounts will contain entries for:
- **Dr**　　Capital withdrawn
- **Dr**　　Goodwill written off
- **Dr**　　Balance c/d
- **Cr**　　Balance b/d
- **Cr**　　Capital introduced (bank, cash or other assets)
- **Cr**　　Goodwill introduced.

Goodwill values the reputation, customer bases and past success of the business. It also rewards existing partners, when new partners are admitted, in the old profit-sharing ratio and is then written off in the new profit-sharing ratio.

CURRENT ACCOUNTS

The profits (and losses) of a partnership are divided between partners. However, the way in which the division is made will depend on the partnership agreement. It may be that each partner shares equally in profits and losses, or there may be some other percentage allocation.

The addition of profits, interest on capital and salaries are credited to the current account of the partner concerned. Unlike the sole proprietor, the partners each have a current account and not a drawings account. This current account also records drawings made by a partner. The current account will be a fluctuating account, as profits and drawings will be added to the account as they are made.

The purpose of preparing a current account is:
- to inform partners of the amount of profit being distributed to each partner in an accounting period and the amount of profit they have taken out during the year. It is assumed that the profit distributed to each partner will be kept in the business as a form of 'capital contribution', therefore current account balances are part of the overall capital of the business
- to separate the capital contribution made by the partner and the profit that each partner receives and withdraws in the form of drawings.

Sometimes, interest is credited to capital accounts – this is especially the case where the capital accounts are not equal. In some cases, interest is charged on drawings. This is the amount taken by the partners in anticipation of profits and is debited to the partners' current accounts. In addition, salaries paid during the year will be credited to the account, which takes into account any year-end adjustments.

At the year or period end, the capital account and current account of each partner must be shown. While the capital account reflects the amount each partner has invested in the partnership, the current account records the share of profit (or loss) and drawings made by each partner.

The capital account is then a fixed capital account when it shows the original amounts that partners have invested in the business or if they have introduced more capital or withdrawn capital from the business. The main advantage of this is that it is easy to see the current capital investment of each partner.

Some partnerships may use a fluctuating capital account that records all entries associated with partners – capital and the appropriation of profit, which is normally entered into the current account. In the examination, you will need to read the question carefully, most use a fixed capital account and a current account for each partner.

Current account entries

Debit (Dr)	Credit (Cr)
Balance b/d	Balance b/d
Interest on drawings	Salaries*
Drawings	Interest on capital
Salaries paid*	Share of profit (if any)
Share of loss (if any)	Interest on partner's loan
Balance c/d	Balance c/d

*the credit entry for partners' salaries are those due to the partner in the current financial period, while the debit entry shows the actual amount paid in the period. Remember, a partner may have salary accrued at the end of the period.

Presentation of capital account and current account in financial statements

Statement of financial position (extract) at xx/xx/xxxx		
Capital	£	£
Capital – A	X	
Capital – B	X	X
Current – A	X	
Current – B	(X)	X

It is possible to have a negative current account balance (in this case, Partner B's current account) if the amount of drawings is bigger than the amount of profit received.

Current account						
	A	**B**		**A**	**B**
Details	£	£	Details	£	£
Drawings	2 000	1 810	Interest on capital	300	200
Interest on drawings	100	90	Salary	5 000	8 000
Balance c/d	10 200	13 300	Profit appropriation	7 000	7 000
	12 300	15 200		12 300	15 200
			Balance b/d	10 200	13 300

STATEMENT OF COMPREHENSIVE INCOME AND THE APPROPRIATION ACCOUNT

At the end of each year, the partnership will prepare a statement of profit or loss and other comprehensive income. The only difference from that of a sole trader is a new section known as the **appropriation account**. It shows how the profit or loss is distributed to each partner according to the terms in the partnership agreement (if there is one).

	Purpose	Effect on appropriation account	Effect on current account
Interest on drawings (+)	To stop partners withdrawing too many funds from the firm, which could result in liquidity problems	Increase (the partners pay interest to the firm)	Decrease (the partners pay the interest from the funds in the current account)
Partnership salaries (−)	To reward partners' physical effort put into the business	Decrease (as a payment to partners)	Increase (the partner receives profit from the business)
Interest on capital (−)	To reward partners for the risk of investing funds into the business	Decrease (as a payment to partners)	Increase (the partner receives profit from the business)
Share of profit (−)	To distribute the remaining profit to partners	Decrease (as payment to partners)	Increase (the partner receive profit from the business)

There are a few rules relating to partnerships, which must be observed.

- Each partner has his/her own capital account as well as a current account.
- The capital account is usually a fixed amount and no additional entries are made to this account in any year.
- If any loans are made by the partners to the partnership, then they are shown separately.
- Interest on these loans is shown in the statement of profit or loss and other comprehensive income before arriving at the profit for the year.
- From the profit for the year, all debits and credits are appropriations of it. The appropriations shown are interest on drawings, current accounts and capital accounts, salaries to partners and allocation of profit or loss for the year.

WORKED EXAMPLE

Green and White are in partnership in their graphic design business. Their agreement states that interest is given on capital accounts at the rate of 10 per cent per annum. As White works for the business, a salary of £6 000 is paid to him before the profits are shared on the basis of 80 per cent to Green and 20 per cent to White. Furthermore, Green lent £20 000 to the firm on the first day of the financial year and the interest is charged at a rate of 5 per cent per annum. No interest had been accounted for.

The business shows a profit of £30 000 for the year prior to any payments to the partners. We will make all the necessary apportionments to give effect to the partnership agreement.

We are told that the capital accounts are Green £80 000 and White £20 000, and profits are shared out in the same ratio as the capital invested.

		£	£	£
Profit for the year (W1)				29 000
Interest on capital	Green	8 000		
	White	2 000	10 000	
Salary	White		6 000	16 000
Residual profit				13 000
Share of profit **(W2)**				
	Green	10 400		
	White	2 600		13 000

W1: Profit for the year = £30 000 − £1 000 (£20 000 × 5 per cent interest on loan from Green) = £29 000 (since the loan interest to partner is treated as an expense).

W2: Profit-sharing ratio, based on Green £80 000: White £20 000 = 4:1.

			Current accounts			
Details	**£**	**£**	**Details**	**£**	**£**
	Green	White		Green	White
Salary paid		6 000	Interest on capital	8 000	2 000
Balance c/d	18 400	4 600	Salary		6 000
			Profit appropriation	10 400	2 600
	18 400	10 600		18 400	10 600
			Balance b/d	18 400	4 600

ACTIVITY 1   SKILLS ▸ ANALYSIS, PROBLEM SOLVING

CASE STUDY: SMITH AND JONES

Smith and Jones decided to go into partnership. Smith would contribute £30 000 and Jones would contribute £20 000. It was agreed that Jones would work in the business and receive a salary of £5 000 per annum. An interest of 10 per cent per annum was to be allowed on the capital accounts and the partners were to share the remaining profit in the ratio of 60 per cent for Smith and 40 per cent for Jones.

1 The business makes a profit of £140 000 in the first year. Show the amount to be credited to each partner.

ACTIVITY 2   SKILLS ▸ ANALYSIS, EXECUTIVE FUNCTION

CASE STUDY: DUN AND SWAIL

Dun and Swail are equal partners. The partnership agreement provides for the annual salaries of Dun at £24 000 and Swail at £23 000. It also provides for interest on capital of 7 per cent per annum and interest on drawings of 3 per cent per annum. The following information relates to the accounting year ending 30 June 2019. The profit for the year shown in the statement of profit or loss and other comprehensive income for the year ended 30 June 2019 was £97 400.

	£	£
	Dun	**Swail**
Capital at 1 July 2018	120 000	80 000
Current account at 1 July 2018	23 850	11 490
Drawings: 1 October 2018	6 000	4 000
1 March 2019	7 000	3 000
Capital introduced: 1 November 2018	24 000	
1 February 2019		36 000

1 Prepare the profit and loss appropriation account, and capital and current accounts at 30 June 2019.

ACTIVITY 3 SKILLS ANALYSIS, EXECUTIVE FUNCTION

CASE STUDY: SINGH AND YATES

Singh and Yates prepare their annual accounts to 31 December 2019. Interest on drawings is charged at 10 per cent per annum, while interest of 8 per cent per annum is allowed on capital account balances. Singh receives a salary of £18 000 per annum. The profit or loss is shared in the ratio of 2:3.

- At 1 January 2019, the balances are:

	£	£
	Singh	Yates
Capital account	£85 000 credit	£60 000 credit
Current account	£11 000 credit	£8 000 credit

- The profit for the year to 31 December 2019 is £80 000.
- The partners' drawings during the year were:

£	£
Singh	Yates
£12 000	£10 000

1 Prepare the appropriation account as well as the ledger accounts of both partners' current accounts.

EXAM HINT

In the appropriation account – clearly state **Plus** interest on drawings and then **Less** interest on capital, salaries and share of profit.

ACTIVITY 4 SKILLS CRITICAL THINKING, REASONING

CASE STUDY: MANIK AND RANA

Manik and Rana have decided to form a partnership. Manik is to contribute £150 000 as capital and Rana, £20 000. Rana is to work full time in the business and Manik will work one day a week. Because Rana has no other income, she expects to make drawings of £1 000 per month from the partnership. Manik expects to make drawings of about £1 000 per quarter (every three months).

1 Using the information above, explain the difference between each of the following ledger accounts in the books of a partnership:
   (a) capital account
   (b) current account
   (c) drawings.

ACTIVITY 5 SKILLS ANALYSIS, EXECUTIVE FUNCTION

CASE STUDY: TANAKA AND WHYTE

Tanaka and Whyte share profits in the ratio of 7:3. The balances on the capital accounts at 1 June 2018 were:

	£
Tanaka	300 000
Whyte	180 000

The partners' current account balances (credits) at 1 June 2018 were:

	£
Tanaka	20 000
Whyte	14 000

During the year ended 31 May 2019, the partners made the following drawings from the partnership bank account:

Tanaka	
	£
Date of drawing	**Amount**
31 July 2018	12 000
30 November 2018	10 000
31 March 2019	12 000
31 May 2019	13 000

Whyte	
	£
Date of drawing	**Amount**
31 July 2018	£6 000
30 November 2018	£2 000
31 March 2019	£6 000
31 May 2019	£3 000

Interest is charged on drawings at the rate of 10 per cent per annum, while interest of 6 per cent per annum is allowed on capital accounts and credit balances on current accounts. Whyte is allowed a salary of £25 000 per annum.

The profit for the year of the partnership for the year ended 31 May 2019 is £126 700.

1 Prepare the partnership appropriation account for the year ended 31 May 2019.
2 Show the current account of each partner at 31 May 2019.

ACTIVITY 6

SKILLS ANALYSIS, EXECUTIVE FUNCTION, INTERPRETATION

CASE STUDY: LEUNG, CHAN AND WEST

The partnership agreement of Leung, Chan and West stipulates that profits should be apportioned in the ratio of 3:2:1 after allowing interest on capital at 6 per cent per annum and crediting Leung with a salary of £28 000.

The following information relates to their first financial year which ended on 31 July 2019. The partners introduced the following amounts as capital on 1 August 2018:

	£
Leung	60 000
Chan	50 000
West	40 000

Cash drawings during the year were:

	£
Leung	7 000
Chan	6 300
West	5 100

The statement of profit or loss and other comprehensive income for the year shows a profit for the year before any partner adjustments of £72 400. No entries had been made in the accounts to record the following:

- During the year, Leung had taken goods for his own use. The cost of those goods was £2 100.
- Included in the travelling expenses account for the year was a payment of £650, which related to Chan's private travelling expenses.

1 Prepare a revised statement of profit or loss and other comprehensive income for the year ended 31 July 2019, to include all partnership adjustments.
2 The partners have agreed to fix their capital accounts at the amounts originally contributed. All other transactions are recorded in their current accounts. Show the current ledger accounts for each partner at 31 July 2019.

ACTIVITY 7

SKILLS ANALYSIS, EXECUTIVE FUNCTION, INTERPRETATION

CASE STUDY: JACK AND FAITH

The following is the trial balance of Jack and Faith at 31 December 2019:

Jack and Faith: trial balance at 31 December 2019

	£ Dr	£ Cr
Capital: Jack		20 000
Capital: Faith		15 000
Current account: Jack	1 900	
Current account: Faith	4 100	
Purchases/revenue	44 823	71 460
Trade receivables/trade payables	6 507	6 561
Building at cost	22 000	
Fixtures at carrying value	7 150	
Salaries	6 004	
Electricity	2 103	
Stationery	460	
Bank interest and charges	64	
Inventory	6 890	
Bank and cash	4 020	
Drawings: Jack, 1 July 2019	4 000	
Faith, 1 September 2019	3 000	
	113 021	113 021

Additional information:

- Inventory at 31 December 2019 was valued at £13 813.
- Electricity accrued at the end of the year was £95.
- Depreciation on fixtures for the year is £1 600.

The partnership agreement provides that each partner is to be credited with interest on capital at 9 per cent per annum and charged interest on any current account debit balances at 5 per cent per annum. No interest is charged on drawings during the year.

Salaries are to be provided of £8 000 per annum for Jack and £6 800 per annum for Faith. The remainder of the profit is to be divided equally between the partners. All adjustments are made to the current account, as the capital account is fixed.

1 Prepare the statement of profit or loss and other comprehensive income, appropriation account for the year and a statement of financial position at 31 December 2019. Your workings must include the current accounts of the partners.

ACTIVITY 8 SKILLS ANALYSIS, EXECUTIVE FUNCTION

CASE STUDY: MICHAEL AND DANIA

Michael and Dania are partners in a gift business. The agreement they have is that profits are shared equally, but interest is paid on their capital accounts. The trial balance of Michael and Dania for the year ended 31 December 2019 is as follows:

Michael and Dania: trial balance at 31 December 2019

	£	£
	Dr	Cr
Fittings and fixtures	22 000	
Provision for depreciation		6 600
Trade receivables	38 700	
Trade payables		21 400
Bank	6 512	
Inventory	93 460	
Purchases	195 220	
Revenue		298 715
General expenses	6 448	
Salaries and wages	43 309	
Irrecoverable debts	1 912	
Allowance/provision for irrecoverable debts		900
Capital account – Michael		67 000
Capital account – Dania		41 000
Current account – Michael		3 144
Current account – Dania		1 102
Drawings – Michael	15 800	
Drawings – Dania	16 500	
	439 861	439 861

The following adjustments have still to be made:

- closing inventory of £132 880
- partnership salary to Michael £2 600
- interest on drawings, Michael £460 and Dania £340
- interest on capital at 10 per cent per annum.

1 Prepare the statement of profit or loss and other comprehensive income and statement of financial position for the year.

CHANGES IN THE PARTNERSHIP

Changes in a business, such as the withdrawal of a partner, a change in profit- and loss-sharing ratios, or the admission of a new partner, result in the termination of the existing partnership agreement and the creation of a new partnership agreement. An important aspect of this is the revaluation of assets at the date of the change. At that point, the capital accounts of the partners are equal to the net worth of the partnership. This net worth is worked out by placing a current value on assets and liabilities. Any increase (or decrease) is transferred to the capital accounts of the partners in the proportion in which they share profits and losses (before any changes).

The purpose of revaluing assets at the time of the retirement or admission of new partners is that the value of assets changes over time. At the point a partner retires, or when a new partner joins the firm, existing partners have the right to share in the gain (or loss) of revaluation.

ADMISSION OF NEW PARTNER

When admitting a new partner it is usual to revalue the assets of the business to reflect a true and fair view of the business. The book value may be lower than the going concern value because of the application of the prudence concept to the value of the assets and the absence of the value of goodwill in the accounts. Goodwill is the difference between the value of a business as a going concern and the carrying value of its separate assets and liabilities. This goodwill value is an intangible asset made up of the reputation of the business, the value of its customer base or other non-physical aspects of the business that can be considered as having a value.

On admission of a new partner, the value of goodwill is temporarily debited to the goodwill account and credited to the existing partners' accounts in the existing profit-sharing ratio. This is to reward the partners' efforts in bringing reputation and customers to the partnership. When a new partner is introduced, the goodwill account is credited with the value of goodwill in the new profit-sharing ratio, which eliminates the goodwill from the assets of the partnership.

This is an application of the concept of prudence. The partners' capital accounts are debited with the value of the goodwill in the new profit-sharing ratio. The treatment would be:

Dr Goodwill
Cr Capital account (existing partners in existing profit-sharing ratio)
Dr Capital account (all partners in new profit-sharing ratio)
Cr Goodwill account

The process is normally to introduce the goodwill, then eliminate it on the admission of the new partner – this then meets IAS standards. If goodwill is to remain in the accounts, the entries would be:

Dr Goodwill account
Cr Capital account (existing partners in existing profit-sharing ratio)

At the same time, the capital introduced by the new partner is recorded on the credit side of the capital account. The capital could consist of bank, cash or assets introduced to the partnership.

WORKED EXAMPLE

Prior to the admission of a new partner, Katie and Dan revalued the non-current assets of their business. The carrying value was £35 000 and they were revalued at £44 000. Before revaluation, the net worth of the partnership was £38 000. The partners share profits and losses equally.

The non-current assets have increased in value by £9 000 (£44 000 – £35 000) and so each partner's capital account is credited with their share of the increase in value of the non-current assets – in this case, £4 500. The debit entry for this transaction would be in the non-current assets accounts and would appear in the statement of financial position.

After revaluation on 2 January 2010, the net worth increased to £47 000.

Capital accounts

Date	Details	£	£	Date	Details	£	£
		Katie	Dan			Katie	Dan
				1/1/2010	Bal b/d	20 000	18 000
				2/1/2010	Non-current asset revaluation	4 500	4 500

WORKED EXAMPLE

At 31 December 2018, a partnership between Ell and Emma existed. They shared profits and losses in the ratio of 3:2. They agreed that because Ell was going to take some time off from the partnership, the ratio would be amended as from the beginning of January 2019 to 2:2.

The annual statement of financial position was prepared at 31 December 2018 containing the following information:

	£	£
	Dr	Cr
Office equipment		9 600
Motor vehicles		3 500
		13 100
Current assets		
Inventory	4 860	
Trade receivables	2 520	
Cash at bank	1 040	
		8 420
Net assets		21 520
Capital account Ell	11 760	
Capital account Emma	7 840	19 600
Trade payables	1 920	21 520

The partners agreed that they will revalue the office equipment at £8 000 and the motor vehicles at £2 000. All the other assets and liabilities are as per the statement of financial position.

The first step is to calculate the amount of the revaluation:

Non-current asset	Original value	New value	Revaluation amount
	£	£	£
Office equipment	9 600	8 000	(£1 600)
Motor vehicles	3 500	2 000	(£1 500)
Total	13 100	10 000	**(£3 100)**

The (£3 100) represents a decrease in the value of the assets and would be credited to the individual asset accounts in the statement of financial position. The corresponding debit of £3 100 is posted to the capital accounts of the partners in their old profit and loss sharing ratio of 3:2, i.e. £1 860 to Ell and £1 240 to Emma.

Office equipment

Date	Details	£	Date	Details	£
31 Dec 2018	Balance b/d	9 600	1 Jan 2019	Revaluation	1 600
				Balance c/d	8 000
		9 600			9 600
1 Jan 2019	Balance c/d	8 000			

Motor vehicles

Date	Details	£	Date	Details	£
31 Dec 2018	Balance b/d	3 500	1 Jan 2019	Revaluation	1 500
				Balance c/d	2 000
		3 500			3 500
1 Jan 2019	Balance c/d	2 000			

Capital

Date	Details	Ell	Emma	Date	Details	Ell	Emma
1 Jan 2019	Revaluation	1 860	1 240	31 Dec 2018	Balance b/d	11 760	7 840
1 Jan 2019	Balance c/d	9 900	6 600				
		11 600	11 600			11 600	7 840
			7 840	1 Jan 2019	Balance b/d	9 900	6 600

In the examination, you will be expected to produce a separate revaluation account. You will also need to revalue assets and possibly liabilities and enter the relevant values in the capital accounts and the statement of financial position.

WORKED EXAMPLE

Sudesh and Sameer are partners sharing profits and losses equally. On 31 October 2018 the capital account balances are Sudesh £75 000 and Sameer £70 000. On 1 November, Nada will be admitted as a partner.
- Nada will introduce capital of £60 000, made up of £40 000 paid into the bank account and £20 000 in non-current assets.
- Goodwill is valued at £60 000 and will not be retained in the business.
- The new profit-sharing ratio will be Sudesh $\frac{1}{2}$, Sameer $\frac{1}{3}$ and Nada $\frac{1}{6}$.

We will prepare the capital accounts for the admission of Nada to the partnership (dates not required).

Capital accounts

Details	£	£	£	Details	£	£	£
	Sudesh	Sameer	Nada		Sudesh	Sameer	Nada
Goodwill	30 000	20 000	10 000	Bal c/d	75 000	70 000	
Bal c/d	75 000	80 000	50 000	Goodwill	30 000	30 000	
				Bank			40 000
				Assets			20 000
	105 000	100 000	60 000		105 000	100 000	60 000
				Bal b/d	75 000	80 000	50 000

As you can see above, Sameer's capital increases by £10 000 (= £30 000 goodwill in the credit side – £20 000 goodwill on the debit side) and this £10 000 is paid by deducting from Nada's capital account.

The goodwill account looks like the following. You may notice that there will be no balance to be carried forward.

Goodwill

Date	Details	£	Date	Details	£
	Capital – Sudesh	30 000		Capital – Sudesh	30 000
	Capital – Sameer	30 000		Capital – Sameer	20 000
				Capital – Nada	10 000
		60 000			60 000

If the partners agree to keep the goodwill account, then the capital account will look like the following:

Capital

Details	£	£	£	Details	£	£	£
	Sudesh	Sameer	Nada		Sudesh	Sameer	Nada
Bal c/d	105 000	100 000	50 000	Bal c/d	75 000	70 000	
				Goodwill	30 000	30 000	
				Bank			40 000
				Assets			20 000
	105 000	100 000	60 000		105 000	100 000	60 000
				Bal b/d	75 000	80 000	50 000

Goodwill

Date	Details	£	Date	Details	£
	Capital – Sudesh	30 000		Balance c/d	60 000
	Capital – Sameer	30 000			
		60 000			60 000
	Balance b/d	60 000			

You can see there will be a balance to be carried forward in the goodwill account. This balance will also be shown in the statement of financial position as an intangible asset.

Statement of financial position (extract) at 31 October 2018

	£	£
Non-current assets		
Goodwill	60 000	

ACTIVITY 9   **SKILLS** ► ANALYSIS, EXECUTIVE FUNCTION, INTERPRETATION

CASE STUDY: ANNA AND BEA

Anna and Bea share the profits in the ratio of 3:2. Anna receives a salary of £20 000 per annum. On 1 January 2019, the capital account balances were:

	£
Anna	17 000
Bea	11 000

On 1 July 2019, Jake was admitted as a partner and the profit-sharing ratio was changed to Anna:Bea:Jake, 5:3:2.

- Jake was to receive a salary of £16 000 per annum.
- At that date, Anna transferred £5 000 from her capital account to a loan account and she was to receive interest on the loan of 8 per cent per annum. The interest was to be credited to her current account.
- Jake brought in machinery to the partnership which was valued at £7 000.

On 31 December, the balances (not taking into account any of the above) were:

	£
Revenue £14 000 per month × 12	168 000
Cost of sales	42 000
Rent	12 000
Wages	17 000
Office expenses	5 000

Machines are depreciated at 15 per cent per annum using the reducing balance method. Assume that the gross profit percentage is fixed and that wages paid were £13 000 for the first 6 months and the balance for the remainder of the year.

1 Prepare the statement of profit or loss and other comprehensive income and appropriation account for the year.
2 Also prepare the current accounts for the partners at year end.

RETIREMENT OF A PARTNER

When a partner retires it will be necessary to calculate the value of the partnership and the amount that the retiring partner is due to receive. This would normally be stated in the partnership agreement. As with the introduction of a new partner, goodwill will be valued, entered into the books, then eliminated on the retirement. The entries will be:

Dr   Goodwill
Cr   Capital accounts (all existing partners in the old profit-sharing ratio)
Dr   Capital accounts (remaining partners in the new profit-sharing ratio)
Cr   Goodwill.

WORKED EXAMPLE

Sudesh, Sameer and Nada are in partnership, sharing profits in the ratio 3:2:1 respectively. Sudesh has decided to retire from the partnership. The remaining partners will share profits, with Sameer receiving 60 per cent and Nada 40 per cent.

- The capital account balances are Sudesh £75 000, Sameer £80 000 and Nada £50 000.

- Goodwill is to be valued at £90 000 and is to be written off after the retirement.
- Sudesh has agreed to leave £50 000 of the amount due as a loan to the partnership, the balance will be paid by cheque.

We will prepare the capital accounts to account for Sudesh's retirement.

Capital accounts

Details	£ Sudesh	£ Sameer	£ Nada	Details	£ Sudesh	£ Sameer	£ Nada
Goodwill		54 000	36 000	Balance b/d	75 000	80 000	50 000
Loan	50 000			Goodwill	45 000	30 000	15 000
Bank	70 000						
Balance c/d		56 000	29 000				
	120 000	110 000	65 000		120 000	110 000	65 000
				Balance b/d		56 000	29 000

It is also possible that assets will be revalued when a partner retires; in which case, a revaluation account will be created and the balance on the account transferred to the credit side of the capital accounts. In addition, a retiring partner may leave an amount in the partnership but convert the capital into a loan. This is often the case when not enough liquid funds are available to settle the amount owing to the retiring partner.

STATEMENT OF FINANCIAL POSITION

Like the statement of profit or loss and other comprehensive income, the statement of financial position for a partnership is very similar to that required for a sole trader. The difference will be in how the capital is recorded. The individual amounts for each partner should be shown as in the example below:

Extract statement of financial position at 31 October 2018

	£	£	£
	Cost	Provision for depreciation	Carrying value
Capital accounts			
Sameer		56 000	
Nada		29 000	
			85 000
Current accounts			
Sameer		25 000	
Nada		(5 000) Dr	
			20 000

Note that, in this example, the current account balance for Nada is a debit balance and so is subtracted from the capital.

ACTIVITY 10   SKILLS   ANALYSIS, EXECUTIVE FUNCTION

CASE STUDY: LANE, WOOD AND JONES

Lane and Wood operate as a partnership selling musical instruments. They share profits equally. They are expanding the business and have invited Jones to become a partner in the business. Jones has agreed to pay £40 000 into the business bank account.

The credit balances on both capital accounts are £35 000. Goodwill has been valued at £30 000 and will not be retained in the accounts. The future profits will be shared equally between the three partners.

1 Prepare the partners' capital accounts when Jones is admitted.

EVALUATE

The decisions to form a partnership by a sole trader or to admit an additional partner to an existing business are significant ones that require a lot of thought and a careful evaluation of the benefits and limitations.

Advantages	Disadvantages
Additional capital for the business	Extension of joint liability. The existing partner/s will be liable for the actions of the new partner. Unlimited liability remains
Expertise and specialist skills may be gained from new partner, leading to better decisions	Decision making may be slower and more difficult as more people are involved in the process
Risks are shared if losses are made	Profits shared amongst more partners can be a disadvantage if profits do not increase after admission of new partner
Workload of each partner is reduced and cover can be provided for holidays or sickness leave	

CHECKPOINT

1 State three differences between a sole trader and a partnership.

2 Explain the term 'jointly and severally liable'.

3 State four rules that apply if there is no partnership agreement.

4 Explain why interest might be charged on the drawings of partners.

5 Explain the difference between a current account and a capital account.

6 Explain the term 'appropriation'.

7 Give two examples of debit entries in the current account.

8 Give two examples of credit entries in the current account.

9 The current account will always be a credit balance. True or false?

10 Goodwill is a tangible asset. True or false?

SUBJECT VOCABULARY

allocation the process of charging costs incurred in a department or cost centre to that department or cost centre

appropriation account the part of the statement of profit or loss and other comprehensive income that records the distribution of profits to partners

current account an account showing the movement of partners' drawings, interest on drawings and capital, salaries and share of profit/loss

fixed capital account when only capital transactions are recorded in the account

fluctuating capital account where all partners' transactions are entered in a single account

interest on capital the use of profit rewarding partners who have invested the most

interest on drawings a reduction in the partners' current account to discourage excessive drawings

legal entity an individual or organisation that has legal rights and obligations

partnership a business with two or more owners

partnership agreement an agreement between partners detailing aspects of the business including rates of interest on capital and drawings, salaries and profit-sharing ratios

partnership salary an appropriation of profit to a partner

EXAM PRACTICE

CASE STUDY: ZOE AND TAYLA

SKILLS ANALYSIS, EXECUTIVE FUNCTION, DECISION MAKING

Zoe and Tayla are in partnership, sharing profits equally. On 31 March 2018, the capital account balances were:

Zoe	£40 000
Tayla	£60 000

On 1 April 2018, Bailey was admitted as a new partner. The partnership agreement stated:

- Bailey would bring in £25 000 in non-current assets and £5 000 cash.
- Goodwill was valued at £27 000 and would not be retained in the books.
- Interest on capital would be paid at the rate of 2 per cent per annum.
- Interest on drawings to be charged on year-end balances at 5 per cent per annum.
- Salaries would be paid to Tayla, £5 000, and Bailey, £4 000.
- Profits and losses would be shared in the ratio – Zoe 3/9, Tayla 4/9 and Bailey 2/9.

At the end of the year, 31 March 2019, the following balances were recorded:

	£
Current accounts at 1 April 2018:	
Zoe	1 200 Cr
Tayla	6 000 Dr
Drawings:	
Zoe	15 000
Tayla	14 000
Bailey	0 000

Additional information at 31 March 2019:
- profit for the year before appropriation = £63 080
- the drawing included the payment of salaries to the partners
- there was no change during the year on the capital accounts.

Q

1. Prepare the capital accounts (in columnar format) of the three partners after the admission of the new partner. **(10 marks)**
2. Prepare the extract of the statement of profit or loss and other comprehensive income for the year ended 31 March 2019, showing the appropriation of profit. **(7 marks)**
3. Prepare the current accounts of the partners for the year ended 31 March 2019. **(9 marks)**
4. Prepare an extract of the statement of financial position at 31 March 2019, showing the capital section. **(5 marks)**
5. Evaluate the use of a partnership agreement. **(6 marks)**

EXAM HINT

Prepare capital and current accounts in columnar format not separate accounts.

Remember to include the partnership salary entries to the current accounts.

15 CLUBS AND NON-PROFIT-MAKING ORGANISATIONS

LEARNING OBJECTIVES

After you have studied this chapter, you should be able to:

- prepare receipts and payments accounts
- prepare income and expenditure accounts for non-profit-making organisations
- understand the need for special treatment of subscriptions and life membership
- account for the loss of inventory or cash
- prepare the financial statements.

GETTING STARTED

Are you a member of a club or society, such as a badminton club or drama society? If you are, do you pay subscriptions or fees to be a member? How do you think the club records this income? Clubs and societies often raise money to support the organisation by carrying out various activities. How might these be recorded and presented to members? How might the financial statements of non-profit-making organisations be different from those of a sole trader or partnership?

The non-profit-making organisations in this group are charities, associations or clubs. Their main purpose is not to trade or make a profit but to operate for the benefit of the members. These organisations receive subscriptions to cover their annual overheads. Although there may be a small profit (surplus) at the year end, this is put back into the organisations' funds for the following year. As such, they do not prepare a statement of profit or loss and other comprehensive income but, as they still need to report to their members, they prepare either an **income and expenditure account** or a **receipts and payments account**.

The latter account is simply a summary of the cash book for the period and only tells members what transactions took place during the year. It is a simple account to prepare and does not deal with the disclosure of any assets or liabilities that the organisation may have at the year end.

Many clubs and other associations have certain assets and liabilities – it may be office equipment, badges, inventory to be sold in the bar, club ties or even outstanding trade receivables. There may also be a liability to the printers for the cost of the report, or for telephone rental or rent.

As such, it is necessary to have a statement of financial position that reveals these assets and liabilities. In addition, the members must also be shown what income and expenditure has been made during the year. Thus, an income and expenditure account is prepared, together with a statement of financial position at year end.

The income and expenditure account is similar to the statement of profit or loss and other comprehensive income, although there is a slight variation in terminology – where we use 'profit for the year' in the statement of profit or loss and other comprehensive income we now use the term '**surplus**'. Conversely, where 'loss for the year' is shown, we use the word '**deficit**'. The surplus or deficit in this account is transferred to the statement of financial position, where it is shown as part of the '**accumulated fund**', which is the term used instead of capital account.

RECEIPTS AND PAYMENTS ACCOUNT

This account is a summarised cash book. It shows where the cash came from and where it has been spent. An example is shown below:

Court Tennis Club: receipts and payments account for the year ended 31 December 2018

Receipts	£	Payments	£
Balance b/d	3 100	Equipment	3 100
Subscriptions	14 600	Wages in café	5 000
Prize draw: tickets sold	3 800	Prize draw: prizes	1 800
Café sales	21 700	Printing	500
		Rent	2 400
		Electricity	700
		Telephone	400
		Repairs to equipment	620
		Purchases for café	16 400
		Balance c/d	12 280
	43 200		43 200
Balance b/d	12 280		

The debit side records all cash and cheque receipts and the credit side shows the cash and cheque payments made during the period. As the account only shows receipts and payments, it doesn't include important accounting information, such as:
- non-cash transactions, for example, depreciation
- accruals and prepayments of income and expenditure
- the distinction between capital and revenue expenditure
- assets and liabilities of the organisation.

CASE STUDY: MILL MUSIC SOCIETY

The Mill Music Society holds meetings and concerts in the local school. It pays £1 200 per annum. This fee was paid in the first week of January 2018 by cheque.

It has 50 members, paying subscriptions of £200 per annum. In 2018 all members paid their annual subscription fees, with five members also paying for the following year.

Ticket sales for concerts were received to the value of £2 000, with associated costs of £1 250 being paid out in cash. Other payments during the year were:
- printing costs £800
- music purchase £250
- heating and lighting £850
- equipment £5 900.

Fundraising activities raised £825 during the year. At the start of the year, the cash and bank balance was £50 Cr.

1 Prepare a receipts and payments account for the year ending 31 December 2018.

TRADING ACCOUNTS FOR DIFFERENT ACTIVITIES

Although we have described these organisations as non-profit-making organisations, there are times when these organisations prepare a trading account. This is when they run a club café or start a project in order to make a profit. This may be a club dance or barbeque, for example. Since the aim of these activities is to generate a profit to improve the organisation, it is appropriate to record the profit or loss made.

For some activities, it is relatively simple to calculate the profit made. For example, for a prize draw it could be simply deducting the cost of prizes and tickets from the revenue made to arrive at a profit for the activity. The profit from the draw would be recorded in the income and expenditure account.

Other trading activities require the preparation of a trading account showing revenue and cost of sales, as it would appear in statement of profit or loss and other comprehensive income. In addition, direct expenses associated with the activity would be deducted to arrive at a profit for the year.

WORKED EXAMPLE

Avenue Sports Club operates a café and the following information is available for the year ended 31 December 2018:

- café revenue £2 900
- inventory at 1 January 2018 £450
- purchases for the year amounted to £1 225
- inventory count at the end of the year valued the café inventory at £250
- wages for staff for the year were £3 600, of which 20 per cent related to staff in the café.

Avenue Sports Club: café trading account for the year ended 31 December 2018

	£	£
Revenue from café		2 900
Opening inventory	450	
Purchases	1 225	
Closing inventory	(250)	
Cost of sales		1 425
Gross profit		1 475
Less expenses		
Café wages	720	
Profit for the year		755

The profit for the year for the café is transferred to the income and expenditure account, being careful not to double record the expenses or revenue in the income and expenditure account.

ACTIVITY 2

CASE STUDY: VALLEY BADMINTON

Valley Badminton have provided the following information for the year ended 31 December 2018:

	£
Bank balance	2 000
Badminton equipment	10 000
Snack bar equipment	3 500
Snack bar inventory at 1 January 2018	105
Snack bar purchases	1 300
Snack bar revenue	4 555
Subscriptions	6 000
Wages: snack bar	1 200

Depreciation on all equipment is charged at the rate of 10 per cent per annum using the straight line method. At the end of the year, £100 was owing for snack bar purchases and snack bar inventory was valued at £55.

1 Prepare a trading account for the snack bar for the year ended 31 December 2018.

SUBSCRIPTIONS ACCOUNT

Subscriptions are the fees members pay to clubs and non-profit-making organisations. Like all revenues, there will be times when subscriptions will be owing, and some will be paid in advance. It is therefore necessary to make the year-end adjustments for accruals and prepayments. To calculate the value of subscriptions to be entered into the income and expenditure account, the following method should be used:

Subscriptions for the year
=
Subscriptions received in the year
(from the receipts and payments account)
plus
Subscriptions prepaid at the start of the year (prepayments)
minus
Subscriptions owing at the start of the year (accruals)
minus
Subscriptions paid in advance at the end of the year (prepayments)
plus
Subscriptions owing at the end of the year (accruals)
minus
Subscriptions written off.

The value of the subscriptions to be entered in the income and expenditure account can also be entered into a **subscriptions account**.

Subscriptions account

Date	Details	£	Date	Details	£
	Balance b/d (subscriptions owing)			Balance b/d (subscriptions prepaid)	
	Income and expenditure account			Subscriptions (received in year)	
				Subscriptions written off	
	Balance c/d (subscriptions prepaid)			Balance c/d (subscriptions owing)	

'Subscriptions written off' is similar to irrecoverable debts. This occurs when subscriptions owing in the last accounting period could not be paid. This will reduce the balance b/d (subscription owing) at the beginning of the year, therefore subscriptions will be credited.

Subscriptions written off does NOT increase the amount of subscriptions, even though it is placed in the credit side of the subscription income account. The credit entry represents the deduction of the balance owing at the beginning of the year (subscriptions in arrears).

The figure for the income and expenditure account is often the 'balancing figure' that you may be asked to calculate and then transfer to the income and expenditure account later in a question. The closing balances would be transferred to the statement of financial position as assets and liabilities. The treatment of subscriptions follows the accruals concept.

ACTIVITY 3   **SKILLS**   ANALYSIS, EXECUTIVE FUNCTION

CASE STUDY: OLD SCHOOL CRICKETERS

The following information is available to the treasurer of Old School Cricketers for the year ended 31 December 2018:

		£
1 January	Subscriptions paid in advance	1 350
	Subscriptions owing	3 000
31 December	Subscriptions owing	2 500
	Subscriptions paid in advance	1 750

Amounts received and banked for subscriptions during the year totalled £24 700. It was agreed that £1 500 of the subscriptions owing at the start of the year was now irrecoverable and would be written off.

1 Prepare the subscriptions account for the year ended 31 December 2018, showing the transfer to the income and expenditure account.

LONG-TERM/LIFE MEMBERSHIPS

Some clubs and non-profit-making organisations may offer life or long-term membership. Members will pay a reduced amount over the duration of the membership as an incentive to pay the money in advance. The organisation will benefit from the membership by receiving many years of membership early, which boosts their cash balances. The payments for these will be entered into a life membership account as a credit entry, the debit entry will be to the bank and cash account.

The payments must be accounted for using the accruals concept – the income must be matched against the accounting period to which it relates. For long-term membership, the amount included in the income and expenditure account will be the fees charged, divided by the number of years the membership is for. For example, a member of a club takes out a 10-year membership for the reduced fee of £700, rather than the annual fee of £100. For each year of membership, £70 will be treated as revenue in the income and expenditure account and the balance will be a liability in the statement of financial position.

For life membership, the accrual rate is more difficult to calculate precisely. Each club and non-profit-making organisation will apply their own rule, but the important thing is that the method chosen will reflect a true and fair view and be consistent over time. A common method would be to transfer a set percentage of the life membership value to the income and expenditure account at the end of each year.

WORKED EXAMPLE

During the year a squash club received £300 in life membership fees. It began the year with a balance of £600 in the life membership account. It has a policy of transferring 12 per cent of the account at the end of the year to the income and expenditure account.

Life membership account

Details	£	Details	£
Income and expenditure*	108	Balance b/d	600
Balance c/d	792	Bank	300
	900		900
		Balance b/d	792

*this is the balancing figure = £900 × 12% = £108

Income and expenditure account (extract) for the year ended 31 December 2019

	£	£
Income		
Subscriptions	X	
Life subscription income	108	

Statement of financial position (extract)

	£	£
Non-current liabilities		
Life membership	792	

LOSSES OF INVENTORY OR CASH

Loss of inventory

When an unknown amount of inventory is missing, whether it is stolen, destroyed or just missing, then it is possible to calculate the value of the missing inventory by using the cost of sales equation. If the value of the cost of sales is given, it is relatively straightforward to calculate the missing inventory figure. The *missing inventory* will be:

> Opening inventory + purchases − closing inventory − cost of sales

However, it may not be possible to work out the value of the cost of sales. In this case, you will need to complete a trading account and use the gross profit margin to calculate the value of the cost of sales from the revenue.

WORKED EXAMPLE

On 7 December 2018, a new employee at the Guangzhou Badminton Club got rid of some of the inventory sold in the club's café by mistake, as the employee believed it was out of date. The club need to find the value of the missing inventory for a possible insurance claim. The following information is available:

- inventory count at 1 December £350
- purchases of inventory for café (1 December– 7 December) = £550
- sales of all food and drink in café (1 December– 7 December) = £1 250
- an inventory count at the end of trading on 7 December was valued at £85
- the gross profit as a percentage of revenue is 40 per cent on all sales in the café.

To calculate the missing inventory, construct a trading account. The revenue is given, as is the gross profit as a percentage of sales, from this we can calculate the gross profit as £500 (£1 250 × 0.4).

The cost of sales can now be calculated as £1 250 − £500 = £750

The figures for opening inventory, purchases and closing inventory can now be entered and the missing inventory value calculated.

Trading account 1–7 December 2018

	£	£
Revenue		1 250
Less cost of sales		
Opening inventory	350	
Purchases	550	
Closing inventory	(85)	
Missing inventory*	**(65)**	
Cost of sales		750
Gross profit		500

*this is the balancing figure from the workings below.

£350 + £550 − £85 − missing inventory (£65) = £750 cost of sales

Loss of cash

If there is a suspected loss of cash, it is necessary to reconstruct the cash account to find the value of the missing amount. Cash receipts and payments will be needed for the period from when the last cash balance was known. These can then be compared to the known cash balance after the loss, the difference being the amount missing.

If missing inventory or cash is insured, it may be possible to claim for the loss. The double entry for the claim would be:

Dr   Insurance company

Cr   Inventory or cash

This journal entry shows the amount owing by the insurance company when the claim is made. When payment is received, the journal entry would be:

Dr   Bank

Cr   Other receivables – insurance claim

WORKED EXAMPLE

While investigating the missing inventory, the Guangzhou Badminton Club discovered some cash was missing from the cash register. The following information is available:

- cash balance at 1 December 2018 = £550
- cash receipts and payments, 1–7 December:

	£
Receipts from bookings	300
Café cash sales	500
Heat and lighting	75
Purchases for café	50
Wages	275

- £300 of cash, held in the safe, was not stolen and was the balance of cash at 7 December.

To find the value of the missing cash, prepare a cash account for the period:

Cash account

Details	£	Details	£
Balance b/d	550	Heat and lighting	75
Receipts	300	Purchases	50
Revenue	500	Wages	275
		Missing cash	650
		Balance c/d	300
	1 350		1 350

The missing cash is considered an expense and should be reported in the income and expenditure account, as follows:

Income and expenditure account (extract) for the year ended 31 December 2018

	£	£
EXPENDITURE		
Cash stolen	650	

INCOME AND EXPENDITURE ACCOUNTS AND STATEMENTS OF FINANCIAL POSITION

The final stage of accounting for club and non-profit-making organisations is the preparation of the financial statements. These are very similar to the financial statements of sole traders, they follow the same concepts and conventions, but have slightly different terminology.

Summary of terminology differences

Sole trader	Clubs and non-profit-making organisations
Cash book	Receipts and payments account
Statement of profit or loss and other comprehensive income	Income and expenditure account
Profit	Surplus/surplus of income over expenditure
Loss	Deficit/deficit of income over expenditure
Capital	Accumulated fund

WORKED EXAMPLE

The London Football Club has the following transactions during the year ending 31 December 2018:

	£	£
Subscriptions for the year	3 547	
Subscriptions in arrears	435	
Subscriptions for 2019	124	4 106
Donations received		1 680
Prize draw: ticket sales		3 500
Dance income		7 340
Total income for the year		16 626
Ground rental	4 800	
Wages for staff	3 750	
Repairs	520	9 070
Band costs for dance	1 800	
Food for dance	1 940	3 740
Telephone charges	310	
Postages	124	434
Prize draw: prizes		2 000
Total expenditure for year		15 244
Opening bank balance	1 950	
Income	16 626	18 576
Expenditure		15 244
Closing bank balance		3 332

While the table above would constitute an acceptable receipts and payment account, it would not show the club assets and liabilities.

The following additional information is available:

- The club training equipment is valued at £11 900 at 1 January 2018. It is depreciated at 15 per cent per annum.
- The office equipment is valued at £5 430 at 1 January 2018 and it is depreciated at 10 per cent per annum.

- Members still owe £1 980 for 2018 subscriptions. The arrears received in 2018 were all amounts due at 31 December 2017.
- The club still has to pay £145 for repairs and £48 for telephone charges. Both these amounts were due at 31 December 2018.

The first step is to prepare a profit and loss account for the dance. This account would show income of £7 340 and expenditure of £3 740, which results in a profit for the year of £3 600 to be transferred to the income and expenditure account:

Dance account

Details	£	Details	£
Band	1 800	Receipts	7 340
Food	1 940		
Income and expenditure	3 600		
	7 340		7 340

London Football Club: income and expenditure account for the year ended 31 December 2018

	£	£	£
Income:			
Subscriptions (3 547 + 1 980)		5 527	
Profit from dance		3 600	
Prize draw ticket income (3 500 − 2 000)		1 500	
Donations received		1 680	12 307
Expenditure:			
Ground costs (9 070 + 145)	9 215		
Telephone charges (310 + 48)	358		
Postage	124		
Depreciation – training equipment	1 785		
Depreciation – office equipment	543		12 025
Surplus of income over expenditure			282

Having determined the surplus for the year, the next process is to prepare the statement of financial position for the members:

London Football Club: statement of financial position at 31 December 2018

	Cost	Provision for depreciation	Carrying value
	£	£	£
Non-current assets:			
Training equipment	11 900	1 785	10 115
Office equipment	5 430	543	4 887
	17 330	2 328	15 002
Current assets:			
Trade receivables	1 980		
Bank	3 332		5 312
Total assets			20 314
Accumulated fund:			
Balance at 1 January 2018*	19 715		
Surplus for the year	282		19 997
Current liabilities:			
Trade payables (145 + 48)	193		
Subscriptions in advance	124		317
Total capital and liabilities			20 314

*The opening balance in the accumulated fund is calculated by taking all opening balances at 1 January 2018. Assets are added together, and all liabilities are deducted. This calculation uses the formula that we have discussed:

$$\text{Assets} - \text{Liabilities} = \text{Capital}$$

In this case, capital is the accumulated fund at 1 January 2018. The calculation is as follows:

£11 900 (training equipment) + 5 430 (office equipment) +
£435 (arrear subscriptions) + £1 950 (bank balance)
= £19 715

It is possible to have the life membership fund in the non-current liabilities section.

You can see from this example that the preparation of these accounts is similar in some respects to those you have done for a sole trader. As with a sole trader, accruals and prepayments are taken into account.

ACTIVITY 4

SKILLS ▶ ANALYSIS, EXECUTIVE FUNCTION, INTERPRETATION

CASE STUDY: VALLEY SPORTS CLUB

The Valley Sports Club closes its financial year on 31 December. The following are the assets and liabilities of the club at year end:

	£	£
	31 December 2018	31 December 2019
Exercise equipment	4 700	6 200
Cash at bank	1 900	11 080
Outstanding amounts:		
Telephone	48	65
Electricity	120	140
Rent	200	300
Purchases for restaurant unpaid	690	950
Restaurant inventory	1 200	1 400

The following are the receipts and payments made for the year ended 31 December 2019.

	£
Receipts:	
Subscriptions	14 600
Prize draw: tickets sold	3 800
Restaurant sales	21 700
Payments:	
Exercise equipment	3 100
Wages in restaurant	5 000
Prize draw: prizes	1 800
Printing	500
Rent	2 400
Electricity	700
Telephone	400
Repairs to equipment	620
Purchases for restaurant	16 400

1 Prepare the income and expenditure account for the year and the statement of financial position at 31 December 2019.
2 As there is a trading section, prepare a trading account for that section.

ACTIVITY 5

SKILLS ▶ ANALYSIS, EXECUTIVE FUNCTION, INTERPRETATION

CASE STUDY: THE TRAINER CLUB

The Trainer Club prepares its accounts at 31 December each year. At 31 December 2018 the following was in the statement of financial position:

	£
Gym equipment	8 900
Café inventory	1 200
Cash at bank	700
	10 800
Accumulated funds	10 800

The receipts for the year to 31 December 2019 were:

	£
Subscriptions for the year	4 730
Subscriptions in advance	260
Café sales	3 980
Prize draw ticket sales	1 200
Competition fees	905
Subscriptions in arrears	240

The payments for the year were:

	£
Rent	2 000
Café purchases	1 250
Wages for staff	800
Repairs to equipment	200
Postage and telephones	140

The café inventory at 31 December 2019 was £1 040 and the gym equipment was to be depreciated at 10 per cent per annum.

In total, £120 of the subscriptions in arrears related to 2016. It is the club's policy to consider subscriptions over one year late as irrecoverable.

1 Prepare the accounts at 31 December 2019 for submission to the members. These should be:
  (a) the café trading account
  (b) the income and expenditure account
  (c) the statement of financial position.

EVALUATE

The receipts and payments account is a summarised cash book. What might be the benefits and limitations of preparing this?

Advantages	Disadvantages
Total receipts and payments available to view	It is not part of a double-entry system
The amount of cash at the end of the period is shown	Does not show accruals or prepayments of income and expenditure
Can be used to verify the accuracy of the cash book	It does not distinguish between capital and revenue expenditure

CHECKPOINT

1 What is the name given to the summarised cash book?

2 State two possible sources of revenue for a non-profit-making organisation.

3 A receipts and payments account shows non-cash transactions. True or false?

4 State one advantage and one disadvantage of a receipts and payments account.

5 Expenses included in the profit and loss of trading activities would also be included in the income and expenditure account. True or false?

6 Explain the accounting treatment for prepaid subscriptions at the start and end of the financial period.

7 Identify an accounting concept that is followed in the preparation of a subscriptions account.

8 State one benefit and one disadvantage of a club operating a life membership scheme.

9 State the term used to show a loss made by a non-profit-making organisation.

10 What is the term used to show the capital of a non-profit-making organisation?

SUBJECT VOCABULARY

accumulated fund the capital account of a club or non-profit-making organisation

deficit the loss incurred by a club or non-profit-making organisation

income and expenditure account the club and non-profit-making organisation equivalent of the statement of profit or loss and other comprehensive income

inventory count the physical verification of the quantity and value of the inventory held in the business

receipts and payments account a record of amounts received and paid in a club or non-profit-making organisation

subscriptions fees paid by members of a club or non-profit-making organisation

subscriptions account the account which records the membership fees of a member of a club

surplus the profit made by clubs and non-profit-making organisations

EXAM PRACTICE

CASE STUDY: KABADDI VETERANS' CLUB

SKILLS ANALYSIS, EXECUTIVE FUNCTION, DECISION MAKING

The Kabaddi Veterans' Club is a non-profit-making organisation. It organises social games and runs a small shop selling sports clothing and other useful items. It holds an annual dinner for members to celebrate achievements made during the year. The treasurer has provided the following information for the year ending 31 December 2018:

	£	£
	1 January 2018	31 December 2018
Property	50 000	50 000
Equipment (at valuation)	2 200	1 900
Subscriptions in advance	300	500
Subscriptions in arrears	600	200
Miscellaneous expenses owing	–	35
Retail shop inventory	1 200	1 500
Life member subscriptions	–	800

Kabaddi Veterans' Club: receipts and payment account for the year ended 31 December 2018

Receipts	£	Payments	£
Subscriptions	3 200	Bal b/d	800
Shop revenue	6 500	Purchase of inventory for shop	3 000
Annual dinner receipts	2 000	Annual dinner expenses	2 300
Life memberships	800	Wages for shop	3 000
		Other wages	1 890
		Miscellaneous expenses	355

Additional information:
A life membership scheme was introduced during the year. The policy is to transfer 15 per cent of the life subscription account to the income and expenditure account at the end of the year.

Q

1 For the year ended 31 December 2018, prepare the following:
  (a) the trading, profit and loss account for the shop
                                       (6 marks)
  (b) the subscription account for the year ended 31 December 2018   **(6 marks)**
  (c) the life membership account   **(3 marks)**
  (d) the income and expenditure account   **(7 marks)**
  (e) the statement of financial position.   **(9 marks)**
2 Evaluate the use of the life membership scheme at the Kabaddi Veterans' Club.   **(6 marks)**

EXAM HINT

Remember to use the correct terminology – the process is very similar to sole trader accounting, but it is easy to forget to change the key terminology.

If the organisation has trading activities, prepare the trading profit and loss account to calculate the profit from the activity. This figure is included in the income and expenditure account. DO NOT enter the figures used to calculate this in the income and expenditure account.

You are often required to prepare a set of financial statements for a non-profit-making organisation from a set of incomplete records (see Chapter 13). In this case, the following workings should have been prepared:

- subscriptions account
- life membership account
- trade receivables (if you are asked to calculate the sales for a trading account)
- trade payables (if you are asked to calculate the purchases for a trading account).

You may also need to calculate the opening accumulated fund from the opening balance of assets and liabilities.

16 MANUFACTURERS

LEARNING OBJECTIVES

After you have studied this chapter, you should be able to:
- prepare manufacturing accounts
- allocate and apportion costs between products and functions
- calculate and account for unrealised profit.

GETTING STARTED

You have been working as a trainee accountant for a retailer who buys and sells books. When you prepared the gross profit, you would have included the purchase of books in the cost of sales. You now work for a business that manufactures footwear from different components, which are bought, modified and assembled in a factory. What figure can you put in the cost of sales? Can you put in the value of the raw materials purchased? Will this reflect the cost of the footwear sold? If it does not, can you think how you would accurately work out the cost of sales?

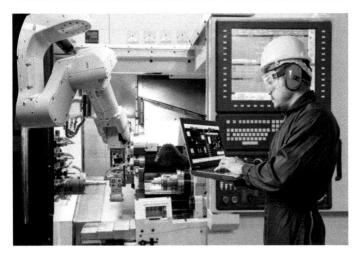

In all manufacturing businesses, the first account that needs to be prepared is the manufacturing account. This is done so that the costs of manufacturing can be transferred to the statement of profit or loss and other comprehensive income. Unlike the latter, the manufacturing account is not published but is, instead, prepared as the first step in working out the cost of sales. The total cost of production, as calculated in this account, is transferred to the trading account section of the statement of profit or loss and other comprehensive income and is shown with other items to make up the total cost of sales.

Therefore, we can see that the manufacturing account shows the costs of producing goods and running a factory. These costs are divided into:
- direct costs, which are expenses that can be attributed to specific cost units
- indirect costs, which are not directly attributed to specific cost units.

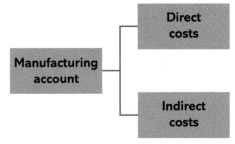

▲ Figure 1 Manufacturing costs

PRIME COSTS

The total of the direct costs, namely raw materials, direct wages and other direct expenses, are called prime costs because they are all costs incurred in the production process. These costs make up the basic costs of manufacturing a product before the addition of factory overhead expenses.

Direct expenses often include royalties, which are sums of money paid for the right to use a product or process that has been invented by another business. Direct costs are those costs which can be directly attributed to a cost unit (a specific product).

Once we have established these costs, we then add to it the indirect costs to arrive at the production cost.

INDIRECT COSTS – FACTORY OVERHEADS

These are costs that are incurred in the factory (sometimes called 'factory overheads'). They are in the manufacturing process but are not directly related to a specific product or cost unit; an example of this is supervisory wages.

A 'cost centre' is a production activity or location to which costs can be allocated. With direct costs there is no problem in allocation, but where the costs are indirect, allocation is not possible. Instead, they are allocated or apportioned to the departments benefiting from this. This is covered in detail in Chapter 19. We know that they are costs of producing the items but do not know which particular item (or cost centre) to charge. It may be that the costs should be spread over all of the items being manufactured.

Examples of these costs are depreciation of non-current assets used in the factory and expenses, such as factory rent, power, insurance, repairs, etc.

INVENTORY

When bringing inventory into account, it is important that the three kinds of inventory are separately identified:
- raw materials – goods purchased by the business
- finished goods – fully completed goods ready for sale
- work in progress – partly finished goods.

The first two are shown in the manufacturing account, while finished goods are shown in the trading account section of the statement of statement of profit or loss and other comprehensive income.

WORK IN PROGRESS

The cost of production is for all goods completed and ready for sale. As business is a continuing operation, this does not always happen. So, at the year end, there are goods that are still in the manufacturing process. They may not have been completely manufactured and are therefore not yet ready for sale – they are termed 'work in progress'. For example, a clothing manufacturer may have spent the past week cutting material for a garment. The manufacturer has all of the cut pieces of material, but they still have to be sewn together to produce the garment.

Therefore, at the end of the year, we add the opening inventory of work in progress and deduct the closing work in progress to arrive at the cost of production.

APPORTIONING EXPENSES

In Chapter 9, rent is shown as an expense in the statement of profit or loss and other comprehensive income, but we also show any factory rent in the manufacturing account as it is a cost of manufacturing. What if we only pay one cheque per month for rent? Where do we show the expense?

In fact, we need to apportion (share) this expense. One way of doing this is to work out the space (floor area) occupied by the manufacturing side of the business and the space occupied by the offices for administration, sales, etc. The rent would then be apportioned on that basis.

There are many other expenses that are apportioned, some between selling expenses and administration expenses (both contained within the statement of profit or loss and other comprehensive income). All apportionments use some basic logical form.

The nature of the expense must be taken into account when deciding how to apportion. For example, heating could be based on floor area, while depreciation of equipment could be based on the book value of each item and where it is used.

WORKED EXAMPLE

Manufacturing account for the year ended 31 December 2018

	£	£
Opening raw material inventory		12 000
Purchases of raw material	13 000	
Less closing raw material	10 100	2 900
Cost of raw material consumed		14 900
Direct labour		10 200
Direct expenses		10 430
Prime cost*		35 530
Factory overhead expenses:		
Indirect costs	9 300	
Wages	8 710	
Depreciation	6 400	
Other factory costs, e.g. rent, rates, etc	3 100	27 510
		63 040
Add work in progress at beginning of year		10 100
		73 140
Less work in progress at end of year		23 060
Cost of production transferred to trading account		50 080

*Prime cost is the total sum of all direct costs incurred in the manufacturing process. All indirect costs are then added to the prime cost to eventually obtain the total production cost.

ACTIVITY 1 | SKILLS | ANALYSIS, EXECUTIVE FUNCTION

CASE STUDY: MARMAX TRADING

Marmax manufacture stationery items such as pens and pencils. You are given the following extract of balances for Marmax Trading at 30 April 2019:

	£	£
Sales		502 000
Revenue returns	2 000	
Inventory at 1 May 2018:		
Raw materials	16 000	
Work in progress	800	
Finished goods	4 800	
Purchases of raw materials	117 000	
Carriage in on raw materials	3 000	
Direct labour	145 000	
Carriage outwards	7 000	
Factory indirect labour	29 000	
Factory indirect materials	1 700	
Factory expenses	20 100	
Plant and machinery	150 000	
Provision for depreciation on plant and machinery at 1 May 2018		90 000
Selling expenses	44 000	
Bank interest	6 000	
Administration expenses	35 000	

At the year end, the closing inventory is:

	£
Raw materials	14000
Work in progress	1000
Finished goods	3900

Depreciation is calculated as follows:

- plant and machinery – 10 per cent on straight line
- property – 2 per cent on cost
- office equipment – 5 per cent on reducing balance.

1 Prepare the manufacturing account for Marmax Trading for the year. (Note: included in the extract are some accounts which are not required in the manufacturing account.)

ACTIVITY 2   SKILLS ANALYSIS, EXECUTIVE FUNCTION

CASE STUDY: CAST MANUFACTURERS

Cast manufactures parts for aircraft. The following balances are taken from its books for the year ended 31 March 2019:

Inventory at 1 April 2018	£
Raw materials	76688
Work in progress	107269
Finished goods	144263
Purchases: raw materials	615000
Carriage on raw materials	17269
Direct labour	996788
Office salaries	175950
Rent and rates	85124
Office lighting and heat	59100
Depreciation: plant and machinery	106125
Depreciation: office equipment	18563
Sales	2402250
Factory fuel and power	134700

Rent and rates are to be apportioned as factory 75 per cent and office 25 per cent. Inventory at 31 March 2019 was:

	£
Raw materials	90788
Work in progress	110213
Finished goods	118069

1 Prepare a manufacturing account for the year ended 31 March 2019.

ACTIVITY 3   SKILLS ANALYSIS, EXECUTIVE FUNCTION

CASE STUDY: EZEE MANUFACTURING

Ezee's factory makes toys for resale. The following balances are taken from their books for the year ended 31 March 2019:

Inventory at 1 April 2018	£
Raw materials	29325
Work in progress	10455
Finished goods	198730
Purchases: raw materials	181475
Carriage on raw materials	1148
Direct labour	193120
Direct expenses	1105
Factory rent	12070
Office lighting and heat	1987
Depreciation: machinery	10030
Depreciation: office equipment	21300
Sales	198761
Factory fuel and power	19210
Indirect wages	76755
Factory insurance	1785
Repairs to factory	4250
General factory expenses	3783

Inventory at 31 March 2019 was:	£
Raw materials	30813
Work in progress	12920
Finished goods	192410

1 Prepare a manufacturing account using the relevant information in the extracts of balances.

ACTIVITY 4   SKILLS   ANALYSIS, EXECUTIVE FUNCTION

CASE STUDY: REEDY MANUFACTURING CO.

Reedy Manufacturing Co. makes biscuits and confectionary. The following balances are taken from its books of account for the year ended 31 December 2018:

Inventory at 1 January 2018	£
Raw materials	10673
Work in progress	9196
Finished goods	14284
Purchases: raw materials	79616
Carriage on raw materials	6633
Manufacturing wages	112101
Rent	11028
Office expenses	5983
Factory lighting and heat	4144
Depreciation: machinery	8208
Depreciation: office equipment	2513
Purchases: finished goods	8144
Sales	344028
Factory fuel and power	5913
Factory expenses	6094
Salaries and wages	76614
Advertising	14127

The following additional information is available to you:

- 50 per cent of salaries and wages and 75 per cent of rent are to be treated as a cost of manufacturing
- inventory at 31 December 2018 was:

	£
Raw materials	15005
Work in progress	12130
Finished goods	32331

1 Prepare a manufacturing account using the relevant information in the extracts of balances.

MANUFACTURING PROFIT

For accountability purposes, some businesses treat their shops and factories as two separate cost centres. As a result, some businesses transfer their products from the factory to the cost of sales in the statement of profit or loss and other comprehensive income at the production cost. This replaces the purchases entry in the cost of sales – remember the manufacturing business has purchased raw materials, NOT finished goods for resale. In this case, the transfer is easy to account for – simply use the figure for cost of production and insert it into the cost of sales after opening inventory of finished goods.

However, some businesses will add an assumed factory profit to the cost of production, calculated in the manufacturing account. This profit is calculated using a percentage mark-up on the production cost. This is then added to the cost of production to obtain a transfer price. It is this transfer price that is now used in the cost of sales calculation in the statement of profit or loss and other comprehensive income. In the worked example from earlier in the chapter, the cost of production transferred to the trading account was £50080. If the business has now decided to add a factory profit of 20 per cent before the goods are transferred, the last entries in the manufacturing account would now be:

	£
Cost of production	50080
Add factory profit (20%)	10016
Transfer price	60096

The transfer price of £60096 is moved to the cost of sales in the statement of profit or loss and other comprehensive income.

ACTIVITY 5   SKILLS   PROBLEM SOLVING

CASE STUDY: EMKOE METAL

Emkoe Metal has calculated that the cost of production for the year ended 31 August 2018 was £160000. The factory profit is based on a mark-up of 25 per cent.

1 Calculate the transfer price of the finished goods.

UNREALISED PROFIT RESULTING FROM GOODS MANUFACTURED

Factory profit

When completing the statement of profit or loss and other comprehensive income, the factory profit included in the closing inventory will have been overstated by the value of the factory profit. Following the accounting concept of realisation, profit cannot be recognised until the product is sold to customers. Therefore, factory profit included in the closing finished goods cannot be recognised because the goods are not sold to customers, but other departments instead. In this case, the finished goods inventory has been overstated because factory profit has been included in the cost.

As a result, we need to prepare an account to inform users how much of factory profit has been included in the finished goods inventory. When we prepare the statement of profit or loss and other comprehensive income, this amount needs to be added to the profit for the year, to ensure that profits are not understated. It is normal to add the factory profit after the calculation for gross profit and the deduction of expenses.

Closing inventory

One other accounting transaction must be completed before we can calculate the profit for the year. Any closing inventory in the cost of sales will contain an element of the factory profit which was added in the manufacturing account. The factory profit that is included in the closing inventory of finished goods is known as the unrealised profit. The closing inventory value will be overstated, so the profit for the year will be overstated.

This unrealised profit must be removed from the statement of profit or loss and other comprehensive income and the overvalued closing inventory must be adjusted in the statement of financial position. The calculation to remove this unrealised profit is:

$$\text{Unrealised profit} = \frac{\text{Mark-up \%}}{(100 + \text{Mark-up \%})} \times \text{Value of closing inventory}$$

WORKED EXAMPLE

After the first year of trading, Barrs Metals had a closing inventory of £24 000. The company add a factory profit of 20 per cent to the cost of production goods. The unrealised profit would be:

$$\text{Unrealised profit} = \frac{20}{120} \times £24\,000 = £4\,000$$

In the statement of profit or loss and other comprehensive income this would be an expense, as it represents an increase in a provision, much like the allowance/provision for irrecoverable debts. In the statement of financial position, it would be recorded as follows:

Current assets	£
Inventory	24 000
Less provision for unrealised profit	4 000
	20 000

At the end of year two, the closing inventory was calculated at £15 000 and the factory profit was 20 per cent. The calculation would be:

$$\text{Unrealised profit} = \frac{20}{120} \times £15\,000 = £2\,500$$

This represents a decrease in the provision for unrealised profit (it was £4 000 and is now £2 500). It is only the difference that is accounted for in the statement of profit or loss and other comprehensive income for the current year. The decrease of £1 500 represents other income and is entered after the gross profit as an addition to profit.

The statement of financial position extract would be:

Current assets	£
Inventory	15 000
Less provision for unrealised profit	2 500
	12 500

The ledger account for the end of year 2 would be:

Provision for unrealised profit on manufactured goods

Details	£	Details	£
Income statement	1 500	Balance b/d	4 000
Balance c/d	2 500		
	4 000		4 000
		Bal b/d	2 500

EFFECT OF FACTORY PROFIT ON STATEMENT OF PROFIT OR LOSS AND OTHER COMPREHENSIVE INCOME

	£	£
Revenue		X
Less: revenue returns		(X)
		X
Less: cost of sales		
Opening finished goods inventory	24 000	
Plus: cost of production	X	
Less: closing finished goods inventory (manufactured)	(16 000)	
Cost of sales		(X)
Gross profit		X
Factory profit	X	
Plus: decrease in provision for unrealised profit	1 500	X
		X

The decrease in provision for unrealised profit increases the total amount of profit earned. Therefore, it should be added to the profit. If the provision for unrealised account balance increases, this means more profit should not be recognised, therefore it will be a loss to the business. This will decrease the amount of profit earned.

ACTIVITY 6

SKILLS PROBLEM SOLVING, REASONING, EXECUTIVE FUNCTION

CASE STUDY: SAMIR

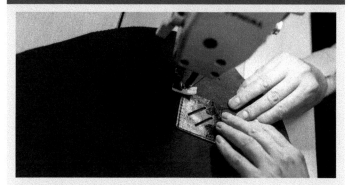

Samir owns a manufacturing business that makes leather goods such as gloves and wallets. Finished inventory is transferred from the manufacturing account to the statement of profit or loss and other comprehensive income at the production cost plus 50 per cent.

The following information for inventory is available for the year ended 31 August 2018:

	£	£
	1 September 2017	**31 August 2018**
Raw materials	105 000	118 500
Work in progress	75 000	70 000
Finished inventory	50 400	74 400

1 Calculate the amount of unrealised profit to be charged to the statement of profit or loss and other comprehensive income for the year ended 31 August 2018.
2 State how the amount would be treated in the statement of profit or loss and other comprehensive income.
3 Prepare an extract statement of financial position at 31 August 2018 showing how inventories and the provision for unrealised profit would be recorded.

STATEMENT OF PROFIT OR LOSS AND COMPREHENSIVE INCOME FOR A MANUFACTURING BUSINESS

The cost of production shown in the manufacturing account, or the transferred price, will be moved to the statement of profit or loss and comprehensive income. Therefore, the statement has the following layout:

Statement of profit or loss and other comprehensive income, year ended xxxx

	£	£	£
Revenue			X
Less: revenue returns			(X)
			X
Less: cost of sales			
Opening inventory – finished goods (manufactured)		X	
Plus: cost of production		X	
Less: closing inventory finished goods (manufactured)		(X)	X
Plus: opening inventory finished goods (purchased)**		X	
Plus: purchases of finished goods**		X	
Less: purchases returns of finished goods**		(X)	
Plus: carriage in of finished goods**		X	
Less: closing inventory finished goods (purchased)**		(X)	X
Cost of sales			(X)
Gross profit			X
Add factory profit			X
			X
Plus: other income			
(List other income)			
Decease in provision for unrealised profit*			X
Less: Expenses			
Increase in provision for unrealised profit*		X	
Profit for the year			X

*If the provision for unrealised profit has increased, this represents an expense to the business and if it has decreased this represents other income (much like the allowance/provision for irrecoverable debts).

**Sometimes a business may purchase finished goods from producers if they do not have the capacity to meet sales from their own factory. Accountants always separate the cost of sales relating to finished goods that the business produces and the cost of sales relating to finished goods purchased from other suppliers.

EXAM HINT

You need to make sure you calculate the prime cost (direct material + direct labour + direct expenses) and label this figure.

Some costs may be direct costs, indirect costs and expenses. Make sure you apportion them in the correct ratio.

Check the headings – in manufacturing accounts, some of these change from those in the financial statements of sole traders.

Factory profit must be added back into the profit for the year.

It is only the difference in provision for unrealised profit that is accounted for in the statement of profit or loss and other comprehensive income.

EVALUATE

Some manufacturers add a factory profit and others do not. So, why is this the case? What might be the benefits of doing this and what might be the limitations?

Advantages of adding factory profit	Disadvantages of adding factory profit
Allows a business to identify the profits made by different cost centres	Profit levels are probably not set with any degree of accuracy
It allows a comparison to be made directly with possible suppliers of the product, as their price would include an element of profit	The factory profit should equate to the profit earned by possible suppliers and this might not be available
Manufacturing profit is separated from the trading operations of the business	Overall profit is no different, so is it a waste of resources?

CHECKPOINT

1 State the three elements of prime cost.

2 State two indirect costs.

3 State two costs that might only appear in expenses.

4 The cost of raw materials consumed would include the purchase of raw materials. True or false?

5 How are opening inventory of work in progress and closing inventory of work in progress treated in the manufacturing account?

6 Where in the statement of profit or loss and other comprehensive income does the production cost of goods manufactured appear?

7 An increase in the provision for unrealised profit is recorded as an expense in the statement of profit or loss and other comprehensive income. True or false?

8 How is the provision of unrealised profit treated in the statement of financial position?

SUBJECT VOCABULARY

cost centre a production or service department
factory overheads indirect costs of manufacture which need to be apportioned on a fair basis to the cost of manufacturing
factory profit the approximate profit added to the production cost of goods completed to arrive at the transfer price
finished goods an inventory classification that consists of fully completed products
prime cost the total of all direct costs, materials, labour and expenses, incurred in the manufacture of a product
production cost the total costs incurred in the manufacture of a product
provision for unrealised profit the profit that is not recognised until the inventory has been sold
raw materials the purchase of inventory waiting to enter the manufacturing process
royalties a sum of money paid to the owner of a product or process for the use of it
transfer price the production cost of manufactured goods plus a mark-up, transferred to the trading account of a manufacturing business
work in progress partly finished goods in a manufacturing business

EXAM PRACTICE

CASE STUDY: YORKE

SKILLS ▸ PROBLEM SOLVING, EXECUTIVE FUNCTION, REASONING

Yorke manufactures gardening equipment. The following information has been extracted from the books of account at 31 October 2018:

Inventory at 1 November 2017	£
Raw materials	9 000
Work in progress	2 250
Finished goods	27 500
Purchases of raw materials	126 000
Wages	
Direct wages	250 000
Factory supervision wages	60 500
Administrative wages	125 000
Indirect expenses:	
Factory	13 000
Office	35 550
Rates	12 800
Royalties	50 000
Machinery at cost	55 000
Provision for depreciation	11 000
Provision for unrealised profit	2 885

Additional information at 31 October 2018:
- Completed production is transferred to the statement of profit or loss and other comprehensive income at cost plus 15 per cent.
- Rates are apportioned in the rate of 75 per cent to the factory and 25 per cent to the office.
- Depreciation on machinery is applied at the rate of 10 per cent per annum using the straight line method.
- Inventory was valued at:
  - raw materials   £10 000
  - work in progress   £3 750
  - finished goods   £28 700.

1. Prepare a manufacturing account for the year ended 31 October 2018. **(15 marks)**
2. Calculate the change in the provision for unrealised profit for the year ended 31 October 2018. Explain how this would be treated in the statement of profit or loss and other comprehensive income. **(7 marks)**
3. Explain why it is necessary to provide a provision for unrealised profit in Yorke's accounts. **(8 marks)**

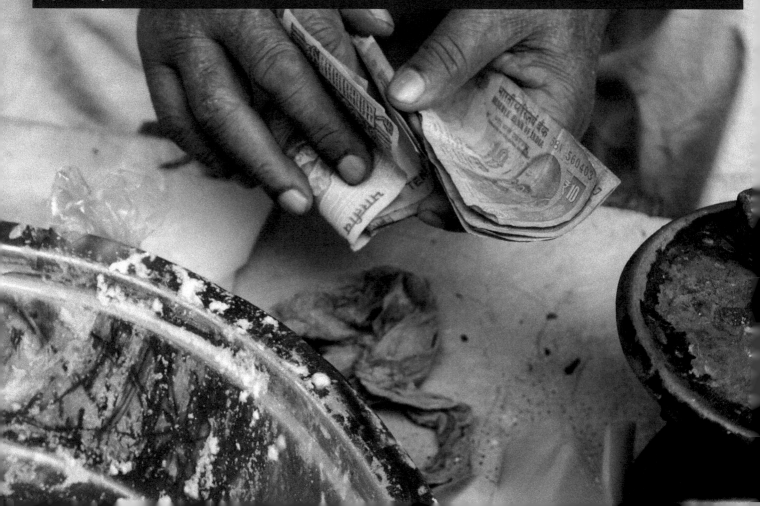

INTRODUCTION TO COSTING

So far, this book has focused on double-entry bookkeeping and the preparation of financial statements for different types of organisation. It has used historic information and provided information mainly for external users. Cost accounting looks to the future and involves the recording, classification and analysis of costs so that business managers can make effective decisions.

Your IAS studies will provide you with an introduction to costing and will cover the valuation of inventory and how labour and overhead costs are determined. You will learn how a business costs specific jobs for customers.

17 VALUATION OF INVENTORY

LEARNING OBJECTIVES

After you have studied this chapter, you should be able to:
- explain the characteristics of the different methods of inventory valuation: net realisable value (NRV), Last In, First Out (LIFO) and First In, First Out (FIFO)
- calculate the value of inventory using the above methods
- calculate the effect on profit and net assets of the different methods of inventory valuation.

GETTING STARTED

Your business has purchased five batches of products during the year, all at different prices. It had some opening inventory from the previous year. How would you value the closing inventory? If the valuation is too high, how will it affect the profit? How would you value inventory if it was damaged and needed to be repaired before being sold? Which accounting concepts will you need to follow?

In Chapter 10 we showed how inventory is treated in the financial statements. The opening inventory is added to purchases and closing inventory is subtracted to arrive at cost of sales in the statement of profit or loss and other comprehensive income. In the statement of financial position, closing inventory is entered under current assets and always appears first, as it is the least liquid of the current assets. In many of the examples given in the activities, as well as in examinations, you will frequently be given a closing inventory figure.

It is appropriate at this stage to examine how inventory is valued. This is important because the method of inventory valuation will affect both the profit and value of a business. This applies to all forms of inventory – raw materials, work in progress or finished goods.

VALUATION METHODS

The methods of inventory valuation are:
- net realisable value (NRV)
- First In, First Out (FIFO)
- Last In, First Out (LIFO).

It is important to remember that these methods relate to the valuation of inventory, they do not reflect the physical movement of inventory within a business.

NET REALISABLE VALUE

International accounting standards require that inventories be valued at the lower of cost or net realisable value (NRV), where:

$$\boxed{\text{NRV} = \text{selling price} - \text{additional costs}}$$

This is an example of the prudence concept. The cardinal rule is that inventory is valued at the lower of cost or net realisable value. The method considers any additional costs that may result in putting the goods for sale into a saleable condition.

The basis of working out whether an inventory is overvalued is to first find out what the selling price is for the inventory. From this, we deduct any costs that will be incurred in order to make the sale. These can include repacking of the goods, new labels, delivery charges to customers, repairs, etc. The final figure is the net realisable value.

If the value is below the cost price of the inventory on hand, it is this value that must be used to value inventory and NOT the cost price. This process ensures that the statement of financial position does not overstate the value of the inventory. The reduction would reduce the value of closing inventory in the cost of sales, increase the cost of sales and so decrease gross profit.

WORKED EXAMPLE

Sachi sells cutlery (knives, forks, spoons, etc.). She has inventory of can openers which were purchased at a cost price of £1.30 each. Because of mass production, it is now possible to purchase the identical openers for 84p each and they are currently being sold for 98p each. To calculate the inventory valuation, we use the formula:

Inventory valuation = the lower of cost or NRV

where NRV = selling price − additional costs

= either £1.30 or 98p

This means that we cannot value our existing inventory at any more than the realisable value, which is 98p each.

However, there is one additional problem. The boxes in which the openers were originally packed have been water damaged and new boxes, costing 11p each, must be provided. This additional cost must be accounted for in our calculation.

NRV = 98p − 11p = 87p each.

As this is lower than the original cost, the inventory of can openers must be valued at 87p each.

ACTIVITY 1

SKILLS ANALYSIS, PROBLEM SOLVING

CASE STUDY: TAVISH FURNITURE

Tavish makes and sells wooden furniture. He has just checked his inventory of finished furniture for the year ended 31 December 2017 and supplied the following information.

His closing inventory was valued at £62 530, based on a physical inventory count. All inventory was correctly valued at cost. However, Tavish discovered that some of the inventory was not in a saleable condition. Tables with a sales value of £28 800 had been damaged in storage. These were recorded at £17 550 cost and Tavish estimated that after repairs they could be sold for £20 800. The repairs would cost £3 540.

1 Calculate the value of inventory to be included in the financial statements at 31 December 2017.

FIRST IN, FIRST OUT AND LAST IN, FIRST OUT

We do not give a cost to each item as and when it is brought into inventory. Often, we continue purchasing the same item during the year and we also sell that item at a fixed price during the year. Therefore, one of the following will occur:

• the inventory is issued to production/sales at the earliest prices – called the First In, First Out system
• the inventory is issued to production/sales at the most recent prices – this is known as Last In, First Out.

(NB – you must remember that inventory valuation relates to the movement of inventory in relation to the cost of the inventory, NOT the actual physical movement of inventory.)

WORKED EXAMPLE

The following are the purchase and sales transactions for can openers.

Date	Goods in		Goods sold
July	Quantity	Price per item	Quantity
5	300	85p	
6			250
8	400	82p	
9			350
11			100
16	500	88p	
19			200
24	800	91p	
28			300

We will calculate the value of the closing inventory using the following valuation bases:
- FIFO
- LIFO.

FIFO

Date	Goods in		Units issued	Inventory in hand		
July	Quantity	Unit price	Quantity	Quantity	Unit price	Value £
5	300	85p		300	85p	255.00
6			250	50	85p	42.50
8	400	82p		50	85p	42.50
				400	82p	328.00
9			350	50	85p	42.50
				100	82p	82.00
11			100	Nil		
16	500	88p		500	88p	440.00
19			200	300		264.00
24	800	91p		300	88p	264.00
				800	91p	728.00
28			300	800	91p	728.00

You may have noticed that in the inventory record, the older inventory is placed first in the balance column. For example, the amount of inventory in hand on 8 July is 450 units, of this, 50 units are the older inventory and 400 units are the newer items.

Using FIFO, the closing balance is 800 units and the value must be equal to the purchase of 800 units at 91p each.

LIFO

Date	Goods in		Units issued	Inventory in hand		
July	Quantity	Unit price	Quantity	Quantity	Unit price	Value £
5	300	85p		300	85p	255.50
6			250	50	85p	42.50
8	400	82p		400	82p	328.00
				50	85p	42.50
9			350	50	82p	41.00
				50	85p	42.50
11			100	Nil		Nil
16	500	88p		500	88p	440.00
19			200	300	88p	264.00
24	800	91p		800	91p	728.00
				300	88p	264.00
28			300	500	91p	455.00
				300	88p	264.00

You may have noticed that in the inventory record, the newer inventory is now placed first in the balance column. For example, the amount of inventory in hand on 8 July is 450 units; of this, 400 units are the newer inventory (which is placed first) and 50 units of older inventory are placed after.

Using LIFO, we see that our closing balance is also 800 units. But now, of these, 500 units are valued at 91p each and 300 units at 88p each.

ACTIVITY 2 — SKILLS ► ANALYSIS, PROBLEM SOLVING

CASE STUDY: SAHAN

Sahan manufactures components for bicycles. He provides the following information:
- He buys 200 units of product ZZ at £1.20 each in April 2009.
- Sahan buys a further 400 units in September 2009 at £1.50 each.
- During the manufacturing process, 300 units of ZZ are issued in October 2009.

1 Using the different methods for the pricing of inventory, show the cost of issues to production.

USING DIFFERENT METHODS

A variation of the final profit for the year is shown by using different methods of inventory valuation. As such, a business must choose one method and consistently use that chosen method. This is an application of the consistency concept.

In some way, the method selected should relate to the type of product sold by the business. If items are perishable or have a short shelf life then FIFO might be more appropriate, but if the product is very durable and will last a long time, for example metals, then it could be argued that LIFO is more appropriate. The main factor determining the choice will relate to the effect the method chosen has on the profit of the business.

Earlier in the chapter we looked at the net realisable value method. Whatever method is normally used by the business there is always the need to ensure that inventory is not overvalued – this is an application of the prudence concept.

PERIODIC OR PERPETUAL INVENTORY VALUATION?

The method of calculating the value of inventory after each transaction is known as the **perpetual inventory valuation**. This method keeps detailed information on inventory levels. The **periodic inventory valuation** method totals up receipts and issues of inventory and calculates a new balance only at the end of the accounting period. The method chosen by a business will depend on the nature of the business and the inventories it holds. In the examination, you might be asked to produce inventory valuations using the perpetual method.

EXAM HINT

When calculating closing inventory, it is quicker to use the periodic method. The most recent purchases of inventory will remain after sales have been deducted from the opening inventory plus purchases.

INVENTORY VALUATION AND THE EFFECT ON PROFIT AND ASSETS

Closing inventory is used to calculate the gross profit and, under the accruals concept, is deducted from purchases to arrive at the cost of sales for that year. Therefore, the choice of method will directly affect the profits reported by a business. In the example earlier, we calculated that, using FIFO, the closing value of inventory was £728. Using LIFO, the value of closing inventory was £719. From this, we can see that a valuation using FIFO would result in a lower cost of sales and therefore a higher gross profit and a higher value of net assets.

However, this is not always the case. In periods of inflation (rising prices), FIFO results in a higher closing inventory, as more expensive inventory is recorded as remaining in the books. This will result in a higher gross profit being reported than if LIFO was used. The value of net assets in the statement of financial position would be higher.

If prices are falling (deflation) then FIFO would record a lower gross profit, as older, more expensive inventory would be issued first, and the closing inventory valuation would be lower. This would reduce the value of current assets on the statement of financial position.

With FIFO, the inventory valuation is based on the most recent purchases of inventory which is therefore nearer the current market values. With LIFO, the inventory valuation is based on the oldest purchases and may not reflect the current replacement cost.

Of the two methods, FIFO would appear to reflect the physical movement of inventory for most businesses, especially those where the inventory has a limited life or might decay quickly, such as food. If prices are rising, many tax authorities do not accept LIFO as a method of inventory valuation as it often leads to lower reported profits.

In the long run, the profits earned by the business will be the same, regardless of the method chosen, as all inventory will be used up at the price paid. It is only in the short term that profit will differ.

ACTIVITY 3   SKILLS   ANALYSIS, PROBLEM SOLVING
CASE STUDY: NAT

Nat purchases 60 boxes of towels in February 2019 for £22 per box. He also buys an additional 30 boxes in April 2019 at £26 per box. In July 2019, he sells 80 boxes for £68 per box. You are told that closing inventory at 31 December 2019 must be valued for use in the trading account of the business.

1 Calculate the value of this inventory using:
  (a) FIFO
  (b) LIFO.

EXAM HINT

Show your workings – marks are still available for these, even if you make an arithmetical error during your calculations.

ACTIVITY 4   SKILLS ANALYSIS, PROBLEM SOLVING

CASE STUDY: MUSICMAN & CO.

Musicman & Co. purchase one model of guitar. The cost of these guitars during the year ending 30 June 2017 varied, but the company sold all the guitars at a fixed price of £800 each. Inventory was taken on 30 June 2016 and this added up to 33 units at a total cost of £6 600.

The following details are for the guitars purchased during the year:

	No. of guitars purchased	Price per guitar £
3 July 2016	120	270
6 Sept 2016	100	300
20 Nov 2016	180	330
25 March 2017	240	390
2 May 2017	120	420

The following were the sales for the year:

	No. of guitars sold
July–Aug	30
Sept–Oct	90
Nov–Dec	150
Jan–Mar	210
Apr–Jun	60

1 Calculate the cost of the inventory at 30 June 2017 using FIFO and LIFO methods.

ACTIVITY 5   SKILLS ANALYSIS, PROBLEM SOLVING

CASE STUDY: SWEET & CO.

Sweet & Co. purchase sugar from a factory for repacking and resale. At 1 January 2018 (the start of the financial year), Sweet & Co. had an inventory of 500 kg, valued at a cost of £1 per kg. During January, the following purchases were made:

	Kg	£ per kg
3 January	800	1.01
13 January	700	1.03
15 January	800	1.05
23 January	500	1.04

During the month, the following sales took place:

	Kg
5 January	900
11 January	100
18 January	400
25 January	600
31 January	900

1 Calculate the value of the closing inventory at 31 January using each of the following methods:
 (a) LIFO
 (b) FIFO.

EXAM HINT

Remember, you are calculating the valuation of inventory, not the physical movement of stock.

EVALUATE

When choosing the most appropriate method of inventory valuation, you should consider the need to give a true and fair view of the financial position of the business. Inventory valuation covers many accounting concepts, from cost and prudence to accruals and consistency. Yet, there is no one way of valuing inventory that applies to all businesses. There are many factors involved in making the decision – it could be one of convenience, choosing the easiest method to calculate; or having a lack of information due to poor or inadequate inventory control procedures.

Both methods have benefits and limitations which need to be analysed and evaluated.

First In, First Out (FIFO)	
Advantages	**Disadvantages**
Closing inventory valuation based on the most recent prices paid for that inventory, so the information is more relevant to users' decision making	The price of inventory issued to manufacturing is likely to be out of date, so selling price might not reflect the most recent costs
Realistic as reflects physical movement of inventory	If prices are rising, it will reduce cost of sales and increase profit, so resulting in higher tax
Acceptable under IAS and tax authorities	Might not conform to the prudence concept by increasing profit and asset valuation
Relatively easy to calculate, thus saving time for the business which can be used for other activities	

Last In, First Out (LIFO)	
Advantages	**Disadvantages**
Selling price will reflect up-to-date costs, as inventory is issued at most recent prices	Not acceptable under IAS and tax authorities
When prices are falling, issues will be close to the current replacement cost	When prices are falling remaining inventory will be overvalued
Fairly easy to calculate, therefore saves time for the business	Identical items of inventory may be issued to production at different costs
	May understate cost of sales and so not be sensible

CHECKPOINT

1 Explain the difference between cost and net realisable value.

2 Which method of inventory valuation uses the most recent prices?

3 Explain the difference between the periodic method and the perpetual method.

4 State one advantage of using LIFO as a method of inventory valuation.

5 State one advantage of using FIFO as a method of inventory valuation.

6 FIFO will always produce higher profits. True or false?

7 State two accounting concepts that apply to the valuation of inventory.

SUBJECT VOCABULARY

First In, First Out (FIFO) a method of inventory valuation where oldest inventory is issued first
Last In, First Out (LIFO) a method of valuing inventory where most recent inventory is issued first
net realisable value (NRV) inventory valuation based on the selling price less any additional costs required to affect the sale
periodic inventory valuation a method of inventory valuation where the inventory is valued at the end of the period
perpetual inventory valuation a method of inventory valuation where a running balance of inventory is recorded after every receipt or issue of inventory

EXAM PRACTICE

CASE STUDY: BIRCHINGTON METALS

SKILLS ANALYSIS, PROBLEM SOLVING

Birchington Metals manufactures aluminium products for the petrochemical industry. The price of aluminium varies during the year. The following information was provided for the year ended 31 October 2017.

Inventory of aluminium at 1 November 2016 was 10 tonnes a £1 500 per tonne.

Date	Receipts (tonnes)	Issues (tonnes)
November 2016–January 2017	10 at £1 400	15
February 2017–April 2017	10 at £1 300	8
May 2017–July 2017	15 at £1 250	14
August 2017–October 2017	8 at £1 200	12

Inventory is issued to production using the First In, First Out perpetual inventory valuation method.

Q

1 Calculate the value of inventory at 31 October 2017 using the First In, First Out perpetual inventory valuation method. **(6 marks)**

The business is considering changing the method of inventory valuation to Last In, First out.

2 Calculate the value of inventory at 31 October 2017, using the Last In, First Out perpetual inventory method. **(9 marks)**

3 Calculate the difference in profit if Birchington Metals had used the Last In, First Out method. **(2 marks)**

18 LABOUR COSTS

UNIT 1
1.4.4–1.4.6

LEARNING OBJECTIVES

After you have studied this chapter, you should be able to:

■ explain what is meant by the term labour productivity
■ evaluate different methods of remuneration: day work, piecework and bonus schemes
■ explain the effects of remuneration schemes on employer costs and employee earnings.

GETTING STARTED

If you ran your own business and employed staff, how would you reward them? Would you pay them an hourly rate regardless of the work done? Would you reward them if they produced more? If you did, how would you calculate this?

LABOUR PRODUCTIVITY

Labour productivity is a measurement of the efficiency of employees within a business. It is calculated by dividing the output produced by the number of employees. The output could be measured in terms of the volume of output (units produced) or the value of the output produced (£). The formula is:

$$\text{Labour productivity} = \frac{\text{Output per period (units)}}{\text{No. of employees}}$$

This would be expressed as output per employee, for example, 500 units per employee per month.

WORKED EXAMPLE

A factory produces 5 000 cardboard boxes per day. It employs 25 workers in the production unit. We will calculate the labour productivity of the production workers:

$$\begin{aligned}
\text{Labour productivity} &= \frac{\text{Output per period (units)}}{\text{No. of employees}} \\
&= \frac{5\,000 \text{ units}}{25 \text{ employees}} \\
&= 200 \text{ boxes per employee per day}
\end{aligned}$$

Labour productivity is important because labour costs are often a significant cost to a business. As a result, it has an impact on profit and profitability. To remain competitive, a business needs to keep total costs and unit costs as low as possible. A more productive workforce will spread overheads over a higher output and reduce the unit costs. This will allow a business to reduce prices and see an increase in demand for its products. Additionally, a productive workforce could lead to performance bonuses for employees and improve their motivation.

Labour productivity could be improved in several ways:

● improved technology/automation, leading to the same output with fewer employees
● training and development of employees, which could lead to greater output with the same level of input (the employees)
● effective employee remuneration methods, which would motivate employees to work more efficiently and thus increase output.

The latter method is the focus of this chapter on labour costs.

METHODS OF EMPLOYEE REMUNERATION

Remuneration is the term applied to payments to employees. It includes wages and other benefits, such as pension contributions or staff uniforms. Employee remuneration is important because it affects the costs of a business and the efficiency and motivation of its workers. The three main methods of remuneration are:

● day work or time rates
● piecework
● bonus or incentive schemes, which can be divided into individual or group schemes.

DAY WORK

Day work is a method where employees are paid a fixed rate based on the amount of time spent at work, regardless of the output produced. It is most often expressed as an hourly rate of pay.

The calculation for the wage cost is:

> Labour cost = hourly wage rate × hours worked

A day rate is often used when it is difficult to measure the output of an employee and where quality might be more important than the quantity produced.

Advantages and disadvantages of day work

Advantages	Disadvantages
Labour costs are easy to plan and budget for	No employee incentive to increase productivity and output
Quality may improve as employee not under time pressure	Rewards all employees equally, regardless of performance
Employees know the level of remuneration in advance	Supervision will be needed to ensure work is completed
Decreased absenteeism (where people are staying away from work)	Inefficient working may require extra overtime working, adding to costs
Costs to operate this method are low	

PIECEWORK

Piecework pays employees based on what they produce. They are paid an agreed amount for each 'unit' of output they complete. In most cases, this will only be a very small component of the product sold by a business. For example, in a clothing factory, an employee could be paid based on the number of shirt collars they produce. Hence the term 'piece rate'. Employees are rewarded on the number of pieces they make – in this case, shirt collars. The calculation is:

> Labour cost = rate per piece produced × quantity produced

Piecework is often used when the quantity of output is important and the work can be divided into small and relatively simple tasks.

Advantages and disadvantages of piecework

Advantages	Disadvantages
Payment of wages linked directly to output	Costs are unpredictable due to different levels of employee output
Employees are encouraged to work hard, leading to improved productivity and output	Quality may suffer – staff may be needed to inspect output
Employees work quicker – less wasted time	Employees cannot plan their income and production issues will affect earnings
More efficient workers earn more	May be difficult to calculate a fair rate for the task, or it could be too generous, therefore increasing costs
	More expensive to operate

BONUS SCHEMES – INDIVIDUAL

Bonus schemes are a combination of day work and piecework systems – they offer an encouragement to employees on a day rate. The employee is paid a set day rate and receives additional payments (the bonus) if output is greater than the standard expected. The bonus element could comprise commission payments for sales staff or profit-related pay for the entire workforce. There are many ways to decide how the bonus payment works. One of the most common methods would be to reward employees for actual output over the planned standard output expected under normal working conditions. The employees would receive an agreed amount for each unit of output above this level. The organisation benefits from increased output and the employee benefits from higher earnings.

The labour cost calculation would be:

> Labour cost = day rate + proportion of time saved

Advantages and disadvantages of individual bonus schemes

Advantages	Disadvantages
Some element of wages linked to output, productivity should increase	Difficulty in establishing bonus rate with staff
Employees will have a minimum guaranteed wage	Quality might suffer
More efficient workers will earn more	
It is an opportunity to encourage non-production staff	Remuneration calculations more difficult and can be costly to operate

BONUS SCHEMES – GROUP

In addition to individual bonus systems, group bonus schemes are sometimes used for employees. This method of remuneration is suitable when employees work in teams and it is more difficult to share output between individual employees. In this case, the bonus payment element of the labour cost would be divided equally amongst the members of the group.

Advantages and disadvantages of group bonus schemes

Advantages	Disadvantages
Increased productivity, leading to greater output. Decrease in unit costs	Less direct incentive than an individual bonus system, so less improvement in productivity
Greater co-operation between workers	Less efficient employees in the team will receive the same bonus as the more efficient ones, therefore affecting the overall team relationship
Could increase employee flexibility within the group	Quality issues remain. Supervision will be needed, further increasing costs
Simpler to operate than individual bonus schemes	

Whatever remuneration method is chosen it should be fair to all staff and must be simple for employees to understand. It should be simple and cost-effective to operate for the business so that the cost benefits obtained by using the chosen method are greater than the costs of operating it.

THE EFFECT ON EMPLOYER COSTS AND EMPLOYEE EARNINGS

The effects of the different remuneration methods on employer costs and employee earnings are summarised in the table below.

Remuneration method	Employer costs	Employee earnings
Day work	Fixed labour costs based on time	Fixed earnings based on hours worked
Piecework	Labour costs increase as output increases. It would be a variable cost	Earnings increase with increases in individual effort and output
Individual bonus scheme	Labour costs will be semi-variable – fixed element from day rate, with element of increased costs for increased output	Minimum fixed earnings plus the ability to increase earnings
Group bonus scheme	Labour costs will be semi-variable – fixed element from day rate, with element of increased costs for increased output	Regular minimum wage is guaranteed plus opportunity to increase earnings, but depends on the efforts of the whole group

ACTIVITY 1   SKILLS   ANALYSIS, PROBLEM SOLVING

CASE STUDY: VILLINGILI HOLIDAYS

Villingili Holidays sells short-break holidays to the Maldives and employs three members of staff. Each member is paid according to the number of holidays they sell. In March 2018, the following information was available:

Employee	No. of sales	Commission paid per sale (£)
Abbas	8	£100
Nasreena	7	£110
Sultan	12	£95

During the month, a customer who purchased a holiday from Sultan cancelled the order. The commission earned, £100, will need to be deducted from earnings made in March.

1 Calculate the labour costs for March.

ACTIVITY 2

SKILLS ANALYSIS, PROBLEM SOLVING

CASE STUDY: KAR KOMPONENTS

Kar Komponents manufactures door handles for the car industry. It pays production workers a day rate, with an additional individual bonus based on any output above the standard of 500 units per week. The following information is available for one week:

Employee	Time rate per hour (£)	Hours worked	Production level (units)	Bonus rate (£)
Osman	11.50	30	510	3.00
Armstrong	12.00	33	490	5.00
Rashid	11.50	32	520	2.00

1 Calculate the earnings of each employee and the total labour costs. Show the cost of issues to production.

EXAM HINT

You should make sure you can clearly distinguish between the different methods of remunerating employees.

EVALUATE

Examination questions usually focus on the advantages and disadvantages of the different methods of remuneration. You should carefully study the tables provided earlier in the chapter. If you are asked to evaluate something, you should not only list the points, but explain in detail two advantages and two disadvantages. If you are asked to recommend a method, choose the most appropriate for the information given, and make a decision.

CHECKPOINT

1 State the formula for labour productivity.

2 Explain why labour productivity is important to a business.

3 Explain the difference between a day rate method of remuneration and a piecework method of remuneration.

4 State two advantages and two disadvantages of a day rate system.

5 State two advantages and two disadvantages of an individual bonus scheme.

6 Explain how labour costs would be calculated in a piece rate system.

SUBJECT VOCABULARY

bonus an additional payment made when work is completed in less than the allowed time or for achieving a given output level
day work payment made by a rate per hour
piecework payment made according to the number of units produced
productivity the measurement of employee efficiency
remuneration payments to employees of wages and other financial benefits

EXAM PRACTICE

CASE STUDY: KIM ELECTRICALS

SKILLS ▶ CRITICAL THINKING, REASONING, CREATIVITY

Kim Electricals manufactures electrical components for audio equipment. The work is relatively low skilled and labour intensive as the business has few non-current assets. It currently remunerates its employees on a day work basis. Kim Electricals has proposed that it change the method to piecework.

1 Explain how a piecework scheme would operate.
(4 marks)
2 Advise Kim Electricals whether it should introduce the new method or stay with the existing method of remunerating employees. (12 marks)

19 OVERHEAD COSTS

LEARNING OBJECTIVES

After you have studied this chapter, you should be able to:

- explain the characteristics of overhead expenses
- account for the allocation, apportionment and absorption of overheads
- account for the apportionment and continuous allotment of service departments
- calculate overhead absorption rates using machine hour and labour rates per hour
- explain over absorption and under absorption of overheads.

GETTING STARTED

Think about the clothes you wear. How much did you pay for them? How much do you think the material cost? How much do you think employees were paid to make them? Is there a large gap between the price you paid and the direct costs? What other costs need to be considered before the total cost of the item of clothing can be calculated?

CHARACTERISTICS OF OVERHEAD EXPENSES

The costs can be classified in different ways, according to the purpose required. In Chapter 16, Manufacturers, costs were classified as either direct or indirect. The direct costs were those costs which could be specifically and accurately attributed to manufacturing.

These were then allocated to the prime cost of the product.

The other classification of cost was indirect costs. These were the overhead costs which could not be specifically linked to an individual product but were needed in the manufacturing process. Examples include rent and rates and supervisory wages. This is the main characteristic of an overhead expense. The business can identify that the expense is required in the manufacturing process, but the cost cannot be linked to an individual unit.

Overhead costs are as much a part of the product cost as the direct material and direct labour. Therefore, they must be accounted for when calculating the total cost of a product and the price the business will charge for the product.

A further characteristic of overhead expenses relates to the change in the overhead expense as the volume of production changes. Overhead expenses do not always remain fixed but change as production activity rises or falls. The classification of costs, based on the level of activity, are:

- fixed costs
- semi-fixed costs
- variable costs
- semi-variable costs.

FIXED COSTS

Fixed costs do not change with the level of activity. This is because they are incurred on a time basis rather than on the level of production output. Examples of fixed costs would include rent and rates, management salaries and interest on loans.

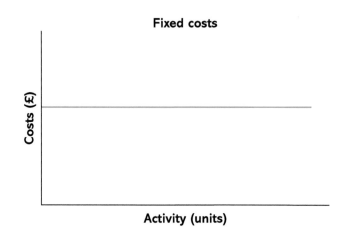

▲ Figure 1 Fixed costs do not change

SEMI-FIXED COSTS

Semi-fixed costs are constant over a range of activity. When that range of activity is reached the costs will increase and then remain constant over the next range of output. They are sometimes referred to as stepped costs (see Figure 2). An example could be supervisory wages – as output reaches a certain level, it may be necessary to employ an extra supervisor. The costs would then increase and remain at the higher level until a further extra supervisor is required.

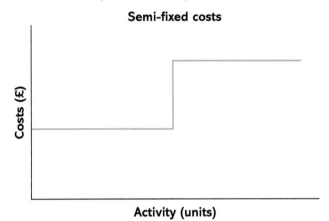

Semi-fixed costs

▲ Figure 2 Semi-fixed costs are sometimes called stepped costs

VARIABLE COSTS

Variable costs change in direct proportion to the level of business activity. These costs include direct material and direct labour.

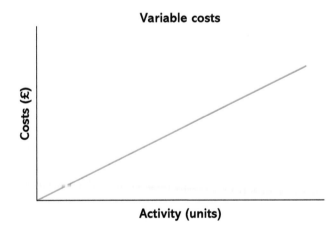

Variable costs

▲ Figure 3 Variable costs change in proportion to activity

SEMI-VARIABLE COSTS

These costs include an element of fixed cost and an element of variable cost. There will be a fixed cost element regardless of the level of activity. As activity increases, the variable cost element will increase in proportion to the increase in activity. An example of a semi-variable cost would be electricity charges. There would be a fixed cost for the standing charge and a variable cost based on the usage of electricity.

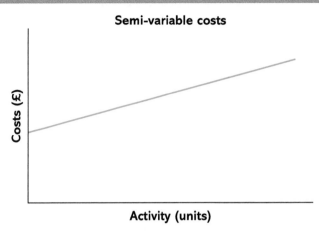

Semi-variable costs

▲ Figure 4 Semi-variable costs change in proportion to activity as well, but even when there is no activity there might still be a fixed cost to cover

ACTIVITY 1   SKILLS CRITICAL THINKING

CASE STUDY: CLASSIFICATION OF COSTS

1 For the following, classify them as either fixed costs, semi-fixed costs, variable costs or semi-variable costs:
  (a) direct labour costs
  (b) factory heating and lighting
  (c) rent and rates
  (d) quality control inspection staff
  (e) management salaries
  (f) factory insurance
  (g) rent on additional factory space
  (h) direct material costs.

ALLOCATION, APPORTIONMENT AND ABSORPTION OF OVERHEADS

The allocation, apportionment and absorption of overheads, often referred to as absorption costing, is the process of ensuring that all factory overheads are absorbed into the total production cost for each cost unit made in the factory. The process consists of three distinct stages:

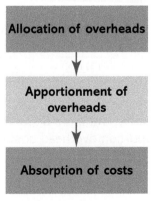

▲ Figure 5 The process of absorption costing

ALLOCATION OF OVERHEADS

The allocation of overheads is the process of charging costs to a cost centre, where the costs are completely associated with that cost centre. An example of overhead allocation would be a machine supervisor who works only in the machine department – these costs should be allocated to that department. Another example could be the rent of a factory space used entirely by one cost centre.

WORKED EXAMPLE

Az Manufacturing has three departments: machining, assembly and painting. For the year ending 31 August 2018, Az incurred the following expenditure:

Expenditure	£
Production materials:	
Machining	120 000
Assembly	37 000
Painting	5 000
Direct labour:	
Machining	65 000
Assembly	30 000
Painting	25 000
Indirect labour:	
Machining	12 000
Assembly	12 000
Painting	6 000
Rent of paint shop building	25 000

We will allocate all costs, both direct and indirect, to the appropriate cost centre (department):

Cost	£ Machining	£ Assembly	£ Painting
Direct materials	120 000	37 000	5 000
Direct labour	65 000	30 000	25 000
Indirect labour	12 000	12 000	6 000
Rent of building			25 000
Total allocated cost	197 000	79 000	61 000

We have collected all of the costs directly incurred by each of the three departments. Next, we need to apportion overhead costs that cannot be allocated.

APPORTIONMENT OF OVERHEADS

Apportionment of overheads is the sharing of overheads between all cost centres that benefit from the overhead expense. Apportioned overheads relate to two or more departments/cost centres and the costs must be shared out between them on the most appropriate and reasonable basis. The reasons for sharing out the overheads will depend on the nature of the expense. Common ones include:

Overhead expense	Basis of apportionment
Rent and rates	Floor area occupied by department
Building insurance	Floor area occupied by department
Heating and lighting	Floor area occupied by department
Maintenance costs	Cost or carrying value per department
Building depreciation	Floor area occupied by department
Depreciation of machinery and equipment	Cost or carrying value per department
Supervisory wages	Number of employees in the department
Raw materials store	Number of requisitions made by department
Staff canteen	Number of employees in the department

When overhead costs are apportioned, they must be done in a ratio so that each department benefits from that cost.

WORKED EXAMPLE

Az Manufacturing has three departments: machining, assembly and painting. We will apportion the cost of buildings insurance and depreciation, determine the ratios in which to share out the costs of building insurance and work out depreciation using the information below.

The following information is now available after the allocation of costs:

- The total buildings insurance for the year is £24 000 and the factory machinery and equipment depreciation charge was £28 000.
- The floor space occupied by each department is:

    Machining   400 m²

    Assembly   600 m²

    Painting   200 m²

- The carrying value of machinery and equipment in each department is:

Machining	£70 000
Assembly	£17 500
Painting	£35 000

- The buildings insurance ratio is machinery : assembly : painting = 2 : 3 : 1, based on the occupied floor space expressed as a ratio. Therefore, the costs apportioned to each department are:

Machining	£8 000
Assembly	£12 000
Painting	£4 000
Total	£24 000

- Depreciation ratio is machinery : assembly : painting = 4 : 1 : 2, based on the carrying value of the machinery. Therefore, the costs apportioned to each department are:

Machining	£16 000
Assembly	£4 000
Painting	£8 000
Total	£28 000

These costs would then be added to the previously allocated costs of the department:

Cost	£ Machining	£ Assembly	£ Painting
Direct materials	120 000	37 000	5 000
Direct labour	65 000	30 000	25 000
Indirect labour	12 000	12 000	6 000
Rent of building			25 000
Allocated costs	197 000	79 000	61 000
Apportioned costs:			
Buildings insurance	8 000	12 000	4 000
Depreciation	16 000	4 000	8 000
	221 000	95 000	73 000

All of the costs of Az Manufacturing have now been allocated and apportioned to the individual cost centres – machining, assembly and painting.

EXAM HINT

In the examination, you will be provided with apportionment bases, but not told which overhead costs they apply to. You should select the most appropriate from the context of the question.

Usually, there is no requirement for a totals column, but it is always useful to check that the total costs after apportionment equal the total costs before the process.

ACTIVITY 2   SKILLS   ANALYSIS, PROBLEM SOLVING

CASE STUDY: THISARA ELECTRICALS

Thisara Electricals manufactures small electronic components. The business has three departments: plastic moulding, electrical and assembly. The following information is available:

Allocated overheads:

	£
Plastic moulding	49 000
Electrical	54 000
Assembly	27 000

Other overheads:

	£
Insurance	14 000
Rent and rates	10 000
Equipment depreciation	14 000
Management salaries	45 000

Additional information:

	Plastic moulding	Electrical	Assembly
Floor area (m²)	300	150	50
Equipment (£)	40 000	200 000	40 000
Employees (no.)	6	10	2

1 Calculate the total overhead cost for the three production departments.

ABSORPTION OF OVERHEADS

Once all of the costs have been allocated and apportioned to a cost centre, the total overhead cost must then be charged to an individual cost unit. This is known as absorption.

To achieve this, a business will use an **overhead absorption rate (OAR)**. It is normal practice to absorb overheads on the basis of budgeted figures rather than actual overheads. This allows a business to calculate the total costs for products and prepare customer quotations for future work. The method of determining the OAR is:

$$OAR = \frac{\text{Budgeted cost centre overheads (£)}}{\text{Budgeted work in cost centre}}$$

The most common methods of budgeted work in a cost centre are:
- labour hours worked
- machine hours.

The choice of method will depend on the nature of the manufacturing process. Labour hours would be used if the manufacturing process was labour intensive; alternatively, if the process was capital intensive then the machine hours approach would be used.

WORKED EXAMPLE

Az Manufacturing, with their three departments of machining, assembly and painting, absorb their overhead expenses on the following basis:
- machining uses the machine hours method of absorption
- assembly uses the labour hours method of absorption
- painting uses the machine hours method.

Az Manufacturing have planned the following budgeted hours:
- machinery = machine hours per annum = 25 000
- assembly = labour hours per annum = 37 000
- painting = machine hours per annum = 10 500

Az Manufacturing have budgeted overheads of:
- machinery = £235 000
- assembly = £110 000
- painting = £68 000

We will calculate the overhead absorption rate (OAR) for each department:

$$\text{Machinery OAR} = \frac{\text{Total overhead cost}}{\text{Budgeted machine hours}}$$

$$= \frac{£235\,000}{25\,000 \text{ hours}}$$

$$= £9.40 \text{ per machine hour}$$

$$\text{Assembly OAR} = \frac{\text{Total overhead cost}}{\text{Budgeted labour hours}}$$

$$= \frac{£110\,000}{37\,000 \text{ hours}}$$

$$= £2.97 \text{ per labour hour}$$

$$\text{Painting OAR} = \frac{\text{Total overhead cost}}{\text{Budgeted machine hours}}$$

$$= \frac{£68\,000}{10\,500 \text{ hours}}$$

$$= £6.48 \text{ per machine hour}$$

ACTIVITY 3   SKILLS   ANALYSIS, PROBLEM SOLVING
CASE STUDY: DASUN

Dasun is an online travel review site which has two departments: A and B. Department A has a total budgeted overhead for the year of £255 450 and Department B has a total budgeted overhead of £144 350.

Department A employs four staff, working 40 hours per week for 48 weeks per year.

Department B employs five staff, working 35 hours per week for 48 weeks per year.

1 Calculate the overhead absorption rate per labour hour for each department.

APPORTIONMENT AND CONTINUOUS ALLOTMENT OF SERVICE DEPARTMENTS

The process of allocating overhead expenses to cost centres is relatively straightforward, since the costs are usually identifiable to a specific department within the business. Where overhead costs are consumed by more than one department, the process is more complex – they need to be shared on a fair basis. We saw earlier, for Az Manufacturing, how this could be achieved with some degree of accuracy with the identification of a basis for apportionment.

REAPPORTIONMENT OF SERVICE DEPARTMENT COSTS

There is, however, one more stage that may be needed before all costs can be absorbed. It is quite common for manufacturing companies to have both production departments and service departments. Service departments do not make products but support production departments. Examples include stores, maintenance and a staff canteen. They may store raw material inventory and possibly work-in-progress inventory for use in the production process.

The costs of operating these service departments must be apportioned to the production departments so that all costs are absorbed. Essentially, the production departments must pay for the services provided by the service departments. As with the earlier apportionment process, a suitable basis needs to be established so that the costs can be shared out. There are three methods used to reapportion service centre costs to production departments.

1 Direct apportionment

This method is used where service departments provide services to the production departments only.

WORKED EXAMPLE

Dinesh has two production departments – machining and assembly. In addition, a small maintenance department supports the work of the two production departments. The following cost information has been recorded after all costs have been allocated and absorbed into the three departments:

	£
Machining	340 000
Assembly	250 000
Maintenance	55 000

The carrying value of non-current assets in each production department is:

Machining	£110 000
Assembly	£66 000

We will reapportion the total overheads of the service department to the production departments.

The basis for the apportionment of the maintenance costs is the value of the non-current assets. It might have been the hours worked by maintenance in the two production departments.

	£ Machining	£ Assembly	£ Maintenance
Apportioned costs	340 000	250 000	55 000
Maintenance apportioned	34 375	20 625	(55 000)
Total	374 375	270 625	NIL

$$\text{Machining} = £55\,000 \times \frac{£110\,000}{£176\,000} = £34\,375$$

$$\text{Assembly} = £55\,000 \times \frac{£66\,000}{£176\,000} = £20\,625$$

We can now see that the total costs are the same (£645 000), before and after the apportionment of the maintenance costs to the production departments. Dinesh can now absorb these costs into the product cost.

This process of reapportionment is relatively straightforward – there is only one service department, so the costs can be shared out in a single step. However, some service departments may provide a service to other service departments. Therefore, some of the cost of one service department may need to be apportioned to another service department, rather than just to the production departments. A second method could be used to achieve this reapportionment.

2 The step-down method

This approach is used when one service department uses the services of a second service department, but the second service department does not use the services of the first department.

WORKED EXAMPLE

Dinesh has expanded his business and now operates a canteen for his employees. The following cost information is available:

	£
Machining	340 000
Assembly	250 000
Maintenance	55 000
Canteen	30 000

The carrying value of non-current assets in each production department is:

Machining	£110 000
Assembly	£66 000

The number of employees in each department is:

Machining	12
Assembly	18
Maintenance	6
Canteen	3

The company apportions the canteen cost according to number of employees in each department.

We will reapportion the total overheads to the production departments using the step-down method.

The first step is to reapportion the costs of the canteen as it does NOT receive any service from the maintenance department. Using the number of employees as the basis for apportionment, we share out the costs as follows:

Canteen cost £30 000, in the ratio of machining : assembly : maintenance = 2 : 3 : 1.

Maintenance costs have now increased by £5 000 and the new total of £60 000 is reapportioned to the two production departments.

Step 1: Apportion the canteen department overhead first, since part of the overhead cost will be apportioned to maintenance department.

Step 2: Apportion the maintenance department overhead because this includes the apportionment of cost from the canteen department. This ensures the overhead cost in the maintenance department is the most accurate.

	£	£	£	£
	Machining	**Assembly**	**Maintenance**	**Canteen**
Apportioned costs	340 000	250 000	55 000	30 000
Canteen	10 000	15 000	5 000	(30 000)
Maintenance	37 500	22 500	(60 000)	
Total overheads	387 500	287 500	nil	nil

Once again, all overhead costs have been apportioned ready for absorption in the cost of the individual profit. Dinesh has apportioned the cost of the canteen into all departments that have used it, including the service cost centre – maintenance – and has then reapportioned the maintenance department costs to the two remaining production cost centres – machining and assembly.

A further complication could take place. It is possible that some service departments could provide services to other service departments and receive a service back from that department. This requires a third method of reapportionment.

Always start with the apportionment from the department that requires apportionment of its overhead cost to service department.

3 The continuous allotment method

This method is used when a service department provides a service to another service department, and the latter responds in kind. This method is also known as the reciprocal method. Using this approach, costs for a service department will be eliminated as they are apportioned to other departments but will receive some cost from the next service department to be apportioned as they use that department and so must share some of the cost. This cost will then be apportioned again, and the process repeated until the balance remaining is immaterial.

In our example, it is probable that the canteen will require the services of the maintenance department in order to function efficiently.

WORKED EXAMPLE

Dinesh had provided some additional information relating to his business. His total overhead costs remain the same at:

	£
Machining	340 000
Assembly	250 000
Maintenance	55 000
Canteen	30 000

The carrying value of non-current assets in each production department has been updated:

Canteen	£ 24 000
Machining	£110 000
Assembly	£ 66 000

The number of employees in each department is:

Machining	12
Assembly	18
Maintenance	6
Canteen	3

We will reapportion the total overheads to the production departments using the continuous method.

First, reapportion the canteen, using the number of employees as the basis for the apportionment – £30 000 in the ration 2:3:1 as before.

Next, reapportion the maintenance costs to the three other departments using the carrying value of non-current assets as the basis.

To calculate each department:

Canteen $£60\,000 \times \dfrac{24\,000}{200\,000} = \underline{£7\,200}$

Machining $£60\,000 \times \dfrac{110\,000}{200\,000} = \underline{£33\,000}$

Assembly $£60\,000 \times \dfrac{66\,000}{200\,000} = \underline{£19\,800}$

Having reapportioned these costs, we find that the canteen now has £7 200 of cost that needs to be reapportioned using the same basis and ratio as before (2:3:1). After this reapportionment, the new maintenance department costs need to be reapportioned, again using the same basis and ratio. Continuing the allotment, the £144 of canteen overhead is once again reapportioned.

The final step would be to reapportion the £24 remaining in the maintenance department. As the figure is not material, it is prudent to just reapportion this to the production departments.

Finally, it is good practice to check the closing totals equal the opening totals. That way you can be sure all costs have been reapportioned.

	Machining £	Assembly £	Maintenance £	Canteen £
Apportioned costs	340 000	250 000	55 000	30 000
Canteen	10 000	15 000	5 000	(30 000)
Maintenance	33 000	19 800	(60 000)	7 200
Canteen	2 400	3 600	1 200	(7 200)
Maintenance	660	396	(1 200)	144
Canteen	48	72	24	(144)
Maintenance	15	9	(24)	
Total overheads	386 123	288 877	nil	nil

Using the continuous allotment method, the figure towards the end of the process will become smaller and smaller. Following the concepts of materiality and prudence, these small amounts remaining in the service departments can be apportioned to the production departments. Finally, some rounding of figure is often required when using the continuous allotment method.

ACTIVITY 4   SKILLS ANALYSIS, PROBLEM SOLVING

CASE STUDY: KUSAL CARPETS

Kusal Carpets manufactures carpets in two production departments – colouring and manufacturing. It has two service departments – stores and maintenance. The following information is available for the year ended 31 December 2019:
- Total overheads for the departments will be:

	£
Colouring	105 000
Manufacturing	75 500
Stores	24 000
Maintenance	36 000

- The use of the two service departments have been estimated to be:

	Colouring	Manufacturing	Stores	Maintenance
Stores	60%	20%		20%
Maintenance	50%	40%	10%	

1 Using the continuous allotment method, reapportion the total overheads of the service departments to the production departments.

OVER ABSORPTION AND UNDER ABSORPTION OF OVERHEADS

Since overhead recovery rates are based on budgeted figures for overhead costs and activity levels, the actual figure will be either higher or lower than planned. If this happens the OAR used will be inaccurate.

In our example, the machinery OAR was £8.84 per hour. A job taking three hours would be charged at 3 × £8.84 = £26.52 for overheads, so £26.52 of overheads would have been recovered (absorbed) by that job.

Over absorption or under absorption is the difference between the total amount of overheads recovered and the total amount spent on overheads in the year. If the overheads absorbed are greater than the actual overheads, then overheads have been over absorbed. If the overheads absorbed are less than actual overheads, this is called under absorption.

WORKED EXAMPLE

For Az Manufacturing, the following information is available for the year for the machinery department:

	Budgeted	Actual
Overheads (£)	£221 000	£229 000
Machine hours	25 000	24 000

The OAR was calculated at £8.84 per hour (£221 000 ÷ 25 000).

Using the actual activity level of 24 000 hours at £8.84 per hour, we can calculate the total overheads absorbed in the period as £212 160. However, the actual overheads were £229 000.

Therefore, under absorbed overheads = £229 000 – £212 160 = £16 840.

WORKED EXAMPLE

Let us look at the example from Dinesh again. The following is available:

	£	£	£	£
	Machining	Assembly	Maintenance	Canteen
Apportioned costs	340 000	250 000	55 000	30 000
Canteen	10 000	15 000	5 000	(30 000)
Maintenance	33 000	19 800	(60 000)	7 200
Canteen	2 400	3 600	1 200	(7 200)
Maintenance	660	396	(1 200)	144
Canteen	48	72	24	(144)
Maintenance	15	9	(24)	
Total overheads	386 123	288 877	nil	nil

The machining department uses the number of machine hours to charge overheads, while direct labour hours are used to charge overheads incurred in the assembly department.

The following additional information is available for the year for the machining and assembly departments:

	Machining (hours)	Assembly (hours)
Budgeted machine hours	100 000	4 000
Budgeted labour hours	5 000	200 000
Actual machine hours	150 000	8 000
Actual labour hours	3 000	220 000
Actual overhead (£)	370 000	320 000

In this case, the overhead absorption rate (OAR) for each department is:

Machining OAR	Assembly OAR
Budgeted overhead ÷ Budgeted machine hours	Budgeted overhead ÷ Budgeted labour hours
£386 123 ÷ 100 000 hours = £3.86 per machine hour*	£288 877 ÷ 200 000 labour hours = £1.44 per labour hour*

*to two decimal places

The actual overhead is:

Machining	Assembly
OAR (machining dept) × Basis for absorption – Machine hours	OAR (assembly dept) × Basis for absorption – Labour hours
£3.86 × 150 000 machine hours = £579 000	£1.44 × 220 000 labour hours = £316 800

From this, we can calculate the over absorption or the under absorption for each department:

Machining	Assembly
Actual overheads – Budgeted overheads	Actual overheads – Budgeted overheads
£370 000 – £579 000 = £209 000 over absorbed overheads	£320 000 – £316 800 = £3 200 under absorbed overheads

The accounting entries for over and under absorption are:

Over absorption:

Dr   Production overheads account
Cr   Statement of profit or loss and other comprehensive income

Under absorption:

Dr Statement of profit or loss and other comprehensive income

Cr Production overheads account

CAUSES OF OVER AND UNDER ABSORPTION

Over absorption:

- the activity level was higher than planned
- the actual level of overhead expense is lower than planned.

Under absorption:

- the activity level is lower than the budgeted plan
- the actual level of overhead expense is higher than planned.

In addition, causes of under and over absorption could include the original rate per hour being based on inaccurate figures.

EXAM HINT

Apply the concepts of materiality and prudence to a small remaining balance in a service department and apportion them to the production departments.

EVALUATE

The allocation and apportionment of overhead expenses appears to be a long process. It is therefore right that we should evaluate the usefulness of this process in determining the full operating costs of production departments.

Benefits of apportionment	Limitations of apportionment
Provides a realistic estimate of usage of costs by each department	The apportionment will only be an estimate of the usage and subsequent cost
Departmental rates can be calculated for pricing and quotations	Might be difficult to decide on a realistic basis for the apportionment so results are arbitrary
The basis for apportionment will ensure a realistic match between usage and the cost	Cost. A skilled accountant may be needed to calculate the apportionments with accuracy
All costs will be covered in any pricing decision	

CHECKPOINT

1 Explain the difference between a fixed cost and a semi-fixed cost.

2 Explain the difference between a semi-fixed cost and semi-variable cost.

3 Fixed costs never change. True or false?

4 Explain the difference between cost allocation and cost apportionment.

5 State three bases for the apportionment of overhead expenses.

6 State two methods of apportioning service department costs.

7 State two methods of calculating the overhead absorption rate (OAR).

8 Explain the meaning of the term over absorbed.

SUBJECT VOCABULARY

absorption the process of charging overhead expenses to cost units

apportionment the process by which overhead expenses are shared between departments

over absorption less overhead costs were incurred than were budgeted for

overhead absorption rate (OAR) the rate at which overhead expenses are absorbed to a cost unit, either direct labour hours or machine hours

production department where the product is manufactured, also referred to as a cost centre

reapportionment the process in which service department overheads are shared out to the production departments

service department a cost centre that supports a production department or other service departments

under absorption more actual overhead costs were incurred than were budgeted for

variable costs expenses that change in direct proportion to levels of activity/output

EXAM PRACTICE

CASE STUDY: MAJA

Maja manufactures components for electric guitars. There are three departments: two production departments – electrical assembly and final assembly – and one service department – stores and shipping. Maja has the following overheads:

- management salaries £20 000
- buildings insurance £10 000
- rent and rates £7 000
- employment insurance £6 000.

Additional information:

	Electrical assembly	Final assembly	Stores and shipping
Floor area (m²)	6 000	3 000	1 000
Direct labour hours (p.a.)	8 000	4 800	3 200

Stores and shipping costs are reapportioned on the basis of 75 per cent to electrical assembly and the rest to the final assembly.

Q

1 Explain the term variable cost. **(2 marks)**
2 Explain the difference between semi-fixed and semi-variable costs. **(4 marks)**
3 Explain the meaning of the term absorption of overheads. **(2 marks)**
4 Calculate the total overheads for each of the production departments. **(8 marks)**
5 Calculate the overhead recovery rate for each production department. **(4 marks)**
6 Evaluate the use of direct labour hours in calculating the OAR. **(6 marks)**

20 JOB COSTING

LEARNING OBJECTIVES

After you have studied this chapter, you should be able to:
- explain the characteristics of job costing
- prepare job costings for batch production and customer orders.

GETTING STARTED

A customer contacts your business for a quotation. How do you calculate the price? What profit will you require? How will you work out the total cost? You might have the direct material costs and the direct labour costs but how do you calculate the cost of the overhead expenses that need to be recovered?

CHARACTERISTICS OF JOB COSTING

Job costing can be defined as a method that divides up and shares out elements of cost to a job being done to a client's specific instructions. This method of costing is used in construction, engineering, printing, car repairs and other similar companies. The main aim of job costing is to identify all the costs associated with completing the order. The characteristics of job costing are:

- It is customer specific. The job or product is made to meet the specific requirements of the customer order. It could be a single unit of product or a batch of identical units.
- Each job is distinguishable. The work undertaken should be clearly distinguishable from other jobs.
- Separate records are maintained. They are often given a unique job number so that the work and costs can be identified as relating to that order. This job account will include direct material, direct labour and factory overheads. Selling and other expenditure will also be charged.
- A quotation is prepared and a job price agreed with the customer. This will include an element of profit.
- Each order will be of a relatively short time period.

JOB COSTING

Job costing effectively makes the product being made for the customer a cost centre to which all costs incurred are charged. Each job will be given a job number so that it can be identified.

The first stage in the costing process would be to identify the **prime cost** of the job. This would include the direct material cost, as well as the direct labour cost. Any direct expenses required for the job are also included. Next, the **overheads** need to be absorbed into the cost of the job using an appropriate overhead absorption rate (OAR) – either direct labour hours or machine hours.

The final stage in the process would be to add the required profit to the costs. This allows you to calculate the price for your customer, as a quotation:

Job cost = prime cost + overheads + profit

WORKED EXAMPLE

B&T Furniture Restorers offers an updating, maintenance and repair service for furniture. They have three departments: upholstery, woodworking and polishing.
- Raw materials are charged at purchase price plus 10 per cent mark-up.
- Labour rates are charged at the following rates:
  - upholstery, £8.00 per hour
  - woodworking, £9.00 per hour
  - polishing, £10.00 per hour.
- Overhead absorption rates (OAR) are:
  - upholstery, £3.50 per hour
  - woodworking, £5.60 per hour
  - polishing, £8.00 per hour.
- B&T operate a system of pricing based on a 20 per cent mark-up of the total cost.

A customer has requested a quotation for the repair and restoration of a piece of furniture. B&T have estimated the following:
- Raw materials: £85
- Direct labour:
  - upholstery 2 hours
  - woodworking 2.5 hours
  - polishing 3 hours.

We will prepare a quotation for the customer:

Quotation

		£	£
Raw materials	£85 + 10% of £85		93.50
Direct labour:			
Upholstery	£8.00 × 2 hrs	16.00	
Woodworking	£9.00 × 2.5 hr	22.50	
Polishing	£10.00 × 3 hrs	30.00	68.50
Overhead:			
Upholstery	£3.50 × 2 hrs	7.00	
Woodworking	£5.60 × 2.5 hrs	14.00	
Polishing	£8.00 × 3 hrs	24.00	45.00
			207.00
Profit	20% of £207.00		41.40
Quotation price			248.40

- Bespoke Furniture estimated the following production times:
  - woodworking 30 minutes per chair
  - polishing 45 minutes per chair
  - assembly 6 hours for the batch.

We will prepare a quotation for the customer and calculate the unit price of a chair:

Quotation

		£	£
Raw materials			2 485
Direct labour:			
Woodworking	£10.00 × 0.5 hr × 20	100	
Polishing	£15.00 × 0.75 hr × 20	225	
Assembly	£7.00 × 6 hrs	42	
			367
Overhead **(W1)***	£8.00 × 31 hrs		248
			3 100
Profit	20% of £3 100		620
Quotation price			3 720

*__W1__ overhead = £8 × 31 hrs total production time (0.5 × 20 + 0.75 × 20 + 6)

Price per chair = £3 720 ÷ 20 = £186

BATCH COSTING

Many businesses will produce their products in convenient batches. The number of products manufactured in a batch will depend on many factors. It may be 200 identical products for a customer, rather than just a single product. Batch costing will involve the cost of making the whole batch; it is very similar to job costing, but the whole batch is treated as single cost unit.

> Unit cost = Total cost ÷ No. units in the batch

WORKED EXAMPLE

Bespoke Furniture manufactures furniture to customer orders. A customer has requested a quotation for 20 original chairs. The business has estimated the following information:
- Materials cost £2 485
- Direct labour cost (per hour):
  - woodworking £10.00
  - polishing £15.00
  - assembly £7.00.
- The overhead absorption rate is £8.00, and the profit is 20 per cent mark-up.

ACTIVITY 1

SKILLS ANALYSIS, PROBLEM SOLVING

CASE STUDY: AERO-PARTZ

Aero-Partz manufactures components for the aircraft industry. A major customer has requested a small batch of a special component for one of their aeroplanes. The following information is available relating to how jobs are costed:
- Direct materials are purchased for the job plus 5 per cent mark-up.

- Direct labour (per hour):
  - machining department £15.00
  - electroplating £6.00
  - assembly £12.00.
- Direct expense – Aero-Partz charge any direct expense to the job at cost plus 20 per cent mark-up.
- Production overheads are recovered on the basis of direct labour at the rate of £22.00 per hour.
- Non-manufacturing overheads are charged at the total cost after production overheads plus 10 per cent.

The following information relates to the customer order:

- Raw material to the value of £2 900 will be purchased.
- The estimates for production time are as follows:
  - machining 8 hours
  - electroplating 7.5 hours
  - assembly 4 hours.
- In order to complete the job, Aero-Partz will hire in specialist tools at a cost of £150.

1 Calculate the total cost of the order.

ACTIVITY 2   SKILLS ▸ PROBLEM SOLVING, ANALYSIS

CASE STUDY: TACKY-TEES

Tacky-Tees make and supply t-shirts. They manufacture them in batches depending on the customer order. They have recently received an order from a music festival organiser, OBB, for 80 t-shirts for their staff.

- The labour costs are:
  - pattern cutting £8.50 per hour
  - sewing £8.20 per hour
  - screen-printing £11.00 per hour
  - finishing £8.00 per hour.
- The overhead absorption rate is a single rate for all departments of £5.36 per hour.
- The company policy is to add a 50 per cent mark-up to the total costs.

After reviewing the order, the following production times were estimated:
  - pattern cutting 1 hour
  - sewing 1.5 hours
  - screen-printing 2.5 hours
  - finishing 30 minutes.
- Material costs were estimated at £1.75 per t-shirt.

1 Prepare a job quotation for OBB for the 80 t-shirts.

EXAM HINT

Read all the information given in the question carefully. Job costing involves many separate calculations, some of which may come from previous calculations, especially the OAR.

EXAM HINT

Examiners will find it easier to mark your work if you arrange your work neatly, label the numbers and show your workings.

EVALUATE

In the examination, you may be asked to evaluate the usefulness of job costing. The following table identifies some benefits and limitations.

Advantages	Disadvantages
Allows for the calculation of profit earned on individual jobs	Requires a great deal of administrative work to keep records of all transactions that relate to the job
Provides a basis for estimating the cost of similar jobs in the future	Overhead absorption rates are based on estimates so may lead to errors when quoting a price for the job
Provides a detailed analysis of all costs for each job	Cannot be efficiently operated without effective production control system and factory organisation
Job costing is necessary for cost-plus orders where the price is worked out by the cost	The costs may be historic and out of date

CHECKPOINT

1 Identify four characteristics of job costing.

2 Explain the difference between job costing and batch costing.

3 State one advantage of job costing.

4 State one disadvantage of job costing.

5 Overheads are not included in the cost of a job. True or false?

SUBJECT VOCABULARY

batch costing a method of costing used when there are a number of identical products being made
job costing a system of costing that allocates and apportions costs to an individual customer order
overheads expenditure on labour, materials and services which cannot be identified with a specific cost unit/product
prime cost the total of all direct costs, materials, labour and expenses, incurred in the manufacture of a product

EXAM PRACTICE

CASE STUDY: PERFECT PRINTERS

SKILLS CRITICAL THINKING, PROBLEM SOLVING

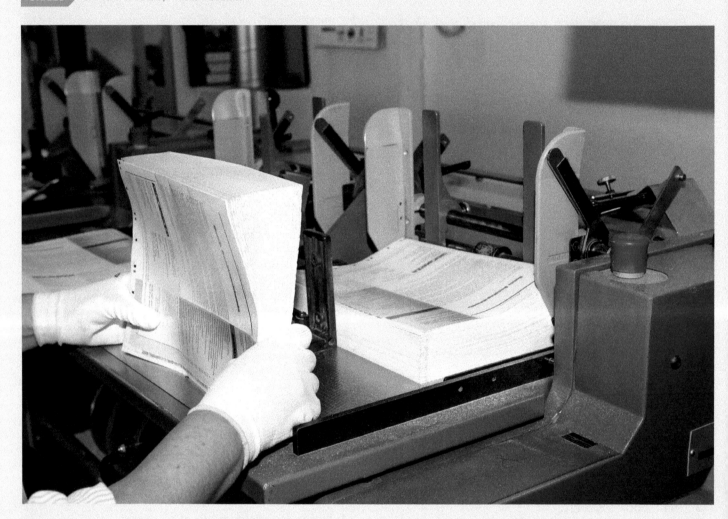

Perfect Printers provide printing services and have been asked to produce a small booklet for a local sports club. The club requires a quotation before an order is placed.

- The material costs are charged at cost plus 15 per cent.
- Labour costs are:
  - printing = £12.00 per hour
  - finishing = £8.00 per hour
- The overhead absorption rate is £8.20 per labour hour.

The estimates for the job are:

- material costs = £100.00
- labour costs:
  - printing = 3 hours
  - finishing = 1.5 hours.

Q

1 What is meant by the term job costing?   **(2 marks)**
2 Calculate the cost of the job.   **(6 marks)**

Perfect Printers normally add a mark-up of 20 per cent to the cost to arrive at a price for the quotation. However, as the club is a new customer, they have decided to reduce this to a 10 per cent mark-up.

3 Calculate the amount of profit Perfect Printers will forgo by reducing the mark-up.   **(4 marks)**

ANALYSIS OF ACCOUNTING STATEMENTS

The purpose of accounting is to record, analyse and communicate information to users (Chapter 1). Much of the information prepared by accountants is in the form of 'absolute' numbers which, in isolation, can be meaningless. If a business makes £50 000 profit in a year, is this good or bad? What use is it to users? If a business has current assets of £20 000, is this useful to a bank looking to lend money to a business? Clearly not. If users are to make sense of accounting information they must look at 'relative' information, which must be analysed before it becomes useful. The bank would want to know the level of current liabilities as well as current assets in order to decide whether the business had sufficient funds to make repayments.

The analysis of accounting statements using ratios allows the different users of accounting information to assess the strengths and weaknesses of a business, according to the needs of the individual user group.

21 RATIOS

LEARNING OBJECTIVES

After you have studied this chapter, you should be able to:
- calculate ratios for profitability, use of assets and liquidity
- apply ratios to the appraisal of sole trader and partnership performance
- use ratios to make future financial projections.

GETTING STARTED

You have some savings and are thinking of investing the money into a business. Your friend has shown you the profit for the year from two businesses that he works with. One made a profit for the year of £50 000, while the other made a profit for the year of £250 000. Which one would you invest in?

Your friend now tells you that the first business had a revenue for the year of £100 000 and had net assets of £10 000. The second business (the one that made a greater profit) had a revenue of several million pounds and has assets in the region of £10 million. Which business would you now wish to invest in? Has this additional information changed your decision?

INTRODUCTION

Ratio analysis is the calculation and comparison of ratios that come from the information in a business's financial statements. The ratios are used to examine the performance of a business over a period of time. They can also be used to compare the current year's performance with a previous year or with the performance of a similar business.

KEY FACTORS IN USING RATIOS

There are certain key factors that apply when using ratios.
- They provide a comparison between two or more variables in the accounts.
- They compare the results from two or more sets of accounts to show the trends and relationships that are not evident from the figures alone (in isolation, ratios provide very little information about the performance of a business).
- They allow us to compare the results with other businesses in the same industry, sector, or even in other sectors.

HOW ARE RATIOS USED?

Many ratios are available, so the question that should be asked is which ratio, or ratios, should be used? Different users have different needs, but the ratios cannot be considered in isolation. Ratios are used by companies, investors, lenders, analysts and competitors to provide additional information to that given in the financial statements.

One aspect of the accountant's work is to interpret statements in order to provide information to management. An important aspect of such interpretation is that ratios must always be considered in relation to other information.

We categorise different types of ratios into groups, because each group looks at a different aspect of behaviour in a business. Companies usually calculate as many ratios as they find useful in order to monitor their own performance. When outsiders look at the performance of a business, they normally use a few of the major ratios. Then, if a particular area seems to require further explanation, they will use other necessary ratios to draw conclusions.

When we compare ratios, there must be a relationship between the figures. They need to be relevant to each other to ensure that the ratio will have meaning. For example, if we compare the profit to cash at bank, there is no relevance in this comparison, and in such a case the ratio is meaningless.

LIMITATIONS OF RATIOS

Ratio analysis is a very useful tool, but it has its limitations.

- The financial statements are historic. The results are old, and things could have improved or got worse since the date of the statements. Take great care when you decide whether historic cost or inflation-adjusted data is used.
- Comparing the results of different businesses can be problematic as there are different methods of measuring charges against profit.
- There are different ways of valuing inventory and tangible and intangible non-current assets. These differences affect the comparative ratios between companies.
- Ratios calculated from information in the published statements may not be comparable. Notes added to the statements may give us information, allowing us to adjust the statements so that the figures are calculated on the same basis as those of another business but, in practice, this is not easy.
- When use is made of financial statements produced in different countries the problem is increased. Valuation methods may be different, and there may not be enough information. This issue has been improved by the introduction of International Accounting Standards.
- An acceptable ratio in some countries would be considered dangerous in others. This applies particularly to liquidity and gearing ratios. Comparison, therefore, must take account of these differences.

The ratios covered can be divided into three separate categories:

- profitability
- use of assets
- liquidity.

PROFITABILITY RATIOS

Profitability ratios measure performance and examine the extent of the profit in relation to the size of the business and the amount of capital invested. They allow an outsider to evaluate the effectiveness of management in the use of the many resources at its disposal.

In your study of this aspect of the course, you need to ensure that you are familiar with the way in which each ratio is worked out. This requires a comprehensive knowledge of the particular formula and an ability to do the calculations.

Gross profit as a percentage of revenue

$$\frac{\text{Gross profit}}{\text{Revenue}} \times 100$$

Using the above formula, we relate the gross profit to the turnover generated. A decrease in the gross profit could mean increased competition, increasing costs of purchases, or a bad pricing strategy. With high profit margins, it is easier to cover the expenses of a business, including interest charges, when there is a decline in income.

A simple example of the gross profit margin is given below.

WORKED EXAMPLE

Alex buys a clock for £25 and sells it for £35. What is the gross profit margin?

We calculate the gross profit by deducting the cost price from the selling price:

Selling price (£35) – cost (£25) = Gross profit (£10)

From this, we can calculate that the gross profit margin is:

$$\frac{10}{35} \times 100 = 28.6\%$$

Often, you are asked to work out the mark-up. In this case, we would use the following formula:

$$\frac{\text{Gross profit}}{\text{Cost of sales}} \times 100$$

Using the example above, we calculate this as:

$$\frac{10}{25} \times 100 = 40\%.$$

In other words, Alex makes a 40 per cent mark-up on the cost price of his goods.

Profit for the year as a percentage of revenue

$$\frac{\text{Profit for the year}}{\text{Revenue}} \times 100$$

This ratio compares the profit to revenue and does vary from one type of business to another. The profit for the year can be influenced by competition, economic climate and type of customer, so no definitive percentage can be set for this ratio.

If the ratio is high (or higher than last year's figure, or figures, from competitors), it may indicate that:
- the business has a good pricing policy, which leads to a higher gross profit margin
- the business has good control over the expenses, which lowers the proportion of expense to total revenue – for example, using energy-saving non-current assets to reduce the cost of electricity.

Return on capital employed (percentage) (ROCE)

$$\frac{\text{Profit before interest (PBI)}}{\text{Capital employed}} \times 100$$

For a sole trader or partnership, the capital employed is calculated as:

$$\text{Capital employed} = \text{Opening capital} + \text{Non-current liabilities (NCL)}$$

This ratio measures the effectiveness of using the owner's funds and long-term loans to produce sufficient profit. If a business has a high ROCE, it suggests that the business has used its funds effectively to generate profit, which means long-term funding providers may continue to provide funds to the business. Perhaps more importantly, it means that the owner or owners of the business are obtaining a good return on their investment in the business and will therefore not be looking to withdraw their funds from the business.

WORKED EXAMPLE

Company A buys and sells furniture. The following information is provided in order to calculate accounting ratios:

Statement of profit or loss and other comprehensive income for the year ended 30 September 2018 (extract)

	£	£
Revenue		120 000
Cost of sales		40 000
Gross profit		80 000
Less expenses		
General expenses	25 000	
Bank loan interest	5 000	
Wages	10 000	40 000
Profit for the year		40 000

Additional information provided:
- capital = £80 000
- bank loan (repayable 2025) = £50 000.

We will calculate the gross profit as a percentage of revenue, profit for the year as a percentage of revenue, and the return on capital employed (percentage). Our workings are shown in the table:

Gross profit as a percentage of revenue:		
$\dfrac{\text{Gross profit}}{\text{Revenue}} \times 100$	$\dfrac{80\,000}{120\,000} \times 100$	= 66.67%

Profit for the year as a percentage of revenue:		
$\dfrac{\text{Profit for year}}{\text{Revenue}} \times 100$	$\dfrac{40\,000}{120\,000} \times 100$	= 33.33%

Return on capital employed (percentage):		
$\dfrac{\text{Profit before interest}}{\text{Capital employed}} \times 100$	$\dfrac{40\,000 + 5\,000}{80\,000 + 50\,000} \times 100$	= 34.61%

USE OF ASSETS RATIO

Ratio of non-current assets to revenue

$$\frac{\text{Revenue}}{\text{Non-current assets}}$$

In this formula, 'non-current assets' means the carrying value of all non-current assets and is expressed as a ratio, for example, 2.5 : 1. It measures how much revenue is generated for every £1 of non-current assets in the business. Using the data above, we are given the additional information: non-current assets carrying value = £50 000.

Non-current assets to revenue:

Revenue / Non-current assets	120 000 / 50 000	= 2.4 : 1

LIQUIDITY RATIOS

This selection of ratios deals with the relationship between assets and liabilities. It measures a business's immediate ability to pay its short-term debts. In calculating the various ratios in this section, we must note that there are certain current assets, such as inventory, which may not be readily convertible into cash. It is for this reason that the quick ratio is used.

The key ratios within this group are:

- current (working capital) ratio
- liquid ratio, or acid test ratio.

Listed opposite are the formulae for calculating the liquidity ratios. Again, you should be familiar with the way in which each ratio is worked out. This requires a comprehensive knowledge of the formula and an ability to do the calculations.

WORKED EXAMPLE

The following information relating to assets and liabilities is available at 30 September 2018:

Statement of assets and liabilities at 30 September 2018 (extract)

	£	£
Inventory	22 500	
Trade receivables	80 000	
Prepaid expenses	10 000	
Trade payables	30 000	
Bank overdraft	15 000	

Our workings are shown in the table below:

Current (working capital) ratio:

Current assets / Current liabilities	$\dfrac{22\,500 + 80\,000 + 10\,000}{30\,000 + 15\,000}$	$= \dfrac{112\,500}{45\,000}$	= 2.5 : 1

Liquid ratio:

Current assets − Inventory / Current liabilities	$\dfrac{80\,000 + 10\,000}{30\,000 + 15\,000}$	$= \dfrac{90\,000}{45\,000}$	= 2 : 1

From the above calculation, we see that current liabilities are covered 2.5 times. Having worked out this ratio, we must consider if this is adequate. An acceptable ratio in one industry is not necessarily acceptable in another, so we look at similar businesses in the same industry to give us a guide. To establish a trend, we also look at the ratio for several past years. If we assume that 2 : 1 is reasonable, then we can make some comment on this ratio.

For the purposes of this example, let us assume that we are given the following ratios for Company A, as well as for the industry average, for the past three years. We are asked to assess how Company A is doing.

	2015	2016	2017
Company A	1.3 : 1	1.4 : 1	1.9 : 1
Industry average	1.9 : 1	1.7 : 1	2.1 : 1

It would appear that in 2018, the company is too liquid and needs to invest some of its surplus funds in more profitable areas. This is demonstrated by the fact that the current (working capital) ratio is increasing all the time.

Current (working capital) ratio

$$\frac{\text{Current assets}}{\text{Current liabilities}}$$

Liquid ratio (acid test)

$$\frac{\text{Current assets} - \text{inventory}}{\text{Current liabilities}}$$

Both these ratios are always expressed as a true ratio, e.g. 3 : 1

Profitability ratios are extremely important, but if a business's cash flow is inadequate, it will not be able to continue trading, no matter how much profit it makes. Liquidity ratios are, therefore, key in understanding the viability of any business.

The differences between current (working capital) ratio and liquid ratio are:

- Current (working capital) ratio measures the ability of repaying current liabilities within the next 12 months from current assets.
- Liquid ratio measures the ability to repay current liabilities that are due in the very short term (one or two months, and certainly within the time taken to collect the amounts due from trade receivables). This ratio provides a safer view of liquidity since inventory is not included. This means if all suppliers were asking for payment in the immediate future, the business can use the acid-test ratio to determine whether there are sufficient liquid assets to pay off those liabilities.

A high liquidity ratio indicates poor management of resources. Adequate working capital is essential, but too much is unnecessary and does not generate extra profits.

The next step is to examine the liquidity situation. If all trade payables demanded payment at once, would Company A be able to meet its obligations? We can answer this by using the acid-test ratio. We can see from our calculation above that the ratio is 2 : 1.

The result is good, as 1 : 1 is normally regarded as the minimum figure required for this ratio. Again, we need to look at the trend to make sure that it is not consistently downwards, as this could eventually prove dangerous to the future success of the business – it could have insufficient liquid funds to pay its immediate debts.

When analysing changes to the current (working capital) ratio, it is important to understand that it will only change due to an increase in current assets or current liabilities, or a decrease in current assets or current liabilities. For example, an increase in current assets could be due to:

- extra capital contribution leading to an increase in bank balance

- having more goods sold either by cash or on credit
- purchasing more inventory
- sale of non-current assets for cash.

If the two ratios are increasing, it would indicate that the business will be able to pay its short-term debts (the trade payables) with ease. However, the increase would also indicate that the business has idle funds in the business (bank and cash) which it is not using to generate profit.

If the ratios are decreasing, it would indicate that the business might be unable to pay its short-term debts. However, it could be argued that it is making better use of its resources to generate profit.

In the examination, it is best to avoid generic answers to liquidity ratio questions. There is no ideal ratio. The most appropriate ratio for a business will depend on many factors. It is important that you use the figures you are given to make a judgement on whether the ratios calculated are good or bad.

EXAM HINT

When writing answers to current (working capital) ratio and liquid ratio calculations always express your answer as **n:1**.

RATE OF INVENTORY TURNOVER

$$\frac{\text{Cost of sales}}{\text{Average inventory}} = \text{Number of times a year}$$

Where average inventory =
$$\frac{\text{Opening inventory} + \text{Closing inventory}^*}{2}$$

*If both inventory figures are not available, use the closing balance figure from the statement of financial position.

The rate of turnover measures how quickly inventory passes through the business. The faster we turn our inventory over, the smaller the amount of inventory we need to hold. This reduces storage costs and releases capital for other forms of investment.

The formula measures the cost of sales against the average inventory of finished goods. Inventory values are always at cost (or occasionally at net realisable value, if lower), therefore, we need to measure average inventory against cost of sales.

If the rate of inventory turnover is increasing, it would indicate that:

- the business is selling more inventory, possibly due to successful marketing activities
- it has introduced a better procedure to purchase inventory to avoid stockpiling too much inventory in the warehouse.

TRADE PAYABLES PAYMENT PERIOD

$$\frac{\text{Trade payables}}{\text{Credit purchases}} \times 365$$

If this increases it may signify cash-flow problems.

TRADE RECEIVABLES COLLECTION PERIOD

$$\frac{\text{Trade receivables}}{\text{Credit sales}} \times 365$$

If the number of days increases, then it could be because of a lack of invoicing, slow payments, irrecoverable debts or market competition forcing increased terms.

In the above calculations, if we multiply by 12 instead of 365, then the collection period is expressed in terms of months. If we multiply by 52, it is expressed in weeks. Always make sure you state exactly what the result is; that is, is it a percentage, a number of days, or the number of weeks? Do not just leave a number without stating what it is.

Ideally, the figures used for trade receivables and trade payables should be an average figure for the year, as the statement of financial position figures may not be representative.

RELATIONSHIP BETWEEN TRADE RECEIVABLES COLLECTION PERIOD, TRADE PAYABLES PAYMENT PERIOD AND LIQUIDITY

The longer the trade receivables collection period, the worse it will affect the cash flow, since it takes a longer time to collect cash from trade receivables. This reveals poor credit control – customers are allowed to purchase goods on credit without the business ensuring prompt payment.

A long trade payable payment period has a positive impact on the cash flow, but it reveals to suppliers that the business has a liquidity problem and, as a result, it may not supply goods to the business on credit anymore. This can lead to an even poorer liquidity result because purchases of inventory may need to be made in cash.

In summary, if the trade receivable collection period is shorter than the trade payable payment period, it will have a positive impact on liquidity. The business also needs to bear in mind that the trade payable payment period should not be too long because this will ensure that suppliers continue to supply the purchases made by the business on credit rather than insisting on cash.

WORKED EXAMPLE

We now use the information for Dula to calculate the ratios discussed above:

- At 1 October 2017, the opening inventory was given as £17 500.
- Credit transactions for the year ended 30 September 2018:
  - sales revenue, £400 000
  - purchases, £285 000

Our workings are shown in the table below:

Dula: statement of assets and liabilities at 30 September 2018 (extract)

	£	£
Inventory	22 500	
Trade receivables	80 000	
Prepaid expenses	10 000	
Trade payables	30 000	
Bank overdraft	15 000	

Rate of inventory turnover:

$\dfrac{\text{Cost of sales}}{\text{Average inventory}}$	$\dfrac{17\,500 + 285\,000 - 22\,500}{(17\,500 + 22\,500) \div 2}$	= 14 times

Trade payables payment period:

$\dfrac{\text{Trade payables}}{\text{Credit purchases}} \times 365$	$\dfrac{30\,000}{285\,000} \times 365$	= 38.42 days

Trade receivables collection period:

$\dfrac{\text{Trade receivables}}{\text{Credit sales}} \times 365$	$\dfrac{80\,000}{400\,000} \times 365$	= 73 days

We now need to interpret the ratios. This is difficult to do in isolation. So, for the purposes of this example, let us assume that we are given the ratios that Dula calculated last year plus the industry averages.

	Dula 2016–17	Industry average 2016–17
Rate of inventory turnover	12 times	12 times
Trade payables payment period	45 days	48 days
Trade receivables collection period	65 days	55 days

The rate of inventory turnover is an important ratio because a great deal of the liquidity of the company depends on the amount of inventory carried in a business. We can see from the figures that Dula has improved the rate and now has a rate that is better than the industry average. A decreasing rate of inventory turnover not only means that holding costs have risen, it may also mean that there is increased competition, or that the demand for products is no longer as great.

Looking at the trade payables payment period, we can see that Dula is paying the trade payables quicker than in previous years and quicker than any competitors. Paying quicker might improve relations with suppliers but may affect the liquidity of the business.

The trade receivables collection period has worsened over the past year and is well above that achieved by Dula's competitors. Additionally, it is over 35 days longer than the trade payables collection period and could indicate future liquidity problems because cash is flowing out of the business and then taking a long time to flow into the business. This could increase the likelihood of future irrecoverable debts.

ACTIVITY 1   SKILLS   ANALYSIS, PROBLEM SOLVING, EXECUTIVE FUNCTION

CASE STUDY: FELIPE

Felipe buys and sell components for motor vehicles. He has provided the following financial statements; all revenue and purchases are on credit:

Felipe: summary statement of profit or loss and other comprehensive income for the year ended 30 November 2017

	£	£
Revenue		75 000
Opening inventory	4 500	
Purchases	54 000	
Closing inventory	4 000	
Cost of sales		54 500
Gross profit		20 500
Expenses		
Bank loan interest	2 000	
General expenses	5 000	
Carriage out	1 000	8 000
Profit for the year		12 500

Felipe: statement of financial position at 30 September 2017

	£	£
Non-current assets: carrying value		30 000
Current assets		
Inventory	4 000	
Trade receivables	5 000	
Bank and cash	5 000	14 000
Total assets		44 000
Capital		8 500
Profit		12 500
Non-current liabilities: bank loan		20 000
Current liabilities		
Trade payables	3 000	3 000
Capital and liabilities		44 000

1 Calculate the following ratios:
   (a) gross profit as a percentage of revenue
   (b) profit for the year as a percentage of revenue
   (c) return on capital employed (percentage)
   (d) revenue to non-current assets
   (e) current (working capital) ratio
   (f) liquid ratio
   (g) rate of inventory turnover (times)
   (h) trade payables payment period
   (i) trade receivables collection period.

APPRAISING FINANCIAL STATEMENTS

It is one thing to calculate a ratio, it is another to be able to interpret the result in the context of business performance. The numbers by themselves are meaningless; if they are to have real significance they need to be compared with a benchmark to decide whether they are good or bad. The benchmark can be:
- a comparison with previous years
- a comparison with competitors.

WORKED EXAMPLE

Ariana Clothing is hoping to expand the business soon and is looking for additional funding. The following ratios have been provided so that an appraisal of the business can be made by potential investors:

Ratio	2018	2017	Sector averages
Gross profit as a percentage of revenue	45	43	55
Profit for the year as a percentage of revenue	25	24	28
Return on capital employed (percentage)	16	17	20
Revenue to non-current assets	2:1	2.1:1	2.2:1
Current (working capital) ratio	2:1	2.5:1	1.9:1
Liquid ratio	1:1	1.5:1	1.2:1
Rate of inventory turnover (times)	21	23	18
Trade payables payment period (days)	36	33	35
Trade receivables collection period (days)	29	35	25

Assessing the performance of Ariana Clothing

In terms of profitability, we can see that both the gross profit percentage and profit for the year percentage have increased, but only slightly. The increase in gross profit percentage may have been the result of higher prices, whilst the increase in profit for the year percentage may have been a result of improvements in controlling expenses. Both can be seen as positives for potential investors. However, both remain below the industry averages, which may indicate room for further improvement. The return on capital employed has fallen, and with the fall the revenue to non-current assets might mean that resources are not being used efficiently within the business.

In terms of liquidity, both the current (working capital) ratio and the liquid ratio appear to be improving and are now much closer to the sector averages. The trade payables payment period has increased by three days which will have helped with cash flow, whilst the reduction in the trade receivables collection period shows a greater control over amounts owed to the business and improved debt collection procedures.

EVALUATING RATIOS

By calculating and analysing financial ratios, trends can be identified. These trends can be used to make future financial projections and forecasts. Examination questions on ratios can be straightforward calculations of ratios, with a brief interpretation of what they mean, or can they can be evaluative, open-ended questions where you are required to make judgements about the performance of the business over two years or more. Depending on the focus of the question, you need to be able to identify the most relevant ratios and evaluate these in the context you have been given. In the example above, Ariana Clothing, perhaps profitability was the most relevant to the situation, as the business was seeking additional finance.

EXAM HINT

In the examination, calculate the ratios to two decimal places unless you are told differently.

As well as describing what has happened to the ratio, explain whether it has improved or worsened.

ACTIVITY 2

SKILLS ANALYSIS, PROBLEM SOLVING, EXECUTIVE FUNCTION

CASE STUDY: CALCULATOR LTD

You are presented with the following information for Calculator Ltd for the year ended 31 December 2019:

Statement of financial position data	£	£
	2018	2019
Non-current assets	9 650	9 530
Current assets including trade receivables	11 470	12 424
Trade receivables included above	4 800	4 200
Current liabilities	4 720	4 954
Trade payables included above	4 420	4 562
Non-current liabilities	6 000	1 200
Capital	5 700	6 028
Profit	4 700	9 772

Profit or loss data	£	£
	2018	2019
Revenue	44 800	52 620
Opening inventory	4 820	6 000
Purchases	37 080	42 840
Closing inventory	6 000	7 400
Cost of sales	35 900	41 440
Gross profit	8 900	11 180
Finance costs	480	130
Profit after interest but before tax	4 345	5 464
Profit for the year	4 224	5 312

The following notes apply to the information above and must be taken into account in your calculations:

- All purchases and sales are made on credit.

1 Calculate (to the nearest one decimal place) the following ratios for the years 2018 and 2019:
   (a) gross profit as a percentage of revenue
   (b) net profit for the year as a percentage of revenue
   (c) return on capital employed
   (d) current (working capital) ratio
   (e) liquid ratio
   (f) inventory turnover
   (g) trade payables payment period
   (h) trade receivables collection period
   (i) revenue to non-current assets.

EVALUATE

Ratio analysis provides many opportunities for the examiner to ask evaluative questions about the financial performance of a business. The best analysis and evaluation of the ratios will not overcome the issue that ratios, as well as having benefits, also come with limitations which should not be ignored. So, just how useful are ratios in working out the performance of a business?

Benefits of ratio analysis	Limitations of ratio analysis
They provide a basis for comparing performance year on year.	They do not consider non-financial factors such as the workforce, social and ethical issues.
They enable comparisons to be made with competitors.	Ratios use historic data, which may not reflect future performance.
They may focus management attention on key areas such as profitability and liquidity.	Some level of expertise is required to accurately analyse and evaluate the ratios correctly.
Ratios will help a business forecast future performance.	Different businesses may use different accounting policies when calculating ratios.
Ratios are useful to external users of financial information who do not require detailed information.	

CHECKPOINT

1 Ratios provide a comparison between two or more variables in the accounts. True or false?

2 Ratios are only used by internal users of accounting information. True or false?

3 What is the difference between a profitability ratio and a liquidity ratio?

4 What does the return on capital employed (percentage) measure?

5 What is the difference between the liquid ratio and the current (working capital) ratio?

6 How is average inventory calculated?

7 State the formula for the trade payables payment period.

8 Cash sales are included in the calculation of the trade receivables collection period. True or false?

9 Explain why an increase in the current (working capital) ratio may not be good.

SUBJECT VOCABULARY

liquidity the ability to convert assets into sufficient cash to meet everyday commitments
profitability ratios a relative measure of the profit generated

EXAM PRACTICE

CASE STUDY: PIERRE

SKILLS ▶ EXECUTIVE FUNCTION, PROBLEM SOLVING, ANALYSIS

Pierre commenced trading on 1 August 2017 selling mobile phone accessories. He started the business with £6 000 of his own savings and a 5 per cent bank loan of £2 000, repayable in 2021. He was able to provide the following information at the end of his first year of trading:

	£
Equipment	3 000
Revenue	30 000
Purchases	16 000
General expenses	6 000
Inventory	2 000

Pierre has decided to depreciate his equipment at the rate of 10 per cent per annum using the straight line method, with a full year in the year of purchase being charged. At the end of the year, all interest owing on the loan was outstanding.

1. Prepare a statement of profit or loss and other comprehensive income for the year ending 31 July 2018. **(10 marks)**
2. Calculate the following ratios:
   (a) gross profit as a percentage of revenue
   (b) net profit for the year as a percentage of revenue
   (c) return on capital employed (percentage)
   (d) rate of inventory turnover. **(8 marks)**

Pierre has been considering employing somebody to help sell his accessories on the days he does not work. He estimates that, if he does, for the following year:
- revenues would increase by 20 per cent, while increasing his selling prices by 10 per cent
- purchases would also increase by 20 per cent, while the cost price would decrease by 5 per cent
- wages for the year would be £6 000
- additional equipment costing £2 000 would be needed
- general expenses would increase by £200 per month
- closing inventory at 31 July 2019 would be 50 per cent higher than the opening inventory.

3. Prepare a forecast statement of profit or loss for the end of the second year of trading. **(8 marks)**
4. Calculate:
   (a) the forecast gross profit as a percentage of revenue
   (b) the forecast net profit for the year as a percentage of revenue. **(4 marks)**

SOCIAL AND ETHICAL ACCOUNTING

In this book, we have looked at the accounting system and costing. The focus of study has been on the financial aspects of accounting, which follow many accounting concepts, including money measurement, prudence and accruals. We have studied the principles of accounting, control procedures, financial statements and costing methods. In Chapter 1, section 1.2 (What is accounting?) you learned that the purpose of accounting is to identify, record, measure and communicate information so people can make informed decisions. Much of the information you have worked with has been quantitative financial information. In this section, we will examine the non-financial factors that need to be considered in the decision-making process.

22 SOCIAL ACCOUNTING AND ETHICS

LEARNING OBJECTIVES

After you have studied this chapter, you should be able to:
- understand the implications of accounting decisions in the wider social context
- understand the significance of non-financial factors in the decision-making process
- evaluate the effect of accounting decisions on different stakeholders
- understand the role of ethics in accounting analysis and decision making.

GETTING STARTED

In August 2018, a profitable UK shoe designer and manufacturer announced plans to close its last UK factory and transfer the production of shoes to India. At the same time in Malaysia, 1 800 jobs were threatened by the introduction of an online auction system for the sale of items to the public. What non-financial issues are raised by these decisions? What groups of people might be affected? How will these groups be affected?

ACCOUNTING DECISIONS

Historically, accounting decisions have been mainly based on numerical data obtained from the accounting system. Only financial factors have been considered in making accounting decisions. Examples of accounting decisions include:
- the acquisition and disposal of non-current assets
- the closure of a loss-making department
- the introduction of a new partner into a partnership
- a change to the method of employee remuneration
- a change to the raw materials used in the manufacture of a product.

All of these decisions can be made using only financial information obtained from the accounting system. The main criteria used in reaching a decision are likely to be the effects on profit and profitability. It is often assumed that profit maximisation is the only objective for the owners of a business. But a business does not and cannot operate in isolation from the wider external environment and must consider the impact of its decisions on other groups. Each of the decisions above will affect other stakeholder groups, as well as the owners of the business. Consideration of these wider effects is often referred to as social accounting.

SOCIAL ACCOUNTING

In the context of social accounting, it is important to understand that the word 'account' refers to the concept of accountability – that is, being responsible to others for your actions. Therefore, social accounting is a term applied when businesses are accountable to society. It involves both financial and non-financial factors and assesses the impact of business decisions on all stakeholders of a business.

There are many situations in which a business will make decisions taking into account the wider social environment. These wider social contexts may include:
- the local community
- the environment
- the workforce
- health and safety
- use of natural resources.

Social accounting recognises that profits may fall if a business fails to meet the needs of the wider external environment. For example, a change in the method of employee remuneration may have a negative effect on the workforce, which might lead to low morale, higher labour turnover and recruitment difficulties.

ACCOUNTING DECISIONS IN THE SOCIAL CONTEXT

Businesses now have to consider the impact of their decisions on the wider community. An increase in global 24/7 media reporting and the use of social media mean that society and stakeholder groups are being constantly updated on the activities of businesses. In order to be seen as socially responsible, businesses increasingly take into account the interests of stakeholder groups when making decisions.

In Chapter 1, we discovered many different users of financial information. These groups of users who have an interest in the activities of a business are known as stakeholders.

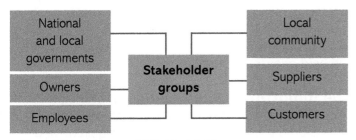

▲ Figure 1 Some common stakeholder groups

Each of these groups is likely to be affected differently by business decisions and it is not unusual to find stakeholders coming into conflict due to their differing objectives. In social accounting it is important for a business to recognise the objectives of all stakeholders.

Stakeholder	Possible objectives
Owners	Growth in profit, high dividends, increased share price
Employees	Higher wages/salaries, job security, job satisfaction, safe working environment
Customers	Value for money, reliable products and services
Suppliers	Timely payment, fair price for product
The local community	Employment opportunities, increased local wealth
National/local governments	Payment of taxes, consumer protection, protection of natural environment

The significance of non-financial factors will vary according to the decision being made. Each decision will be unique in terms of its impact on social accounting. Stakeholders will be affected in different ways and each social context will be different.

THE EFFECTS OF ACCOUNTING DECISIONS ON STAKEHOLDERS

Businesses should consider the implications of their decisions in the wider social context and the effects these have on stakeholder groups. Some possible social accounting decisions are detailed below.

Stakeholder affected	Possible social accounting consequences
Owners/ shareholders	The press and the local community are likely to have a negative view of the closure of a factory, because it will result in a loss of jobs. The bad publicity this creates will have a negative impact on the company's reputation, which could lead to a fall in share price.
Employees	Employees will be affected by the loss of jobs. Other employees at the company may have concerns about their job security, which could lead to low morale.
Local community	Due to the loss of jobs, there will be higher local unemployment. The unemployed will not have wages with which to buy goods and services, so the local economy might suffer. It is possible there will be a fall in living standards.
Suppliers	Suppliers of goods and services to the business might be concerned about reduction in sales to the business. This could negatively impact their own profitability, their workforce, etc.

▲ Table 1 The closure of an unprofitable department/factory

Stakeholder affected	Possible social accounting consequences
Employees	Loss of jobs, lack of job security, effect on health and safety from operating machinery
Owners/ shareholders	Bad publicity, cost of redundancies, introduction of capital
Customers	Possible change in quality of product from hand-made to machine-made

▲ Table 2 Replacement of workforce by new technology

Stakeholder affected	Possible social accounting consequences
Owners	Bad publicity might affect share price
Customers	Pressure groups might organise protests against expansion, advise customers to stop buying the product
Local community	Damage to the local environment
Government	Concern at rapid reduction of a scarce resource for future generations

▲ Table 3 Expansion resulting in overuse of scarce natural resources

This is only a small sample of accounting decisions and their possible effects on stakeholders. When answering examination questions, you will need to select one or two considerations and explain them in detail, rather than simply listing all stakeholders affected and all the consequences.

ACTIVITY 1 — SKILLS: CRITICAL THINKING, ANALYSIS

CASE STUDY: FACTORY CLOSURE

Global Garments produces clothing in many different countries. It has recently announced plans to close an unprofitable factory in Bangladesh. The factory is in an economically deprived area of the country with few alternative employment opportunities.

1 State four social contexts that affect accounting decisions.
2 Explain the non-financial factors that Global Garments needs to consider before making a final decision.

EXAM HINT

When answering evaluative questions relating to a business decision, you can use social accounting issues to support or argue against the decision. You can use these non-financial arguments alongside the financial data given.

ACTIVITY 2 — SKILLS: COMMUNICATION, REASONING

CASE STUDY: STAKEHOLDER DEBATE

1 As a class, decide on a topical accounting decision.
2 Define the term 'stakeholder'.
3 Identify the stakeholder group that is likely to have the objective of profit maximisation.
4 Identify a likely objective of the workforce.
5 Divide the class into groups of four or five students. Each student within a group should adopt the role of a different stakeholder and present arguments for and against the decision.

ETHICS IN ACCOUNTING

What is ethics?

Ethics can be defined as a set of moral principles or values. Ethics tells us how to behave well and what bad behaviour looks like in a situation. In our case, the context is accounting: the process of identifying, recording, measuring and communicating accounting information to different users. Businesses should report with honesty, issue correct statements and should not withhold relevant information.

The importance of ethical accounting

Accountants need to maintain a high level of ethical behaviour in their work. A fundamental requirement of financial reporting is that financial statements give a 'true and fair' view of the company's financial position. The users of accounting information rely on this information to make important decisions – for example, relating to savings and investment, education and retirement.

Unethical accounting

Unethical accounting often happens when a business does not follow the generally accepted accounting principles and concepts or IAS rules. In 2001, it was discovered that the US multinational company Enron had not shown a true and fair view of their financial statements. They had kept huge liabilities off their statement of financial position and had falsely increased revenues. In 2009, it was discovered that Indian IT services company Saytam had falsely claimed revenues of $1.5 billion and that $1 billion claimed in cash assets did not exist.

Both these examples show that unethical accounting can be on a huge scale and involve vast sums of money. However, not all unethical behaviour is on this scale. It can occur in many of the accounting transactions you have studied.

Unethical practices include:

- inflating revenue by recording sales which have not yet taken place
- treating revenue expenditure as capital expenditure or the other way round
- overstating the value of closing inventory by not writing down inventory that is not in use any more
- overstating the value of trade receivables by not accounting for irrecoverable debts or not providing an allowance/provision for irrecoverable debts.

You will be aware that many accounting concepts and conventions are intended to ensure that financial statements show a fair and true view of a company and that ethical accounting has been maintained.

ACTIVITY 3   SKILLS   ANALYSIS, CREATIVITY

CASE STUDY: CODE OF ETHICS FOR ACCOUNTANTS

The Institute of Chartered Accountants in England and Wales has a Code of Ethics for accountants that has five fundamental principles. The first two are:

- Integrity – to be straightforward and honest in all professional and business relationships.
- Objectivity – to not allow bias, conflict of interest or undue influence of others to override professional or business judgments.

Source: ICAEW Code of Ethics

1 Research the other three fundamental principles and produce a poster to show them and their meaning.
2 The ICAEW is the professional body for accountants in England and Wales. Research whether another such body exists in the country where you live. Do they have their own code of ethics? What differences are there between that code and the ICAEW's?

CHECKPOINT

1 What do you understand by the term 'social context'?

2 Identify two accounting decisions affected by social accounting.

3 Identify four stakeholder groups.

4 State one stakeholder group and one possible objective of this group.

5 Explain the difference between financial factors and non-financial factors.

6 What is ethics?

7 Accounts should give a true and fair view of a company's financial position. True or false?

8 It is ethical for a company to include in its trade receivables account amounts owing from a customer who has gone bankrupt. True or false?

EVALUATE

When answering evaluation questions on social and ethical accounting, it is important to show your reasoning and consider both positive and negative arguments, before reaching a justified conclusion. Let us look at the following scenario: a business plans to close an unprofitable department.

The social accounting issue could be the workforce. It could be argued that closing the department will lead to a loss of jobs – this would be an argument against the decision. However, it could also be argued that closing the loss-making department will give the remaining employees greater job security.

Arguments for	Arguments against
Greater job security for the remaining workforce	Loss of jobs – negative impact on local community
Increased profits for owners	Bad publicity for the owners
Suppliers are confident that the business will continue to operate and they will continue to make some sales	Suppliers might be concerned about reduction in sales to the business

▲ Table 5 Arguments for and against plans to close an unprofitable department

As with all evaluative questions, there is no right or wrong answer. Your decision will be based on the specific arguments you have made.

SUBJECT VOCABULARY

ethics a set of moral principles or values that tell us how to behave well in a situation
social accounting a type of accounting used by businesses which takes into account both financial factors, such as profit, and non-financial factors from a social context, such as the impact on the local community and the environment
stakeholder user of financial information who has an interest in the activities of a business

EXAM PRACTICE

CASE STUDY: EXPANSION PROPOSAL

SKILLS CRITICAL THINKING, INTERPRETATION, REASONING

Agri Products grows and produces a variety of agricultural products, including rice and coffee for export. Due to an increase in demand, it is considering expanding by purchasing more farmland from local farmers. It is forecast that the expansion would increase the net profit margin from 5 per cent to 20 per cent. Due to the extensive use of technology, few additional workers would be required. In addition, the expansion would require the use of vast amounts of water from the local river.

EXAM HINT

The terms social accounting and ethical accounting are often used incorrectly in general conversation. As an accounting student, you need to be able to distinguish between the two concepts. They are not the same thing and the terms are not interchangeable.

Q

1 Explain the difference between social and ethical accounting. **(4 marks)**
2 Evaluate the expansion proposal of Agri Products. **(12 marks)**

APPENDIX

COMMAND TERMS

In the examinations, the questions asked will use one of the command terms below. You should learn what each of these terms means to help you answer the question being asked. There is more information on the term 'Evaluate' on page ix of this book.

Calculate This will involve working out a numerical problem using mathematical processes and formulae, showing relevant working.

Comment The answer must include a simple statement based on the scenario and also a summary of why/how that statement is important to the scenario.

Complete This requires the completion of a table or structure. This may include a calculation which will then be required to fill the incomplete table/structure.

Define To state the precise meaning of an accounting term and/or provide a description.

Evaluate This will involve reviewing information and then bringing it together to form a conclusion, drawing on evidence including strengths, weaknesses, alternative actions, relevant data or information. A supported judgement/decision will be reached in relation to its context.

Explain This requires a linked justification/exemplification of a point.

Identify This requires information to be selected from a range of possibilities, list or given stimulus.

Prepare This will involve arranging financial information into a standard format.

Recommend This will involve suggesting a solution/decision by reviewing information from a scenario and providing a justification/exemplification for that choice.

State This requires the recall of one or more pieces of information.

FORMULAE

The formulae below will not be supplied in the examinations, so you will need to learn them. Please note that a formula may be applied in more than one section.

Profitability

1 Gross Profit as a Percentage of Revenue (sales margin) $= \dfrac{\text{Gross Profit}}{\text{Revenue}} \times 100$

2 Percentage Mark-up $= \dfrac{\text{Gross Profit as a Percentage of Revenue}}{\text{Cost of Sales}} \times 100$

3 Net Profit for the Year as a Percentage of Revenue $= \dfrac{\text{Net Profit for the Year}}{\text{Revenue}} \times 100$

4 Return on Capital Employed (percentage) $= \dfrac{\text{Net Profit Before Interest (NPBI)}}{\text{Capital Employed}} \times 100$

   For a sole trader or partnership Capital Employed = Capital + Non-current Liabilities (NCL)

5 Return on Capital Employed (percentage) for Corporate Bodies $= \dfrac{\text{Net Profit Before Interest (NPBI)}}{\text{Capital Employed}} \times 100$

   For a Company Capital Employed = Issued Shares + Reserves + Non-current Liabilities

Liquidity

6 Current Ratio $= \dfrac{\text{Current Assets}}{\text{Current Liabilities}}$

7 Liquid Ratio (Acid Test) $= \dfrac{\text{Current Assets} - \text{Inventory}}{\text{Current Liabilities}}$

8 Rate of Inventory Turnover $= \dfrac{\text{Cost of Sales}}{\text{Average Inventory (Times per Accounting Period)}}$

9 Trade Payables Payment Period $= \dfrac{\text{Trade Payables}}{\text{Credit Purchases}} \times 365$

10 Trade Receivables Collection Period $= \dfrac{\text{Trade Receivables}}{\text{Credit Sales}} \times 365$

Use of assets

11 Revenue to Non-current Assets $= \dfrac{\text{Revenue}}{\text{Non-current Assets}}$

Investment

12 Gearing Ratio $= \dfrac{\text{Fixed Cost Capital (Debt)}}{\text{Total Capital Employed (Debt + Equity)}} \times 100$

13 Earnings per Share $= \dfrac{\text{Net Profit after Tax} - \text{Preference Share Dividend}}{\text{Number of Issued Ordinary Shares}}$

14 Price Earnings Ratio $= \dfrac{\text{Market Price per Share}}{\text{Earnings per Share}}$

15 Dividend per Share $= \dfrac{\text{Total Ordinary Dividend Paid}}{\text{Number of Issued Ordinary Shares}}$

16 Dividend Yield $= \dfrac{\text{Dividend Paid per Share}}{\text{Market Price of Share}}$

17 Dividend Cover $= \dfrac{\text{Profit after Tax} - \text{Preference Dividends}}{\text{Total Ordinary Dividend Paid}}$

GLOSSARY

absorption the process of charging overhead expenses to cost units

accounting the process of recording, classifying, analysing and communicating financial information

accounting concepts guidelines for the treatment of accounting transactions

accruals the concept that income and expenditure for goods and services is matched to the same accounting period when calculating profit

accumulated the total to date

accumulated fund the capital account of a club or non-profit-making organisation

allocation the process of charging costs incurred in a department or cost centre to that department or cost centre

allowance/provision for irrecoverable debts an amount put aside from profits for possible irrecoverable debts

apportionment the process by which overhead expenses are shared between departments

appropriation account the part of the statement of profit or loss and other comprehensive income that records the distribution of profits to partners

assets resources that are owned and used by the business

batch costing a method of costing used when there are a number of identical products being made

bonus an additional payment made when work is completed in less than the allowed time or for achieving a given output level

books of prime entry where transactions are classified and recorded before posting to the ledger accounts

bring down (or carry down) the amount entered as the opening balance in the next accounting period, which is the balancing figure calculated for the current financial period. It is entered on the opposite side in the new financial period, this maintains the double entry

business entity only the transactions relating to the business are recorded in the books of account for the business

capital investment (cash, resources or other assets) provided by the owner of the business

capital account the fixed account of a partner showing capital introduced or withdrawn

capital expenditure spending on non-current assets or their improvement

capital income receipts from the sale of non-current assets

carriage inwards the expense incurred in the transporting of items into the business

carrying value (net book value) the current value of a non-current asset after accumulated depreciation is deducted

cash book a book of prime entry in which all cash and bank transactions are recorded. It is also part of the double-entry system

cash discount a reduction in the amount owing in return for early payment of the debt

consistency the concept that after a business has adopted a particular policy for recording financial transactions, the policy should not be changed without a valid reason

contra entry (or set-off) an entry in the control accounts which cancels a debit balance with a credit balance

control accounts accounts which prove the transactions of a set of accounts: the trade receivables control account and the trade payables control account

cost centre a production or service department

cost of sales (cost of goods sold) the direct costs related to the manufacture or purchase of a product that is sold to a customer

cost unit a unit of production or service that absorbs the overhead costs

credit entry (Cr) an entry on the right-hand side of the ledger account

current account an account showing the movement of partners' drawings, interest on drawings and capital, salaries and share of profit/loss

current assets resources which are converted to cash within one year

current liabilities amounts owed that are payable within one year

day work payment made by a rate per hour

debit entry (Dr) an entry on the left-hand side of the ledger account

deficit the loss incurred by a club or non-profit-making organisation

departmental records financial statements that show the profits made by different sections of a business

depreciation the loss in value of a non-current asset over its useful economic life, which is apportioned to the accounting periods that benefit from its use

determine to work out or decide

discount received the cash discount a business obtains for early payment to a trade payable

dispose to remove an asset from the books of accounts. This could involve selling the asset, or scrapping the asset if it has no resale value

drawings resources removed from the business by the owner; these could be cash or inventory

ethics a set of moral principles or values that tell us how to behave well in a situation

expenses cost incurred by the business in generating revenue

external user a person outside the business organisation

factory overheads indirect costs of manufacture which need to be apportioned on a fair basis to the cost of manufacturing

factory profit the approximate profit added to the production cost of goods completed to arrive at the transfer price

financial accounting the recording and presentation of past financial information to external users for their decision making

financial statements (final accounts) produced by the business to provide a summary of the performance of the business (the statement of profit or loss and other comprehensive income) and the financial position of the business (the statement of financial position)

financial transaction a business event or action that has a monetary impact on the business

finished goods an inventory classification that consists of fully completed products

First In, First Out (FIFO) a method of inventory valuation where oldest inventory is issued first

fixed capital account when only capital transactions are recorded in the account

fixed costs costs that do not vary with output or activity levels

fluctuating capital account where all partners' transactions are entered in a single account

general ledger a book containing all impersonal accounts

going concern the assumption that the business will continue to trade in the foreseeable future

goodwill an intangible non-current asset reflecting the value given to the reputation of the business

gross profit the difference between the revenue and the cost of sales

historic cost this concept states that transactions should be recorded in the books of account using the actual cost at the time the transaction took place

income and expenditure account the club and non-profit-making organisation equivalent of the statement of profit or loss and other comprehensive income

incurred a term used in accounting to show that a business transaction has taken place and needs to be recognised in the books of accounts

intangible asset a non-physical asset that cannot be touched or seen, such as goodwill or a brand name

interest on capital the use of profit rewarding partners who have invested the most

interest on drawings a reduction in the partners' current account to discourage excessive drawings

internal user a person inside the business organisation

International Accounting Standards (IAS) accounting standards, which apply globally, enabling users of accounting information to make reliable judgements and decisions about businesses from a range of countries

inventory (stock) raw material, work in progress and finished goods held by a business

inventory count the physical verification of the quantity and value of the inventory held in the business

irrecoverable debt amount deducted from a trade receivable when the amount owed is not recoverable

job costing a system of costing that allocates and apportions costs to an individual customer order

Last In, First Out (LIFO) a method of valuing inventory where most recent inventory is issued first

ledger account an account containing the double entry

legal entity an individual or organisation that has legal rights and obligations

liabilities the debts of a business owed to others

liquidity the ability to convert assets into sufficient cash to meet everyday commitments

management accounting the preparation of past and future, financial and non-financial information for internal users

margin gross profit in relation to revenue

mark-up gross profit in relation to the cost of sales

materiality allows for the correct accounting treatment to be ignored if the amount involved is insignificant relative to the size of the business

money measurement items should only be recorded in the books of accounts if they can be measured in monetary terms

net realisable value (NRV) inventory valuation based on the selling price less any additional costs required to affect the sale

non-current assets (fixed assets) assets held by a business for more than one year

non-current liabilities (long-term liabilities) amounts owed with a repayment date greater than one year

other operating income (sundry income) revenue from non-trading activities

other payables (accruals) amounts owed at the end of the financial period which match to the revenue for that period

other receivables (prepayments) amounts paid in one financial period that will match with revenue earned in the next financial period

over absorption less overhead costs were incurred than were budgeted for

overcast entering an amount greater than the correct amount into an account

overhead absorption rate (OAR) the rate at which overhead expenses are absorbed to a cost unit, either direct labour hours or machine hours

overheads expenditure on labour, materials and services which cannot be identified with a specific cost unit/product

overstate to state more than the actual sum

partnership a business with two or more owners

partnership agreement an agreement between partners detailing aspects of the business including rates of interest on capital and drawings, salaries and profit-sharing ratios

partnership salary an appropriation of profit to a partner

periodic inventory valuation a method of inventory valuation where the inventory is valued at the end of the period

perpetual inventory valuation a method of inventory valuation where a running balance of inventory is recorded after every receipt or issue of inventory

piecework payment made according to the number of units produced

prepayments revenues or expenses relating to the next accounting period

prime cost the total of all direct costs, materials, labour and expenses, incurred in the manufacture of a product

production cost the total costs incurred in the manufacture of a product

production department where the product is manufactured, also referred to as a cost centre

productivity the measurement of employee efficiency

profitability the ability of a business to generate profit

profitability ratios a relative measure of the profit generated

profit for the year (net profit) the amount revenue is greater than all expenses

provision an expected future liability or future expectation of expenditure that is uncertain

provision for depreciation account the account where the accumulated depreciation is recorded

provision for unrealised profit the profit that is not recognised until the inventory has been sold

prudence states that accounts should reflect a cautious view of the business, that losses should be accounted for as they are anticipated, but profits should not be recognised until realised

purchases inventory bought for resale

quotation a document prepared in response to an enquiry from a customer detailing the price that will be charged for the product or service requested

raw materials the purchase of inventory waiting to enter the manufacturing process

realisation the concept that revenues should only be recognised when the exchange of goods and services has taken place

reapportionment the process in which service department overheads are shared out to the production departments

receipts and payments account a record of amounts received and paid in a club or non-profit-making organisation

reconciliation the process of comparing two different accounting records to ensure that they agree with each other

reducing balance method of depreciation a method of depreciation based on the carrying value of the non-current asset

remuneration payments to employees of wages and other financial benefits

residual value the value of a non-current asset at the end of its useful economic life

revaluation method a method of calculating the annual depreciation charge based on a year-end annual valuation of the assets

revenue (or income) the monetary value of sales made by a business

revenue expenditure spending on the day-to-day running expenses of the business

revenue income receipts resulting from the normal trading activities of a business

royalties a sum of money paid to the owner of a product or process for the use of it

sales inventory sold in the normal course of business to customers

schedule of non-current assets a summary of the movement of non-current assets over the accounting period

schedule of trade receivables a list of outstanding trade receivables by the age of the debt

service department a cost centre that supports a production department or other service departments

set-off a contra entry between control accounts

social accounting a type of accounting used by businesses which takes into account both financial factors, such as profit, and non-financial factors from a social context, such as the impact on the local community and the environment

sole trader a business owned by a single person

stakeholder user of financial information who has an interest in the activities of a business

statement of affairs a basic statement of financial position used to find missing values in the accounting equation

statement of financial position one of two financial statements that shows the assets, capital and liabilities of a business

statement of profit or loss and other comprehensive income one of two financial statements which shows the profits or losses of the business

straight line method of depreciation a method of calculating annual depreciation based on the cost of the non-current asset

subscriptions fees paid by members of a club or non-profit-making organisation

subscriptions account the account which records the membership fees of a member of a club

subsidiary book another term for the books of prime entry or day books

surplus the profit made by clubs and non-profit-making organisations

suspense account a temporary account used to balance the trial balance until errors are found and corrected. It is used to record the elimination of errors

total assets non-current assets plus current assets

trade discount reduction in the invoice total given to a customer

trade payables the total of all the individual persons and businesses that a business owes money to and will pay within one year

trade payables ledger a ledger containing individual personal accounts of credit suppliers

trade receivables the total of all the individual persons and businesses that owe money and will repay within one year

trade receivables ledger a ledger containing the accounts of the individual credit customers

trading account the part of the statement of profit or loss and other comprehensive income that calculates the gross profit from trading activities

transaction a business event, such as the sale of inventory, which can be measured in monetary terms and which must be recorded in the books of accounts

transfer price the production cost of manufactured goods plus a mark-up, transferred to the trading account of a manufacturing business

trial balance a summary of all the balances extracted from the ledgers of a business

under absorption more actual overhead costs were incurred than were budgeted for

undercast entering an amount lower than the correct amount into an account

understate to state less than the actual sum

variable costs expenses that change in direct proportion to levels of activity/output

work in progress partly finished goods in a manufacturing business

INDEX

Page numbers in **bold** denote entries in subject vocabulary.